MINING
CALIFORNIA

MINING CALIFORNIA

An Ecological History

ANDREW C. ISENBERG

Hill and Wang

A division of Farrar, Straus and Giroux

New York

Hill and Wang
A division of Farrar, Straus and Giroux
19 Union Square West, New York 10003

Copyright © 2005 by Andrew C. Isenberg
All rights reserved
Distributed in Canada by Douglas & McIntyre Ltd.
Printed in the United States of America
First edition, 2005

Maps on pages 5, 40, and 141 copyright © 2005 by Jeffrey L. Ward. Map of Sacramento
and vicinity, 1855, on page 61 provided by the Sacramento Archives and Museum Collection
Center. "Sacramento, 1849," on page 59, courtesy of the Eleanor McClatchy Collection, City
of Sacramento, History and Science Division, Sacramento Archives and Museum Collection
Center, catalog number 82/05/1343. Photograph of Modoc band chief Keintpoos on page
133 courtesy of Western History Collections, University of Oklahoma Library. All other
images courtesy of the California History Section, California State Library:
Photograph Collection.

Library of Congress Cataloging-in-Publication Data
Isenberg, Andrew C. (Andrew Christian)
    Mining California : an ecological history / by Andrew Isenberg.— 1st ed.
        p. cm.
    Includes bibliographical references and index.
    ISBN-13: 978-0-8090-9535-3
    ISBN-10: 0-8090-9535-1 (alk. paper)
        1. California—Environmental conditions—History. 2. Nature—Effect of human beings
on—California. I. Title.

GE155.C2184 2005
333.7′09794—dc22

                                                                                    2004025564

Designed by Jonathan D. Lippincott

www.fsgbooks.com

1   3   5   7   9   10   8   6   4   2

For Joan and Wesley Isenberg

Contents

MINING
CALIFORNIA

Introduction: The Political Economy of California Industrialization

C alifornia is a most beautiful country," wrote John Eagle in 1852, shortly after his arrival in the gold-mining town of Auburn Ravine. Many of the argonauts who migrated to California following the discovery of gold on the south fork of the American River in 1848 shared Eagle's sentiments. The rivers, valleys, forests, and wildlife moved John Kincade to describe the region as "a land that is lovely above all others."[1] Lorenzo Sawyer, later the chief justice of the state supreme court, wrote in December 1850, shortly after his arrival in California, that "beauty, grandeur, sublimity characterize every lineament of this vast scene."[2] However beautiful, the environment that Eagle, Kincade, Sawyer, and others encountered in the 1850s was hardly pristine. For thousands of years, Native Americans, whose population in the mid-eighteenth century may have been as high as 300,000, had fished, hunted, gathered, and selectively burned large swaths of the land between the Pacific Ocean and the Sierra Nevada mountains. Spanish and Mexican settlement beginning in the mid-eighteenth century had introduced Old World livestock and plants to California, altering the environment still further. These changes notwithstanding, the California landscape was striking in its diversity and beauty when, in midcentury, tens of thousands of prospectors arrived there from eastern North America, Mexico, South America, Western Europe, and East Asia.[3]

California's environment in 1850 was, moreover, one of the most complex, distinctive, and dynamic in North America. The environment that midcentury emigrants such as Kincade, Eagle, and Sawyer encountered was largely isolated by the Pacific Ocean to the west, the Colorado and Mojave deserts to the south and southeast, the Sierra Nevada to the east, and the Klamath and Cascade mountain ranges to the north. Because of this relative isolation, many plant and animal species in California evolved in ways that diverged from other patterns in North America. Emigrants encountered distinctive plant species that varied from the massive redwoods of the northern coast to the stunted chaparral of the Coast Range. They found dozens of animal species including the tule elk, the California mule deer, and the California condor endemic only to the state. Although the emigrants could not have known it, California's eight thousand species of plants, nearly two hundred mammals, and over five hundred birds contained more unique species than any other state in the continental United States.[4]

Although some naturalists have exaggerated California's uniqueness, it would be difficult to overstate the diversity of the mid-nineteenth-century California environment. The landforms of the state vary from the peaks of the Sierra Nevada and Coast Range to the grasslands of the Central Valley and the deserts of the south. California's environments range in altitude from 282 feet below sea level in Death Valley to nearly 14,500 feet above sea level atop Mount Whitney in the Sierra. As a transitional zone between the humid coastal Pacific Northwest and arid Baja California, the climate is likewise diverse: the Mojave Desert receives less than five inches of average annual precipitation, while parts of the redwood rain forests to the northwest receive five feet or more.[5]

These diverse environments are prone to change. Geologically, California is one of the youngest and most rapidly changing regions in the world. Its landforms, including the Sierra Nevada, are relatively recent formations born of the collision between the Pacific and North American tectonic plates. The Owens Valley earthquake of 1872 and the infamous San Francisco earthquake of 1906 (both of which would have registered an estimated 8.3 on the Richter scale) were testaments to the continuing effects of that ongoing collision.[6] Likewise, eruptions of Shastina near Mount Shasta in 1786 and Lassen Peak in 1914 indicated continuing volcanic activity.

Similarly, the California climate has been an unpredictable source of change in the region's human history. Dendrochronological records indicate that California suffered two prolonged droughts in the last millennium, first between 890 and 1100 and again between 1210 and 1350.[7] Climatic records in the last century and a half indicate continued dramatic fluctuations of

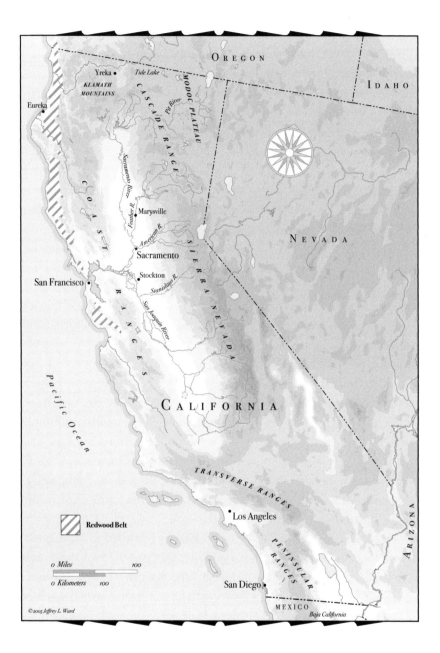

OREGON

IDAHO

Yreka •   Tule Lake
KLAMATH
MOUNTAINS

Eureka •

CASCADE RANGE

Pit River

MODOC PLATEAU

Sacramento River

Feather R.

Marysville •

American R.

★ Sacramento

Stockton •

San Francisco •

Stanislaus R.

San Joaquin River

COAST   RANGES

SIERRA   NEVADA

NEVADA

CALIFORNIA

Pacific Ocean

TRANSVERSE RANGES

• Los Angeles

PENINSULAR RANGES

ARIZONA

Redwood Belt

0 Miles   100

0 Kilometers   100

San Diego •

MEXICO
Baja California

© 2005 Jeffrey L. Ward

temperature and rainfall, often but not always caused by warm-water El Niño currents in the Pacific Ocean. Such fluctuations have precipitated unpredictable droughts and floods. Even in the absence of El Niño disturbances, temperature and rainfall are unpredictable. As the California writer Mike Davis has noted, while Los Angeles averages fifteen inches of annual precipitation, in only 17 of the last 127 years has the actual annual rainfall been within 25 percent of the average. Fire has also been a dynamic force in the ecology of the state, especially in southern California, where low-temperature shrub and grass fires caused by hot, dry seasonal air currents initiate new growth in local plant species. Yet these low-temperature fires occasionally erupt into major wildfires.[8]

The complex interplay of fire, drought, and flood has altered habitats unpredictably, causing significant fluctuations in plant and animal populations. The region's environment, in short, was not an Eden; in many respects, its volatile ecology made it a tenuous place for its varied plant and animal species.

While historic plant and animal populations fluctuated in California's dynamic environments, the state was characterized by both a diversity and a density of plant and animal species. An estimated 20,000 sea otters once inhabited the coastal waters. Millions of salmon clogged the rivers every year as they migrated upstream to spawn. Perhaps 500,000 tule elk and even larger numbers of deer and pronghorn antelope inhabited the prairies and shrublands. In 1850, redwoods, which have a greater above-ground biomass than almost any other plant species, covered over two million acres along the northern coast. In short, California before the gold rush was composed of changeable yet productive biomes capable of supporting dense plant and animal populations.[9]

The abundance of flora and fauna in California was in large part the product of deliberate management by natives. The Indians of California set fires in both the fall and spring to clear brush and litter from forests and to promote new growth of shrubs favored by browsing mammals such as deer. Controlled burns created large, open areas beneath high forest canopies. They also lessened the likelihood of catastrophic forest fires—thus an ancillary effect was the preservation of California forests.[10] On the Pacific, Indian harvests of mollusks increased the supply of kelp and thus the populations of coastal fishes. While Indian resource strategies were by and large sensible and practical, the Indians were not ecological saints: archeological evidence suggests that some coastal communities may have been forced to disperse after exhausting local shellfish supplies, for example. As the environmental historian Arthur McEvoy has noted, natives developed their resource management strategies over a long period, a process that likely included such errors as the depletion of shellfish.[11]

Most European and Euroamerican immigrants to California were oblivious to the agency of Indians in the management of the region's environment. For the new arrivals, the rich environment was a natural cornucopia that offered the prospect of great wealth. Boosters, nineteenth-century promoters of western economic growth, touted the natural advantages of California as sure signs of future prosperity. The *Stockton City Directory and Emigrants' Guide* of 1852 reported not only an abundance of wild game that were "strangers to the crack of the rifle," but so many fish in the San Joaquin River that "children stand on the city wharves, and fill their baskets with the smaller finny tribe, in the course of an hour."[12] To these paeans to the area's natural wealth, early nineteenth-century observers such as Richard Henry Dana added claims that the climate was disease-free and conducive to good health.[13] According to the boosters, California was a rare place that promised its inhabitants both prosperity and the pristine.

Most Californians believed that by tapping natural resources, they transformed the beautiful but unproductive wilderness into a garden. Writing in 1853, Kincade reflected scornfully on the condition of California in 1848, when "Indians swarmed throughout the country gaining their subsistence by taking game, feeding on Acorns, Roots, grass, &c." By contrast, Kincade boasted that "the progress of the Anglo-Saxon has been rapidly onward. . . . The wild cattle are fast being consumed, the Horses subdued, the Indians receding, Cities and Towns, Churches and Schools, Mills &c. are interspersed throughout every portion like unto other countries of a century's growth." Kincade did not exaggerate: San Francisco's population multiplied from one thousand in 1848 to fifty thousand in 1856. In those eight years, it had become one of the largest cities in the United States.[14] The *Placer Herald*, an Auburn, California, newspaper, summed up this view of the changes in the California environment in the quarter-century since the discovery of gold: "A desert in '49, a garden in '74."[15]

Yet a few observers were less certain that the rapid transformation of the environment was entirely benign. "Young as California was," lamented

J. D. Borthwick in 1857, "already it could show ruins and deserted villages" where gold claims had proved to be unproductive. John Eagle excepted the mining country from his description of the beauty of California scenery. "Among the mines is the roughest and most barren looking places a person can conceive of," he wrote. He observed "the ground dug up for miles in some places to the depth of twenty or thirty feet."[16] Likewise, Sawyer wrote in 1850 that miners had despoiled the gold country: "Cast your eye along those vallies, Deer creek, Little Deer creek, Gold run and many others, see their beds to a great depth thrown up, behold the pine, the fir, the cedar, the oak, these monarchs of the forest undermined, uprooted. . . ."[17] While Borthwick, Eagle, and Sawyer could only deplore cosmetic changes to the scenery, they intuited that the extraordinary mineral wealth that California produced in the years after the discovery of gold exacted staggering environmental costs.

The economic demands of mining spurred a host of other economic activities including commercial agriculture, hunting, and fishing; these, too, took their toll on the nonhuman natural environment. Between the discovery of gold and the end of the nineteenth century, Californians decimated fish and game populations. By 1858, according to the *Sacramento Daily Union*, because of overfishing and pollution from the mines, the yield of commercial salmon fisheries on the Sacramento–San Joaquin river system had declined to "a nominal amount."[18] In 1877, 116 citizens of Siskiyou County in northern California complained to the state government that "a few years ago deer and kindred game were plentiful in our mountains and valleys," but that "owing to the wanton destruction of these animals" by market hunters, they "will soon become extinct."[19]

Californians also cut large numbers of trees, primarily to build cities to house the state's growing population. In Sacramento in 1853, according to one observer, lumber was purchased "with an avidity that could scarcely be conceived." The demand for lumber by city builders contributed to the deforestation of one-third of California's available supply of timber by 1872.[20] The cities, overcrowded and constructed in haste, became centers of epidemic disease. Sacramento suffered an epidemic of cholera in 1850 and endemic typhoid and dysentery in succeeding decades. Sanitation and health problems in California cities persisted in the nineteenth century. As late as 1888, engineers hired to construct a sewer system for Stockton reported with evident disgust that the existing sewage system was "frightfully unsanitary."[21] The cities were also centers of industrial pollution. The economic demands of mining and logging fostered industrial enterprises in California that ranged from the mercury furnaces of New Almaden to the iron foundries of San Francisco and Sacramento. The factories emitted large amounts of toxins into the air, water, and soil.

The transformation of the California environment in the nineteenth century through mining, city-building, and industry is at odds with the agrarian paradigms of nineteenth-century western history. The overtaxed urban environment fits poorly into the ideal of the pastoral frontier first articulated in 1893 by the historian Frederick Jackson Turner.[22] By the mid-twentieth century, many historians had recognized the inadequacies of Turner's thesis. By the 1940s, under critical examination by such historians, Turner's frontier had retreated from the Far West to the Upper Midwest. For most western historians, Turner's frontier, with its characteristic free land, agrarian prosperity, and political liberty, became an exceptional rather than general explanation for western settlement.[23] Nonetheless, Turner's frontier thesis has proved remarkably resilient. It is like a century-old manor, dilapidated but still grand; every few years a western historian inspects the place and declares that all it needs is a few modern renovations to make it habitable again.[24]

As mid-twentieth-century historians of the American West cast about for an alternative to Turner's frontier thesis, Walter Prescott Webb's definition of the West as a semiarid region of defeated expectations emerged as the dominant interpretation of the field.[25] Whereas Turner had argued that the process of transforming a cornucopian "wilderness" to "civilization" had produced both liberty and prosperity, Webb's West was a region of exception, oddity, and failure; a land characterized by desert and depression. But California's nineteenth-century history fit as poorly into Webb's depopulated, provincial West as it had into Turner's frontier. Although the region suffered a devastating drought in 1863–64, Webb's paradigm only partly applies to California, where the environment is too complex and diverse to fit neatly into his simple regional generalization: while parts of southern California are desert, parts of the northern coast are a temperate rain forest. Thus, like Turner's frontier before it, the extent of Webb's region has receded as historians have found exceptions to it. In recent years some "New

Western Historians"—largely followers of Webb's regional interpretation—have excluded California from the West entirely.[26]

Donald Worster, Webb's chief intellectual heir, has extended the paradigm of the desert West to California by characterizing the state as a "hydraulic society," a modern Mesopotamia of bureaucratically centralized irrigated agriculture.[27] As a description of modern California, Worster's vision is apt. Yet irrigated agriculture in California began only fitfully in the last quarter of the nineteenth century. Gold-mining companies in California sought to control and divert rivers but their purpose was not, at first, agricultural but rather industrial. If Turner's vision of nineteenth-century California folded the state back into the agricultural settlement of the trans-Appalachian West in the eighteenth and early nineteenth century, Worster's pressed it forward into the irrigated landscape of the twentieth-century West. A distinct nineteenth-century California disappears from both of these conceptions of the West.

Webb's climatic paradigm for western history was the dominant intellectual path for midcentury historians, but it was not the only trail leading away from the frontier thesis. Another group of historians, including Rodman Paul, Samuel Hays, Earl Pomeroy, and J. Willard Hurst, marked out another route. They saw the West less as a distinct region whose history was dictated by a unique climate and geography, than as an integral part of the nation. They looked to the concerns of national historians—industrialism, labor, national politics, and the law—for their clues to understanding the West. For Paul, in particular, the West was an industrial place. Nineteenth-century California—industrial, economically diverse, urban, and densely populated—exemplified Paul's West. His 1947 study, *California Gold*, dismissed the Turnerian interpretation of the gold rush as a triumphal story of individuals wresting fortunes from the wilderness. Instead, he noted how individual prospectors quickly gave way to corporate hydraulic mines and stamp mills. Yet Paul's account of industrial California shared the celebratory perspective of Turner's frontier thesis. Paul applauded the industrialization of California, contrasting "the exuberant youth of 1848–49 and the sober maturity of the early seventies." In large part because of this triumphalism, Paul's industrial paradigm of the West never acquired the stature of Webb's more critical depiction of the region as a desert province.

Despite a number of studies of industry in the nineteenth-century West by Mark Wyman, William Deverell, David Igler, and Kathryn Morse, among others, and a recent call by Igler to conceive of the Far West in the late nineteenth century as an industrial place, most historians of the nineteenth-century West have treated industry as a curious exception in a place they consider to be best described as a frontier or semidesert.[28] The work of these relatively few western historians on technology, industry, and mining demonstrates how the competing paradigms of Turner and Webb shared at least one characteristic. For both scholars, the West was primarily an agrarian place. The Homestead Act of 1862, which offered potential settlers 160 acres of land in the West, epitomized both perspectives. Turner viewed the Homestead Act as a salient example of his core argument that Americans' settlement of "free land" was the key to prosperity and democratic political development. Turner's frontier thesis reconstructed John Locke's main ideas: Americans' contact with wilderness—a "State of Nature"—created American liberty; the reduction of wilderness to property created American civilization. In contrast, Webb and his followers pointed to the high failure rate of Homestead Act farms.[29] The legislation was thus for Webb a prime example of his essentially Malthusian core argument that much of the western environment was too dry and sterile to support farmers.

Whether Lockean or Malthusian, farmers were not the only Euroamericans in the nineteenth-century West. Enterprises that extracted natural resources, such as mining and logging, were a significant part of the western economy, particularly in the second half of the nineteenth century.[30] Large-scale ranching, while an agricultural enterprise, resembled mining and logging rather than family farming in its reliance on forced or proletarian labor and its exploitation rather than cultivation of forage. Big ranches and farms were heavily dependent on industrial technology. They relied on steam-powered agricultural machinery to mow hay and reap and thresh wheat, and on railroads to ship their products to urban markets. This style of "bonanza farming," as the historian of technology Carroll Pursell has called it, emerged earliest in California before diffusing eastward.[31]

Extractive industries and the expanding rail network on which these industries depended in turn spurred the growth of urban centers across the West. Despite the enduring image of the late-nineteenth-century West as a rural province, the West at the end of the century was, though less heavily populated, as fully urbanized as the rest of the nation. By 1900, when 40.4 percent of Americans lived in cities of 2,500 people or more, 52.3 percent of

Californians and 40.7 percent of the residents of the West—defined as the states or territories of Washington, Oregon, California, Nevada, Idaho, Utah, Arizona, New Mexico, Montana, Wyoming, and Colorado—lived in such urban places. Cities were not simply by-products of the industrial exploitation of western natural resources. They were themselves economic enterprises, founded by land speculators who anticipated fortunes in real estate development. Cities organized vast spaces in the West, drawing to themselves capital, labor, and resources and dictating economic enterprises in far-flung hinterlands.[32]

Urbanization, industrialization, and the rise of mechanized farming in the West occurred as the United States became an industrial power in the second half of the nineteenth century: the United States' relative share of world manufacturing output rose from a mere 7 percent in 1860 (when it ranked behind Britain, France, China, and India), to 14 percent in 1880 (when it was second only to Britain), to 24 percent in 1900 (when it was the world leader).[33] Like all industrializing nations, the United States achieved its economic growth through the combined exploitation of the three so-called factors of production: capital, labor, and natural resources.[34] Remarkably, the United States achieved its extraordinary economic growth between 1860 and 1900 despite being chronically short of the first two of these three ingredients of industrial growth—capital and labor. To finance industrial growth, nineteenth-century Americans relied heavily on foreign investment, primarily from Britain; for example, the British invested $34 million in Great Plains cattle ranching between 1870 and 1900.[35] By 1900, foreign investors owned $3.3 billion in American securities, an amount equal to 36 percent of the total capital invested in U.S. industries. Similarly, the chronic shortage of labor in the expanding American economy drew immigrants to the United States. Eleven million immigrants entered the country between 1870 and 1900, drawn by the high price of labor in the American market. By 1910, one in five American laborers was an immigrant.[36]

Conditions in the West exacerbated the chronic shortages of capital and labor in industrializing America. Of the nearly $525 million invested in manufacturing in the United States in 1850, only a little over $1 million was invested in the West—all of it in California. By 1900, over $9.7 billion was invested in American industry but only $330 million, or just under 3.5 percent, was invested in the West. Shortages of labor in the nineteenth-century West accounted for the large immigrant population of the region. Between 1860 and 1890, the percentage of foreign-born residents of the West ranged between 25 and 30 percent, exceeding the percentages even in the industrial Northeast. California workers exemplified the transient foreign-born laboring population of the West. The discovery of gold attracted not only American citizens to California but migrants from Europe, Latin America, and East Asia. As a result, 39 percent of the state's residents were foreign-born in 1860. That percentage had declined only to 30 percent by 1890.[37]

While the United States was chronically short of capital and labor (and American industrialists in general thus paid a premium price for them), it had an abundance of natural resources, primarily minerals and timber. Industrialization in the nineteenth-century United States was thus heavily dependent on natural resource exploitation. In large part, American economic historians have devoted relatively little scholarly attention to the exploitation of natural resources, concentrating instead on the other two factors of production, capital and labor. In a typical instance, the economic historian Robert Gallman, in his introduction to the encyclopedic *Cambridge Economic History of the United States*, defined natural resources narrowly (and, like Turner and Webb, in agrarian terms) as the "land supply," and concluded that it contributed little to nineteenth-century American industrial growth.[38] Gallman, like most economic historians, shied away from Gavin Wright's provocative 1990 article "The Origins of American Industrial Success, 1879–1940," which located the roots of American industry in the exploitation of nonrenewable natural resources.[39] In the East, those resources notably included Pennsylvania coal and oil, Minnesota and Alabama iron ore, and Michigan copper. By 1900, the United States mined one-third of the coal in the world, most of it from a belt of deposits between Pennsylvania and Illinois. The Mesabi Range in Minnesota alone produced one-sixth of the iron ore in the world.

California, with limited deposits of these two primary natural resources of nineteenth-century heavy industry—coal and iron ore—would seem an unlikely place for the development of industry.[40] Yet throughout the West, where capital and labor were still scarcer and more expensive than elsewhere in the United States, the exploitation of all natural resources, and not merely coal and iron ore, assumed great importance.

While resources in the East were largely in private hands, in the West the federal government controlled them. The industrialization of the West was therefore hardly an autonomous economic development. Beginning with the discovery of gold in California in 1848, state and federal authorities enacted legislation that liberalized access to mineral resources on western public lands. The law permitted miners—first independent prospectors and later industrial mining companies—to enter upon the public domain to dig, tunnel, log, and dam in their search for gold.

The example of the gold rush prompted the federal government to open more land in the West to industrial development. In the years after 1862, the federal government enacted several industrial versions of the Homestead Act in order to accelerate the development of natural resources in the West and to compensate industrialists for the high costs of capital and labor. These included the Pacific Railway Act (1862), the first of a series of railroad land grants that financed the building of lines; the Mineral Resources Act (1866) and the General Mining Law (1872), which opened mineral resources on public lands to private exploitation at a nominal price; the Timber and Stone Act (1878), which did the same for forestlands, and the Desert Lands Act (1877), which disbursed large tracts of rangeland to ranchers. These laws and others like them funneled natural resources from western public lands into the control of industrial entrepreneurs.[41] In California and elsewhere in the West, state and federal courts facilitated the transfer of natural resources in the public domain to the control of private industrialists through a series of friendly rulings.

By the end of the nineteenth century, railroads and extractive industries such as mining, logging, and large-scale ranching had largely triumphed over small farmers. The agrarian West of the 1890s was characterized by depopulation, tenancy, and political radicalism directed, in scattershot fashion, at the banks, railroads, and other representatives of triumphant industry.[42] Several generations of labor historians have taken account of this process of industrialization and proletarianization in the nineteenth-century West.[43]

Yet few such studies took more than passing notice of the natural environment.[44] Precisely because western industry was disproportionately dependent on the exploitation of cheap natural resources, it exacted heavy environmental costs. It was this industrial damage to the environment that Eagle, Borthwick, and Sawyer first observed in the 1850s. The consideration of those costs was missing from Paul's study of California, as well as from Robert Kelley's like-minded 1959 study of the political conflict between hydraulic miners and California farmers.[45]

Industry and the western environment have come together in the work of the historian William Cronon, who has argued in his landmark 1991 study, *Nature's Metropolis*, that much of the nineteenth-century West was remade by industrialization. Railroads, logging technology, barbed wire, and commercial agricultural machinery produced in eastern cities enabled the exploitation of trees, grain, and livestock in the Great Plains and Upper Midwest. According to Cronon's paradigm, however, industry was located firmly east of the Mississippi River. It exerted its transforming, neocolonial power over the West from a distance. Cronon's nineteenth-century West was an underdeveloped colony, locked in a pattern of debt and dependency with the industrial world to which it supplied natural resources. It was a place remade by industry, but not itself industrial.[46]

By contrast, this book explores some of the industries and other economic activities that were indigenous to California: hydraulic placer mining in the Sierra foothills, logging in the redwood forests, city-building in the Sacramento Valley, and large-scale ranching in the extreme southern and northeastern corners of the state. The study certainly could have encompassed more: lode mining and stamp mills, silver mining across the border in Nevada, logging in the Sierra, fishing, sheep raising, and wheat farming–indeed, the analysis might have been extended to include oil exploration in early-twentieth-century California. Rather, this book focuses on those transformations of nature that emerged early and proved to be portable to other parts of the West. Hydraulic mining, urban development, and industrial logging and ranching proved successful enough endeavors that they inspired the further exploitation of nature both within and outside the state.

Whether industrial demands for resources were local or extralocal, nowhere in North America was industry free simply to draw upon whatever resources it desired. The environment's supplies of minerals, timber, and grass were not just passive resources to be consumed–wisely or wastefully– by American industry. In nineteenth-century California, miners, ranchers, lumberers, and city builders had to adapt themselves to a capricious environment capable of extensive and maddeningly frequent upheaval. Flood, disease, and drought repeatedly forced California industrialists and urban residents to alter their plans to exploit the state's resources.

The western environment was not simply a storehouse of industrial resources. Environments are composed of numerous and complex interconnections. In the natural world, everything–soil, air, water, plants, and animals—is linked through dynamic cycles of chemicals and energy. The naturalist John Muir captured this interconnectivity when, in 1911, he wrote, "When we try to pick out anything by itself, we find it hitched to everything else in the universe."[47]

As Californians sought to shape the environment to their advantage, they often found that their actions worked to their disadvantage: hydraulic mining, for instance, polluted the rivers flowing from the Sierra to the Central Valley with debris. The accumulation of debris raised riverbeds, leading to floods which caused millions of dollars of damage to farmers and city dwellers. Certainly, nineteenth-century Californians understood the environment less well than a twenty-first-century ecologist. Nonetheless, the state's industrialists were not unaware of these problems. There was copious evidence in the nineteenth century that the wealth that mining companies, to say nothing of loggers and ranchers, extracted from the California environment took an enormous ecological toll. Certainly many Californians, beginning with Eagle, Borthwick, and Sawyer in the 1850s, were plainly aware of the costs.

Yet the profits produced by the exploitation of gold and other resources in California overrode such concerns in the 1850s and 1860s. Only gradually in the 1870s and 1880s did an alliance of farmers, railroads, and nascent preservationists emerge to contest the most destructive effects of mining and logging. At the same time that these Californians voiced their doubts over the benefits of industrial resource use, the California example was encouraging further trials of the industrial exploitation of nature in the West: in the gold mines of Colorado, Idaho, Montana, South Dakota, and Alaska; in the silver mines of Nevada and Arizona; in the timberlands of the Pacific Northwest; and in the rangelands of the Great Plains. The technology of hydraulic mining led directly to the creation of hydraulic systems for irrigation, power, and municipal water in the West.[48] These spasms of industrial exploitation provided the "boom and bust" pattern of economic development that has characterized the economic history of the West.[49] Rather than the exception to western history that Turner, Webb, and other western historians have thought nineteenth-century California to be, California during and after the gold rush exemplified the industrializing West. In short, in their exploitation of natural resources, California and the West exemplified industrializing America.

PART I

THE NATURE OF INDUSTRY

In a 1938 essay on environmental degradation in North America, the geographer Carl Sauer wrote that Americans "had not yet learned the difference between yield and loot."[1] Sauer's perspective profoundly influenced the emergence, decades later, of the new subfield of environmental history.[2] Indeed, in his 1983 study of colonial New England, one of the seminal works of environmental history, the historian William Cronon endorsed Sauer's view in his description of the colonists' exploitation of New England's timber, furs, and fish.[3] That characterization has persisted through most scholarly and popular histories of the capitalist consumption of natural resources in North America before 1900. In more recent years, some such characterizations have become more pronounced, depicting American settlers, loggers, fishers, miners, and particularly hunters as willfully, at times gleefully destructive of nature. Like Vandals or Visigoths, they are described as ravaging the North American environment, seemingly more interested in laying waste to nature than in the profit they might gain from the extraction of commodities.[4]

Yet were such spasms of violence against nature typical of North American resource exploitation? Capitalism in nineteenth-century North America was not merely a license to plunder. Rather, what distinguished the culture of capitalism, particularly before 1900, from other forms of economic organization was its avoidance, even repugnance, for waste, and its tendency toward abstemious reinvestment. As an economic system, nineteenth-century capitalism, even in its relationship with the nonhuman natural environment, tended toward systemization. Despite the popular image of the California gold rush as a mad scramble for treasure, investors in mining and logging companies sought the regular flow of profits from nature. In other words, most nineteenth-century North American capitalists engaged in the exploitation of natural resources were not like Herman Melville's Captain Ahab, single-mindedly bent on the vengeful destruction of a particular whale, but rather like Ahab's first mate, Starbuck, who efficiently slaughtered whales for his livelihood.

In an economy in which capital and labor were scarce and expensive, Californians turned their efforts at systemization on the environment. Such economic systemization took little account of nature's intricate ecological interconnections. Pure capitalism sees nature as a collection of commodities—and there was no purer capitalism than that brought to California in the 1850s by gold-hungry argonauts: James Beith, a Scottish immigrant, wrote in 1857, "If the Gates of Hell were hinged with Gold a Yankee would go there and take them."[5] Extracting those commodities required planning, investment, and order, including technological innovation and favorable legislation, among other things. Yet the commodification of nature does not by itself explain the systematic exploitation of California's natural resources. To understand the intensity of resource extraction in California one must take into account the place of natural resources in the nineteenth-century economy as a whole. Resources were part of a broader economy that included relatively expensive labor and capital. In short, the system nineteenth-century California investors constructed exploited cheap resources to subsidize the development of California's industrial economy.

The first step in this development was the imposition of economic order upon the dynamic environment. Until the late 1850s, investors avoided gold mining in California, wary of the expense and volatility of labor-intensive panning for gold in the river valleys of the Sierra Nevada. To attract investment, mining companies constructed a parallel hydraulic system to the Sierra foothills' unpredictable rivers, diverting snowmelt into ditches and reservoirs. They piped the water from those reservoirs into hydraulic water cannons that washed auriferous gravel into flumes that collected the gold.

Like mining, logging required technological innovation to tame the old-growth redwood forests and attract capital. Steam technology, in the form of engines to haul and saw logs and railroads to transport them, revolutionized the California lumber industry. In the wake of these technological innovations, investors poured in additional funds. Likewise, California city builders ordered the land by laying regular grids of city lots upon riverbanks, transforming forests and prairies into valuable commercial and residential properties. To protect their investments from flooding—a prospect made more likely by logging and the advent of hydraulic gold-mining technology upriver—city builders built levees, dams, and canals.

Altogether, in mining, logging, and urban development, the intervention of technology in the form of steam and hydraulic engineering stabilized and ordered a dynamic nature. Once the environments had been pacified—or once investors thought they had been—further investment capital streamed into these enterprises.

Yet the forest, valley, and river environments transformed by industrial technology in the mid-nineteenth century were not so readily pacified. The dynamic and unpredictable environments possessed a complex ecological order of their own. When Californians felled trees and dammed rivers, ecological changes rippled through the interconnected environments. The environmental historian Arthur McEvoy has put the matter cogently, by turning the language of commodification on its head. "Nature is a very careful accountant," McEvoy wrote in 1986. "Every change in one part of an ecosystem sooner or later has some effect, however minute, on every other part."[6] Or, as Melville put it in *Moby-Dick*, "It's a mutual, joint-stock world." Nineteenth-century industrialism ultimately affected every part of California's environments.

1

The Alchemy of Hydraulic Mining:
Technology, Law, and
Resource-Intensive Industrialization

B etween 1849 and 1858, California produced over $550 million in gold. This mineral wealth drew tens of thousands of prospectors: in 1848, the non-Indian population of California was a mere 14,000; by 1860, the new state had a non-Indian population of 380,000. Yet despite the booming economy, many argonauts had slipped into poverty by the late 1850s. According to one estimate, a miner's average earnings for a day's work fell from $20 in 1848 to a mere $3 by 1856.[1] The latter figure represents only the wages of those who earned enough in the gold country to remain there. Many earned far less; these disappointed prospectors drifted into other sectors of the economy. One such failed prospector, Sullivan Osborne, lamented in 1857 that after six years in California he "lived and fared like a dog." He recorded in his diary that in 1851 he had been "young full of high hopes and bright anticipations of the future." Those dreams, however, "have long since perished and with them every fine ambition [and] all I've thought or wished to be."[2]

Like many emigrants to California, Osborne had embarked for the Far West believing that gold was a free good easily available in nature, obtained by independent laborers and simple means. Within a few years of the discovery of gold on the American River, however, labor-intensive means of exploiting readily accessible deposits known as placers—panning, rockers, and makeshift dams to divert rivers and dig at the streambed—had given way to hydraulic mining.[3] Using this technology, in which high-pressure water cannons washed hillsides into sluices constructed to trap gold but let soil and gravel wash away, California continued to mine large quantities of gold after

1858: between 1859 and 1874, the state produced $400 million in gold. In these later years, even fewer independent prospectors took part in the exploitation of California's mineral wealth than in the 1850s. One observer, John Kincade, wrote in 1871, "Mining is no longer generally prosecuted by those having a will to work, but is conducted by the few having capital to invest. All that class of mining that was easily discovered and worked has passed away."[4]

The emergence of hydraulic mining and the decline of independent prospectors were not coincidental. Hydraulic mining was a relatively old and simple technology; the Romans had employed it in Iberia. Yet it was not for its simplicity that hydraulic mining emerged in California. However accessible the technology, constructing a hydraulic mining system—dams, reservoirs, distributing flumes and aqueducts, pipes and nozzles, tunnels, and sluices—was a massive undertaking that required the outlay of significant amounts of capital, a scarce commodity in the nineteenth-century West. For investors, the benefits of hydraulic mining justified its initial costs for two primary reasons. First, the investment in the technology of hydraulic mining reduced the high costs of labor in the gold country. Hydraulic mines initiated the transformation of the gold country from a locale dominated by independent prospectors to an industrial place characterized by wage laborers. The key to this transition was the replacement of *tools* such as pans, picks, and shovels, which were owned and used by independent laborers, with the *machines* of hydraulic mining, which were owned and controlled by investors.[5]

Second, the hydraulic system extended a measure of human control over the dynamic hydrology of the California gold country. The effort to impose control over the nonhuman natural environment is a hallmark of large technological systems.[6] The unpredictable environment—floods one season, drought the next—made the use of water to wash gold-bearing gravel unreliable. Investors were wary of committing capital to California placer mining until the industry had tamed the volatile environment. By attracting capital investment as well as reducing labor costs, hydraulic mining technology compensated for chronic shortages of capital and high costs of labor—the two most expensive factors of production in nineteenth-century America.

The historian Richard White has analyzed the intersection of nature, technology, labor, and culture in his study of the Columbia River. White argued that nineteenth-century Americans used technology not to change nature and forms of labor but to realize them "in a new form." He grounded his argument largely in a reading of the New England transcendentalist Ralph Waldo Emerson, who "reconciled" a spiritual nature with a productive capitalism. In their approach to nature and capitalism, White wrote, "Americans were Emersonians." On an intellectual level, this may have been true, although other historians, such as John Kasson, have suggested that Emerson's view of machines and nature was more ambivalent. In either case, hydraulic mining engineers in California certainly did not understate the transformative power of their technology: for them, it radically changed the economic and natural environments, taming nature and laborers alike and thus making placer mining an attractive investment.[7] Industrial technology was for them a sign of economic power, much as European nations used technology to impose power on their colonial possessions in Africa and Asia.[8]

While hydraulic mining had substantial benefits for investors, it had significant environmental costs. The sluices flushed tailings into the streams that flowed out of the Sierra. By the mid-1860s, debris from hydraulic gold mining had fouled and flooded rivers that drained into the Sacramento River, and ultimately into San Francisco Bay, destroying both fish and farmland. Hydraulic mines used large amounts of mercury, a toxic mineral mined and processed near San Jose, as an amalgam in their sluices. Much of this mercury also found its way into the riverine environment. In short, as Californians transformed the environment in the pursuit of wealth, they created costly environmental problems. Yet the legal environment that made natural resources available cheaply also protected industry's right to dispose of wastes in public waterways—at least until a coalition of opposing agrarian and industrial interests formed to challenge the hydraulic mines in the 1880s. By that time, however, much of the environment of the gold country—its hydrology, its ecology, and its very geology—had been irrevocably altered. California had become an industrial place.

The mercury and gold deposits of California were the products of millions of years of geological change. The Sierra Nevada, a 400-mile mountain chain rising to nearly 14,500 feet, extending from the Mojave Desert in the south to the Cascade Range in the north, owes its origin to the convergence of tectonic plates, the continental- and oceanic-sized pieces forming the outer layer of the earth. Tectonic plates are not fixed in place; they slowly drift atop a more viscous layer below. The Sierra began to form 200 million years ago as the westward-drifting North American plate collided with the Pacific plate. As the two plates abutted, the ocean floor of the Pacific plate squeezed beneath the North American plate at an oblique angle, in a process geologists call subduction. The intense pressure of the subduction created heat sufficient to form magma, or molten rock. The magma eventually cooled to become an enormous block of granite called a batholith. Succeeding pulses of magma intruded into the batholith, causing it to rise.[9]

Beginning ten to twelve million years ago, and particularly in the last three million years, the Sierra batholith has lifted up rapidly. In 1872, an earthquake in the Owens Valley raised the eastern front of the Sierra by twenty-five feet. To borrow an analogy from the geologists Edward Tarbuck and Frederick Lutgens, the batholith acted like a heavy but buoyant log floating high in the water in isostatic balance with the mass below it.[10]

The magma that became the granite of the Sierra forced to the surface hot water containing gold in solution. The presence of gold in solution is not itself remarkable: many rocks and even seawater contain minute amounts of gold. What was notable was that in California the silica solution settled in fissures in the granite to form gold-bearing quartz veins. Here it would have remained, largely inaccessible, were it not for millions of years of fluvial erosion. In the first phase of erosion, occurring between forty and sixty million years ago, long before uplift, broad rivers flowed across the hills that preceded the Sierra, eroding the quartz veins and disbursing the gold along gravel riverbeds. Subsequently, volcanic activity over tens of millions of years buried these ancient riverbeds in lava and ash. In the second phase, after uplift, mountain streams on the western slope of the Sierra eroded the sedimentary and volcanic accretions that had covered the gravel deposits. When argonauts arrived in California in 1849, therefore, this second phase of erosion had left much gold relatively accessible. In 1849, in certain places in the streambeds of the Feather, Yuba, American, Mokelumne, Stanislaus, Tuolumne, and Merced rivers, flakes and nuggets of gold were visible to the naked eye.[11]

The riverine environments of the western slope of the Sierra were the ecological centers of the gold country. The riverlands were unique environments in the otherwise dry climate of the foothills and Central Valley. In contrast to the coniferous forests of the mountains and the grasses of the valley, the riverlands supported dense forests of cottonwoods, willows, Oregon ash, California black walnut, oaks, sycamores, and alder on the natural levees created by centuries of sedimentary deposits. These types of trees, with bright green, large leaves, are rare in the dry region west of the Rocky Mountains, an area without native elms, beeches, or hickories.[12]

The geologist Jeffrey Mount has called the rivers of California products of a contest between the mountains and the erosive effects of the oxygen- and water-rich atmosphere. Water flowing in the rivers begins as moisture in air currents flowing eastward from the Pacific, that is until they meet the western slopes of the California Coast Range. The coastal mountains cast a "rain shadow" over the low-lying Central Valley, causing much of the region to receive less than twenty inches of annual precipitation. Moisture-bearing air currents that are high enough pass over the Coast Range and encounter the higher elevations of the Sierra. Precipitation there, however, is uneven: 50 percent of upper Sierra annual precipitation falls as snow between January and March. Less than 3 percent of annual precipitation falls during the summer. As a consequence, the flow of water in the streams on the western slope of the Sierras is torrential in the spring, as winter snow melts, but a comparative trickle in the summer.[13]

River flow alternately impeded and permitted miners' search for gold. High water in the spring prevented miners from scouring the auriferous gravel of the riverbeds for treasure. In the summer, when the streams had receded, companies of miners sought to dam or divert streams to search the riverbeds for dust, flakes, and nuggets. In a letter home in 1850, Joseph Pownall described this backbreakingly labor-intensive process:

> You have come to the conclusion it may be that we can pick up a chunk of gold whenever we choose on the surface anywhere. This is a gross mistake. Imagine to yourself a stream between two mountains full of rocks and trees and stones and grass. . . . What is there to be done? Why you have to strike for the rocky bottom or ledge on which the stream runs and on which the gold is deposited . . . which often requires a tremendous deal of extremely laborious work. Picture to yourself your humble servant pulling at one end of a pump endeavoring to keep a hole free while some 3 or 4 companions are at work in it.[14]

Despite their labors, dams and ditches collapsed frequently, forcing miners to begin their work again. Maddeningly, if too much water obstructed the miners' access to gold, so did too little. Miners relied on flowing water to wash gravel through long wooden sluices designed to separate gold from lighter soil and gravel; low water made it impossible for miners to wash their gold.[15]

The unpredictability of the river valley environment impeded not only the search for gold but the search for outside capital investment to support mining in California. One of the ironies of gold rush California was that, despite producing roughly one-third of the world's gold in the 1850s, far from being awash in capital, the state was chronically short of it. Once the most obvious and accessible gold deposits had been exhausted, few investors from outside the state were willing to commit capital to the speculative venture of California placer mining.[16] Indeed, because so many goods were imported, bullion flowed out of California in the 1850s; Californians relied on a currency of gold dust, nuggets, and foreign coins. In 1854 much of the California economy operated on credit, and in early 1855 several California banks closed.[17] The investment climate worsened at the end of the decade, when the discovery of silver deposits in Nevada siphoned off most of the available capital.[18]

To make up for this shortfall, California, like most of industrializing America, looked to British investors, who underwrote much of the industrialization of North America and Western Europe.[19] Most British investors regarded California placer mining as too risky a venture to commit to, however. In the first few years after the discovery of gold, a handful of investment companies formed in London to raise capital for California gold mining. Most of these companies did little more than formally incorporate, however, and none stayed in existence longer than two years.[20]

So in the early and mid-1850s, when miners began to build reservoirs and canals to control the unpredictable river flow of California, they sought not only to regularize the environment and thus gain easier access to placer deposits, but to attract capital investment by imposing predictability on the rivers.

Encountering the same natural obstacles as placer mining, the construction of reservoirs and ditches proceeded fitfully. In December 1851, A. H. Gilmore wrote to his brother in Indiana of the impressive scale and potential profit of the Mokelumne Hill ditch: capitalized at $175,000, the ditch was eighteen miles long, including at one point a 1,000-foot-long aqueduct spanning a ravine seventy-two feet deep. The work was not completed, however. "Our canalling operations are not coming on as well as was anticipated, the rainy season having set in rather early [*sic*] than usual. All operations on the works have necessarily been suspended until next spring, so there will be no profit reaped from this source for the time being."[21]

Once completed, early reservoirs and ditches were shoddy and unreliable. A reservoir near the settlement of Independence Hill in Placer County broke in January 1855, causing water to sweep down the ravine, killing three people. Eventually, with the help of capital investments from within the state, the reservoirs became more stable. Pownall, seeing the centrality of the control of water to mining operations and perhaps weary of laboring in the mines, joined a group of investors that eventually called itself the Tuolumne County Water Company. Beginning in 1853, the company constructed a system of reservoirs and ditches on the Stanislaus River. By June 1855 it had built four large dams at a cost of $140,000. The largest reservoir had a capacity of nearly 200,000 cubic feet. A system of distributing ditches supplied water—for a fee, of course—to mining camps in the area. A typical agreement with a miner in California was for 10 percent of the net proceeds arising from the use of the company's water.[22]

Amos Parmalee Catlin, a lawyer from Duchess County, New York, who had migrated to Sacramento in 1849, had still less desire than Pownall to labor in the diggings himself. In December 1851 he and his partners posted a claim on the South Fork of the American River: "Notice is hereby given that a company under the name of Natoma Water Company has been formed for the purpose of taking water by means of a canal from the south fork of the American River and conveying it thence on the southerly side of said South Fork down to the placers in the vicinity of Mormon Island." The company's dam washed out after one year, but the reconstructed dam succeeded in siphoning water from the South Fork of the American River just above Salmon Falls into a ditch running parallel to the river's southern bank. The ditch delivered water to such mining camps as Rhodes Diggings, Prairie Diggings, and Willow Springs Diggings, proving so profitable that in 1853 Catlin and his partners were able to reorganize the company with a capital stock of $600,000.[23]

In succeeding years, hydraulic systems, constructed in part by immigrant Chinese laborers, became more extensive.[24] By the 1870s the Natoma Water

Placer flumes (*Pictoral Union*, 1855)

Company's ditches totaled forty miles.[25] By 1883 the largest reservoirs in California covered hundreds of acres; the largest dams were between eighty and ninety feet high. Some, however, were no sturdier than those constructed in the early 1850s. In 1876, Hamilton Smith, Jr., one of the leading hydraulic engineers in California, warned that the English Dam, one of the largest dams in the state, was near collapse.[26] Indeed, the dam washed out in 1883.

However unstable, hydraulic systems were vast. By 1876 the Eureka Lake and Yuba Canal Company had spent $1,074,242 building its extensive system of reservoirs and ditches; its reservoirs had a capacity of 1.13 billion cubic feet. The South Yuba Hydraulic Mining Company impounded 1.8 billion cubic feet of water; the North Bloomfield Company and the El Dorado Deep Gravel Mining Company each stored just over one billion cubic feet. Altogether, California hydraulic mining companies impounded 7.6 billion cubic feet of water in 1883, an amount equal to about 50 percent of the maximum capacity of the later, infamous Hetch Hetchy Reservoir in Yosemite National Park. Ditch construction cost between $4,000 and $17,000 per mile.[27] In 1883, six thousand miles of ditches, constructed at a cost of $15 million, supplied water to the hydraulic mines.[28]

In short, hydraulic mining companies constructed an extensive system of reservoirs and ditches that paralleled the mountain lakes and streams of the Sierra, channeling water in regular, manageable amounts directly to the goldfields, where miners used it to wash gravel.

California gold mining was not primarily the work of independent prospectors; the era of successful panning lasted only a few seasons, as unfortunates such as Sullivan Osborne discovered to their dismay. Over the long term, gold mining became a technology-driven enterprise sustained by the systematic control of water. By the twentieth century, of course, throughout the semiarid West, irrigation and hydropower came to dominate agriculture and industry.[29] This hydraulic West, one of the dominant themes of twentieth-century western history, had its origins not in the irrigation campaigns of the early twentieth century but in the industrial landscape of the nineteenth-century California gold country.

The emergence of the state's extensive hydraulic system required an amenable legal environment. Through the 1850s and early 1860s, California judges were eager to extend the protection of the law to hydraulic miners. To do so, they had to transform a legal system initially constructed to protect the rights of independent prospectors. California's earliest mining laws were improvised by prospectors themselves, borrowing, perhaps, from the tradition of the so-called claim clubs of the Upper Midwest. In 1849, riverbank prospectors could stake out claims to the minerals below the earth without holding title to the land; most of the land in question belonged to the federal government. Prospectors' claims were bounded, of course, by certain restrictions. They were both limited in extent (from fifteen to one thousand square feet, depending on the locality) and number (usually no more than one). If unworked, a prospector's claim lapsed entirely. The regulations thus embraced and supported the mid-nineteenth-century notion of free labor: each prospector was entitled to a single claim of limited extent so long as he labored at it.[30]

So important was mining to California's economy in the 1850s that state law raised the rights of independent miners above those of agriculturalists. Yet here, too, California law aimed to distribute the riches of the gold country among ordinary free laborers. With few exceptions, prospectors had the right to enter public lands settled by farmers or ranchers, stake out a claim to the minerals below the surface, and search for gold. In permitting miners "to go upon public lands occupied by others," the state, according to one jurist, "has legalized what would otherwise be called a trespass." Without such an extraordinary right, California judges feared "the entire gold region might have been enclosed in large tracts, under the pretense of agriculture and grazing and eventually, what would have sufficed as a rich bounty to many thousands, would be reduced to the proprietorship of a few."[31]

As early as January 1855, when hydraulic mining had just begun to take hold, the California Supreme Court extended to hydraulic miners the same rights enjoyed by prospectors, ruling "that however much the policy of the State, as indicated by her legislation, has conferred the privilege to work the mines, it has equally conferred the right to divert the streams from their natural channels." In effect, Californians such as Amos Catlin could establish a claim to the water of a river much as they could stake a claim to underground minerals. Hydraulic miners were bound only to respect the rights of prior appropriators of a river's water. In an October 1855 case, for instance, the California Supreme Court forced the Spring Creek Water and Mining Company to compensate the owner of a downstream lumber mill in the amount of $1,000. The mill, which had been established one year before the mining company began its diversion, had a right to the undisturbed flow of the river under the doctrine of prior appropriation, which declared "first in time, first in right" (*qui prior est in tempore, potior est in jure*). While in this particular case a mining company lost its suit, the ruling established that prior appropriators, who in many other cases were miners or mining companies that succeeded to rights first established by others, acquired a "*quasi* private proprietorship" to the use of a river.[32]

In several cases, California jurists eroded the ability of lawyers to categorize hydraulic miners' ditches, which frequently overflowed and flooded neighbors' lands, as nuisances. Such a categorization would have required the hydraulic mines' investors to compensate those injured by broken ditches. In January 1855 the California Supreme Court ruled that county courts had no jurisdiction over suits involving the abatement of nuisances. The ruling, which emerged from a lawsuit brought by a farmer whose lands had been flooded because of a broken ditch belonging to the Tuolumne County Water Company, prevented landowners from seeking the closest legal redress for their injuries.[33]

In 1858 the California Supreme Court overturned a District Court ruling that had awarded damages to plaintiffs whose lands had been flooded by another break in a Tuolumne County Water Company reservoir. In overturning the lower court's ruling, the state supreme court held that the lower court judge had erroneously instructed the jury to hold the water company to ideal standards of construction and safety. The judge had told the jury that "if they believe that the dam was improperly or inartificially constructed, or that the defendants could have constructed it in a better or more substantial manner as to prevent its breaking, then they are liable." Such standards, the court argued, imposed impossibly high burdens on water companies and hydraulic miners. Instead, they ruled that water companies were required only to construct their dams using the far weaker and more nebulous standard of "*ordinary* care and diligence." It was not a question, they decided, of what the company "could have done," but rather, "what discreet and prudent men should do."[34]

Later that same term, the state supreme court overturned another District Court ruling in a similar case against the St. Louis Independent Water Company, in which the company's flume had collapsed in a storm, flooding neighbors' lands. The judges of the California Supreme Court charged that the lower court judge had improperly instructed the jury to find the company liable unless it had built its flume to the standards of a "*very prudent* man" rather than merely the standards of "ordinarily prudent men."[35] Such rulings made it nearly impossible for injured parties to demonstrate a mining or water company's negligence.

The rulings friendly to hydraulic mining were extensions of a process of legal change that had started in the Northeast decades earlier. Judges shifted away from reliance upon the English common law, which largely protected agricultural uses of land and rivers and discouraged industrial development. They came to regard the law not as a body of immutable principles but as a social tool that could promote change. By the middle of the nineteenth century court decisions increasingly favored industrialists, reflecting industry's increasing economic weight. The Kentucky Supreme Court expressed the emerging judicial favor for industry in an 1839 ruling that reversed an injunction that had barred the Lexington and Ohio Railroad from running through the city of Louisville on the grounds that the railroad was a nuisance. "The onward spirit of the age must, to a reasonable extent, have its way. The law is made for the times, and will be made or modified by them," the court wrote.[36] California's legal transformation likewise paralleled the economic trans-

formation of the state: from independent prospectors to technologically sophisticated industries. Yet the legal change did not merely reflect the industrialization of mining. Rather, its relationship to economic change was
reciprocal. Broader legal privileges for water and mining companies not only
were the product of ecological and economic change, but also furthered those
changes.

Liberated by friendly state court rulings, a process that the legal historian
J. Willard Hurst has termed "the release of energy,"[37] hydraulic mines were
free to build reservoirs and ditches. Impounding water, in turn, was a necessary precondition for the development of the single most important technology in the exploitation of placer deposits: the machinery of hydraulic mining.
As early as 1852, the engineer Edward Mattison used pressurized water in a
canvas hose to flush gravel into a sluice. By 1853, hydraulic miners had begun
making improvements on Mattison's innovation. Canvas hoses lasted only a
few months. Miners tried leather and rubber before the development of the
"crinoline hose" in the early 1860s, which wrapped the fabric of the hose with

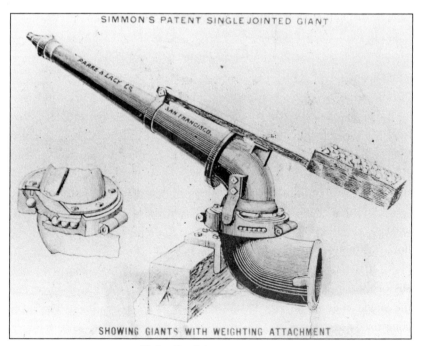

Hydraulic mining water cannon

iron bands.[38] The crinoline hose eventually ceded its place to sheet iron hoses, just as, by the mid-1860s, miners replaced the simple nozzle with the water cannon, called the monitor.

The monitors emitted water at tremendous speed. At the North Bloomfield mine, which by the mid-1870s was the largest in California, water shot from the monitor at a speed of 150 feet per second, or over 100 miles per hour.[39] By the early 1880s, large hydraulic mines kept the monitors running and sluices flowing day and night, using waterpower to generate electricity that flooded the mines with light.[40] Every week or two, the miners briefly stopped the flow of water to "clean up" the sluices, in other words to extract the gold. In the early 1860s in Nevada County, the center of the hydraulic mining country, cleanups every eight or ten days yielded from $1,000 to $3,000 worth of gold.[41]

The emergence of hydraulic mining technology furthered the commodification of water as an essential component in the production of gold. One hydraulic mine's annual report to its stockholders put the matter succinctly: "The great agent in this is water, and the value of mining property . . . depends on the present or prospective water supply."[42] By 1878, the authors of a prospectus inviting investment in the Excelsior Water and Mining Company could argue that "the cheapness and effectiveness of hydraulic power . . . render the calculation of the results of hydraulic mining susceptible to almost absolute certainty."[43] In short, the regularization of water flow regularized the production of gold. The unpredictability of placer mining that had discouraged investment in the mid-1850s had been vanquished.

By the late 1850s, gold mining was no longer a matter of individual fortitude or luck. Capital and industrial technology had transformed the search for gold into a regular extraction of mineral wealth. Predictable profits, in turn, attracted greater amounts of capital. While British investment in California mining had been minimal in the 1850s, it mushroomed in the late 1860s and early 1870s. Between 1870 and 1873, British investors poured over £4 million into California placer mining.[44]

Gold mining dominated the California economy. The manufacturing census of 1860 reveals a geography of capital in which gold production was the single most important determinant of industrial wealth. Gold mining comprised nearly 60 percent of manufacturing establishments in California, employed 56 percent of California's manufacturing workforce, and had drawn to itself 40 percent of the capital invested in California manufacturing. Yet the mining industry was not dispersed evenly throughout the state: of the forty counties in California in 1860, the ten wealthiest, measured in terms of the value of their manufacturing production, contained 92 percent of the gold-mining establishments in the state, 93 percent of the capital invested in gold mining, and 91 percent of gold-mining employees.[45]

Despite the dominance of gold, hydraulic mining technology helped to spur other industrial production in California, particularly iron foundries to produce pipes, nozzles, and monitors. California manufacturing excluding gold mining rose from a value of $3.8 million in 1850 to $116 million in 1880. During that same period the number of ironworking establishments rose from 42 to 994; the value of iron products rose from $1.1 million to $10.8 million.[46] Iron ore within California came primarily from the Sierra Iron and Mining Company, which controlled two thousand acres of land containing iron ore deposits in Plumas and Sierra counties on the California-Nevada border. Coal to fire forges came from the Mount Diablo mines in Contra Costa County, on the east side of San Francisco Bay. Mount Diablo coal was generally of poor quality, but the various mining companies working the deposits produced 50,000 tons in 1864, 100,000 in 1867, and over 170,000 in 1872.[47]

Sacramento, located midway between the coal mines of Contra Costa and the iron ore deposits of the Sierra, was a notable example of a city where the gold industry spurred industrialization. Sacramento's first iron foundry opened in 1850. By 1853, the largest, Bowstead and Co., consumed 600,000 pounds of iron ore annually. By the 1880s the foundry's consumption of ore had doubled.[48] Other leading manufacturers of iron piping for the hydraulic mines were located between Sacramento and the gold country in Nevada City and Dutch Flat.[49] Altogether, by 1860, Sacramento County contained 221 factories that employed over seven hundred workers. That year, the county produced over $2.2 million of manufacturing products, an amount exceeded only by the larger industrial center of San Francisco and the gold-producing counties of Nevada and Tuolumne. By 1870, the number of manufacturing employees in Sacramento was over one thousand and the value of Sacramento's products was nearly $4 million—figures second only to San Francisco. Indeed, throughout the nineteenth century, Sacramento County, with its close ties to the gold-mining industry, remained among the largest industrial centers in California, consistently among the leaders in the number of manufacturing establishments, manufacturing employees, and the value of manufacturing products.[50]

These factories were the sources of considerable urban pollution. In addition to slag, the solid waste that was produced as a by-product of the iron-making process, iron foundries emitted poisonous clouds of heavy metals. When they burned coal to heat the iron ore, foundries emitted carbon particles, tars, hydrocarbons, carbon monoxide, methane, and sulfur dioxide. Employees and neighbors of the foundries were thus exposed to intensely polluted air. Sulfur dioxide and carbon particulates are leading contributors to tuberculosis and other respiratory illnesses because they damage the respiratory system and make it more liable to an active infection by *Mycobacterium tuberculosis* and other germs. Gases from foundries also contain carcinogens.[51] Considerable amounts of lead escaped from the furnaces of nineteenth-century lead smelters; in the twentieth century, pollution from lead smelting was found to cause neurological damage and gastrointestinal cancer.

Industrial pollution helped make Sacramento among the unhealthiest places in the state. In the early 1870s, Sacramento's death rate was just over 20 per thousand, well over the state average of 17 deaths per thousand for its twenty-six largest cities.[52] The findings of public health officials, which recorded the causes of death in urban California, pointed to industrial pollution as the leading factor in urban mortality. Tuberculosis and other lung diseases caused over 60 percent of deaths in California in the early 1870s. Many of these deadly respiratory illnesses were likely the consequence of California's airborne industrial pollution from iron foundries and lead and silver smelters. By comparison, stomach and bowel diseases resulting from inadequate urban sanitation accounted for between 14 and 18 percent of deaths; malaria, the most common disease in the Central Valley, caused between 12 and 13 percent of deaths.[53]

While industrial pollution shortened some laborers' lives, the technology of hydraulic mining reduced wages. Hydraulic mining was astonishingly successful in reducing the costs of labor. According to the *Marysville Herald* in 1854, hydraulic mining allowed one laborer to do the work of six.[54] John Kincade agreed in 1856, estimating that three laborers—one to direct the water cannon and two to run the sluice—accumulated as much gold as twenty workers with shovels. Likewise, in 1854 the *Sacramento Daily Union* marveled at both the transforming power and the minimal labor requirements of the Iowa Hill hydraulic mine. When the hoses were turned on the hillside, "it melts before them, and is carried away through the sluices with almost as much rapidity as if it were a bank of snow." The sluices, according to the *Daily Union*, were from five hundred to one thousand feet long: "Cobblestones and small boulders when thrown into them go tumbling and rumbling their entire length." The report concluded: "No such labor saving power has ever been introduced to assist the miner in his operations."[55]

An 1873 study of mining techniques calculated that handling a cubic yard of auriferous gravel cost $15.00 employing a pan, $3.75 with the rocker, $.75 with the long tom, and a mere $.15 with the hydraulic process. Reports of hydraulic mining companies invariably repeated these figures. Hydraulic mining effectively shifted the exploitation of placer deposits from a labor- to a technology-intensive endeavor. "Canvas towns" of independent prospectors, concluded John Kincade in 1856, "are now only to be read of."[56]

Despite the decline of the laboring population in the mining districts, the systematic control of water made possible the expansion of mining beyond the river valleys. While hydraulic mining remained centered in three counties—Placer, Nevada, and Sierra—that overlay the "Yuba Ridge," a spur of the Sierra containing particularly rich gold deposits, aqueducts allowed mining to transcend the valleys.[57] In 1856, Kincade wrote, "Five or six years ago mining was mostly confined to Rivers and Ravines. Now the surface of the country is being washed away."[58] By 1871 the North Bloomfield Gravel Mining Company had built forty-one miles of ditches to carry water from its reservoirs to its mines.[59] An auriferous deposit atop a plateau opposite Oroville, "known to be exceedingly rich," had been largely unexploited as late as 1858 because of the unavailability of sufficient water. The claimants to the Oroville goldfield resolved to rectify this deficiency, investing over $250,000 to construct an aqueduct made of iron pipes across a canyon 9,000 feet wide and 800 feet deep.[60] The ambitious scheme, which proved to be beyond the technological capacity of engineers in 1858, "startled even mining engineers of note," according to one observer. The two-mile-long aqueduct was not completed until 1870.[61]

In 1875, the Spanish Hill Hydraulic Mining Company took an alternative route to deliver water from their reservoir to their gold deposits: they bored a

500-foot tunnel through the crest of a hill.[62] Aqueducts and tunnels to carry water to the goldfields, according to a Marysville newspaper, the *California Daily Express*, "enable experienced miners to work to great advantage places that, a few years ago, were deemed relatively worthless."[63] The expense of tunnels and aqueducts was more than offset by their return. In 1873, for example, the Blue Point Gravel Company completed, after over three years of construction, a 2,270-foot-long tunnel at a cost of $146,000. The tunnel opened up a rich deposit of auriferous gravel. The company recouped the tunnel's expense in the first three months of hydraulic operations and anticipated a tenfold profit on the investment over three years.[64]

Given such prospects, by 1873 hydraulic mining attracted considerable investment.[65] In 1878, Hamilton Smith, Jr., a civil engineer who had worked since 1870 in the hydraulic mines, estimated that between $35 million and $50 million had been invested in the hydraulic mines throughout the state. According to Smith, the value of those mines in 1878 was $100 million. He further estimated that the hydraulic mines produced between $18 million and $19 million worth of gold annually.[66] Testifying before a committee of the California legislature that was considering a bill to force miners to limit their dumping of debris into the state's rivers, Smith was probably inclined to inflate his estimates of the mines' productivity. More objective calculations in 1878 estimated that hydraulic mining contributed between $10 million and $15 million annually to California's economy.[67] Whatever the exact figure, by the late 1870s hydraulic mining companies had transformed the volatile gold country, pressing its environment and its laborers into the systematic production of gold.

The wealth that hydraulic mining produced came at significant environmental cost. The changes that hydraulic mining wrought upon the environment were wide-ranging. The industry consumed large amounts of timber. Water cannons carved craters out of the Sierra foothills and flushed debris into streams, poisoning water supplies for people and livestock as well as destroying fish habitats. By the 1860s, hydraulic mining consumed one million pounds of mercury annually. The production of mercury near San Jose and its use in the Sierra diffused toxins into the California environment.

If, as the geologist Jeffrey Mount maintained, the rivers of the Sierra foothills are the results of a geologic contest between the mountains and the erosive ef-

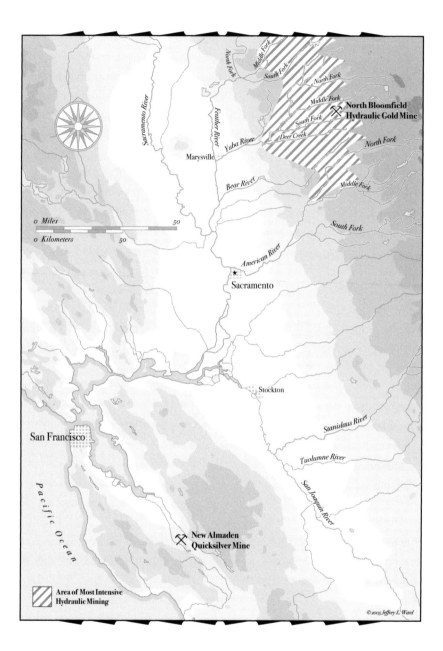

Sacramento River

North Fork

Middle Fork

South Fork

North Fork

Middle Fork

North Bloomfield
Hydraulic Gold Mine

Feather River

South Fork

Deer Creek

North Fork

Marysville

Yuba River

Bear River

Middle Fork

0 Miles   50

0 Kilometers   50

South Fork

American River

★
Sacramento

Stockton

Stanislaus River

San Francisco

Tuolumne River

San Joaquin River

Pacific Ocean

New Almaden
Quicksilver Mine

Area of Most Intensive
Hydraulic Mining

© 2005 Jeffrey L. Ward

fects of the water-rich atmosphere, then hydraulic mining tipped the balance of that contest decidedly in favor of erosion. At the mines, water cannons left the landscape blasted and worn. To reach deep deposits of gold, large mines first washed away the uppermost level of gravel, then sunk a shaft from 100 to 200 feet deep to the channel of gold. Miners then dug a nearly horizontal tunnel called an adit, graded slightly downward, from the bottom of the shaft to the bank of the nearest river. In the adit, which could be several hundred feet long, the miners constructed a plank sluice. For valuable mines, the adit was wide enough to accommodate two sluices side by side, so that miners could clean up one sluice while continuing to flush gravel through the other. If the ground could not be loosened by the power of the water cannons alone, the miners detonated several hundred kegs of blasting powder at the bottom of the shaft.[68]

The wilderness advocate John Muir observed that as a result of these labors in the gold country, "the hills have been cut and scalped and every gorge and gulch and broad valley have been fairly torn to pieces and disemboweled, expressing a fierce and desperate energy hard to understand."[69] Titus Fey Cronise was likewise horrified by the appearance of the mines. He wrote in 1868 in his survey of California's natural resources:

> By no other means does man so completely change the face of nature than by this process of hydraulic mining. Hills melt away and disappear under its influence. . . . The desolation that remains after the ground, thus washed, is abandoned, is remediless and appalling. The rounded surface of the bed rock, torn with picks and strewn with enormous boulders too large to be removed, shows here and there islands of the poorer gravel rising in vertical cliffs with red and blue stains, serving to mark the former levels, and filling the mind with astonishment at the changes, geologic in their nature and extent, which the hand of man has wrought.[70]

Hydraulic mines also consumed or destroyed large amounts of timber. The mines needed large supplies of wood for flumes and sluices. The extent of the miners' demand was indicated in 1852 in G. L. Gilley and S. D. Merchant's specifications to the Natoma Water Company for the size of the flume for their mine: 47,520 feet long, six feet wide, and three feet high. The completed flume cost the miners $197,500.[71]

North Bloomfield hydraulic mine

The demand continued once the flumes and sluices were constructed. Wooden blocks used to pave the sluices were replaced every few weeks. "The forest-timber, growing on the surface of a hydraulic mine, is, consequently, rapidly destroyed to supply blocks for riffling," according to a journalist in 1883. That same journalist also noted that the reservoirs that supplied the mines with water submerged whole forests. "In the construction of these mountain reservoirs no effort is made to remove the timber growing within the valley to be inundated. The great forest trees are left standing, and when the waters rise well up to their upper branches they soon wither and die."[72] According to the State Agricultural Society, by 1870 one-third of the "accessible timber of value" in the state was already gone.[73]

The environmental costs of hydraulic mining were not confined to the mines. Thousands of tons of debris—boulders, soil, sand, and gravel—traveled through the sluices to be deposited in the river valleys directly below the mines. Large clay boulders rolled through the sluices, carrying off significant amounts of gold.[74] One mining engineer, Rossiter Raymond, estimated in 1873 that hydraulic mines failed to capture 20 percent of their precious metals in the sluices.[75] Indeed, owing to the inefficiency of the sluices in capturing gold, the debris contained such large amounts of precious metal that enterprising engineers contracted to mine it. Debris prospectors included Thomas Edison, who formed a company to mine tailings in 1879.[76]

Edison and other debris prospectors had ample material with which to work. In 1928, at a time when the state of California briefly considered reviving hydraulic mining after banning it over forty years earlier, one observer calculated that the amount of debris deposited in the ravines of the Sierra between the mid-1850s and 1885 was 885 million cubic yards. That figure represents a volume over three and one-half times greater than that excavated for the Panama Canal. Of that amount, 648 million cubic yards, or 73 percent of the total, was deposited in the mountain or piedmont belts of just four rivers, the Yuba, Bear, American, and Feather.[77] An Auburn newspaper, the *Placer Herald*, reported in 1872 that eighty feet of debris had accumulated in parts of the Bear River. "Tall pine trees, formerly far above the stream, have been gradually engulfed season after season, until now only the top branches appear above the current," according to the report.[78] Observers attested to similar damage on the Yuba River. In 1878 the farmer W. H. Drum, who had settled on the Yuba in 1851, claimed that at certain points along the river, tailings had covered twenty-foot-tall telegraph poles so fully that only

Hydraulic mining reservoir. Note the submerged timber.

Hydraulic mine, Dutch flat

the top four to six feet remained above the surface.[79] Smaller streams were filled as completely. The Alturas Gold Mine filled the Slate Creek with forty feet of debris.[80]

While larger pieces of debris accumulated in the higher ravines, the current carried still more tailings in the form of smaller, lighter amounts of sand and soil farther downstream. The total amount of lighter debris was, according to one estimate, over one and one-half times the amount of the heavier tailings that lodged in the upper valleys.[81] The lighter debris filled river channels, transforming the swift, clear rivers flowing from the Sierra into slow, murky, broad effluents. One observer, A. T. Arrowsmith, testifying before a California legislative committee in 1878 on the effects of hydraulic mining, claimed that in 1851 the Bear River was between 150 and 200 feet wide and between 15 and 20 feet deep. However, enormous amounts of sediment from the mines—4.5 million cubic yards annually—had "obliterated" the river. "There is probably no channel of Bear River now," Arrowsmith testified, "the water just spreads itself." James H. Keyes, who settled on a farm along the Bear in 1856, agreed. Keyes described the Bear River in 1856 as "a clear, running stream, with well-defined banks." After 1860, however, the bed began to fill.

The sediment "has entirely obliterated the channel, running over the bottom-lands in every direction." J. H. Jewett, a Marysville banker, described the Yuba River of 1850 as "a bright, clear stream, with pebbly bottom." By 1878 the river had filled with twenty-five feet of sediment and the valley was "a perfect desert." Joseph Johnson, a civil engineer, testified that the channel of the Yuba was filled so completely with hydraulic mining sediment that the stream ran a mile away from its original course.[82]

The raised riverbeds of the Yuba, Bear, Feather, and American caused spring freshets to overtop the natural levees of the rivers, inundating riverine farmlands with a watery mixture of sand and gravel that farmers dubbed "slickens." The mixture was poisonous to both animals and soil. It was high in alkali and deficient in phosphorus and nitrogen; nothing would grow in it. Water carrying even the finest sediment from the hydraulic mines contained roughly 5 percent "earthy matter," according to an 1879 complainant, rendering the water unfit for irrigation or consumption by either people or animals.[83]

On the Yuba River, slickens covered one farmer's bottomlands with over eight feet of sediment. He estimated that twelve thousand acres of farmland between the mouth of the Yuba and the Sierra foothills had been similarly destroyed. A farmer on the Bear River described similar destruction for a ten-mile segment of the river below the Sierra. Altogether, farms along one hundred miles of rivers in the Sacramento Valley were significantly affected.[84] Many of the ruined farms had been among the most productive in the state. James Keyes estimated that farms along the Bear River, once valued at $60–$75 an acre, had declined in value to $15 per acre. H. M. Larue had farmed on the American River until 1870, when slickens covered the soil. He sold the farm for less than one-quarter of what he had paid for it.[85] A federal study in 1891 reported that over forty thousand acres of farmland on the Feather, Bear, and Yuba rivers, valued at $2,597,634, had been destroyed by slickens.[86]

In order to confine the waters of the spring freshets, farmers raised the levees. As new deposits of sediment accreted on the riverbeds, they raised the levees further. By 1878, stretches of the Bear River's bed were actually higher than the surrounding countryside. Only the walls of the levee kept the waters of the river from overflowing. Levees, however, were expensive. According to one estimate, the complete system of levees on the Sacramento and its tributaries cost over $2 million, nearly 80 percent of the value of the farmland destroyed by tailings. Levees created new problems. Water seeped through them, and, with nowhere to drain, pooled alongside them. Salts leached to the surface of the saturated soil, salinating the topsoil and rendering it unfit for cultivation.[87] Moreover, levees were liable to break. According to George Ohlyer, who settled on the Feather River in 1852, the levee along that river "breaks almost every time we have a first-class flood," a frequency of "every year or two."[88]

Debris covering the beds of the Sacramento and its tributaries destroyed the spawning grounds of millions of Pacific salmon. Salmon is an anadromous species (from the Greek *anadromos*, "running upward"), so called because it migrates from the ocean upriver to spawn. In the 1850s, the annual California salmon run was immense. According to one estimate, Indians of the Central Valley harvested nine million pounds of salmon, or roughly 650,000 fish, each year. The salmon were abundant because the streams of the Sierra provided an ideal spawning habitat. Salmon's reproductive success depended on the coarse gravel of the river bottoms in which to bury eggs as well as cold, clean water for the eggs to hatch.[89]

In the early years of the gold rush, those conditions persisted, and newspapers reported a great number of salmon in the Sacramento River and its tributaries during the fall runs.[90] As hydraulic mining sediment accreted in California rivers, however, it covered the gravel beds with tailings and muddied the water. As debris destroyed the spawning grounds of salmon and other species, their populations declined precipitously. The Yuba River, for example, was once "a swift and clear mountain torrent; it is now a turbid and not rapid stream," according to Charles Nordhoff in his 1872 California travelogue, *California for Health, Pleasure, and Residence.* "It once contained trout, but now I imagine a catfish would not die in it."[91] By 1872, the California Commissioners of Fisheries reported that salmon, once plentiful in the Feather, Yuba, and American rivers, had disappeared from those streams. In 1878 the commissioners reported that hydraulic mining debris had destroyed half of the salmon habitat in the state.[92]

Mining sediment poisoned the environment not only for salmon but for humans. By the mid-1870s, the water of the American and Sacramento rivers carried so much silt from the mines upstream that it was unfit to drink. Hydraulic mining companies sought to profit from the Central Valley cities' lack of clean drinking water. In 1873, the mining engineer Francis Bishop wrote to

John P. Clough, one of the owners of the Eureka Water Company, that "in consequence of the extensive mining" of "nearly all the tributaries of the Sacramento River," the river was filled "with fine particles of earth and it specially passes Sacramento City in a most affective condition. . . ." Indeed, for "three months of each year the river becomes turbid with silt." As Bishop noted, Sacramento was trying, albeit ineffectively, to purify its water supply by letting the river water sit in tanks to allow the sediment to settle. According to one observer, however, "even at its cleanest stage . . . six inches of mud are deposited monthly in the reservoir."[93] Bishop proposed that the owners of the Eureka Canal sell "pure water" to the city, from the same mountain reservoir that supplied the mines.[94]

Bishop's suggestion was not unheralded. In 1872, an engineer proposed to the Board of Supervisors of San Francisco that the city tap Lake Tahoe for its water supply—an idea that foreshadowed San Francisco's construction of the Hetch Hetchy Reservoir in Yosemite National Park and Los Angeles's appropriation of the water of Owens Valley.[95] By 1874 some residents of Sacramento were already supplied with water by a so-called sanitary water pipe. On the order of the State Board of Health, however, the use of the pipe, made of a composite containing lead, was discontinued when seventeen people who drew water from this source were found to be suffering from severe lead poisoning.[96]

Sediment poured all the way to the mouth of the Sacramento River and beyond. Steamboat pilots reported in 1878 that Suison Bay, at the mouth of the Sacramento, had accumulated so much sediment that the bottom showed at low tide. Richard Thompson, the secretary of the Navy, reported shoaling by the late 1870s at the naval base on Mare Island in San Pablo Bay.[97] Sediment discolored the water of San Francisco Bay so extensively that in the 1870s it was visible in the Golden Gate.[98]

While hydraulic mining brought the soil and minerals of the Sierra to the Pacific, the mining of quicksilver returned the minerals of the Coast Range to the gold country. The subduction of the Pacific tectonic plate beneath the North American plate created not only the Sierra Nevada but the California Coast Range, which extends four hundred miles along the Pacific shore. While the convergence of tectonic plates created both ranges, the Sierra and the Coast Range emerged because of very different geological processes and as a result are quite unalike. The larger Sierra, a magmatic batholith born of enormous pressure and high temperature, is composed primarily of granite.

The Coast Range, by contrast, is a formation known as a mélange. It was created as the Pacific plate, squeezing below the North American plate, folded its uppermost crust, containing a variety of minerals, against it. As the term "mélange" suggests, this process left the Coast Range with a diversity of mineral deposits.[99]

Among the minerals of the Coast Range were vast deposits of mercuric sulfide, a dark red ore that contains mercury. Euroamericans began to exploit the mercuric sulfide deposits of the Coast Range in 1845, when California was still a Mexican province. By the 1870s California had not only become a leading producer of gold, but mined one-third of the mercury in the world. Much of the mercury came from the New Almaden mine outside of San Jose in Santa Clara County. Smaller amounts came from Fresno and Napa.[100] The production figures of New Almaden's Quicksilver Mining Company from 1850 to 1885 show an average yearly production of over 1.7 million pounds. The New Almaden production site was an extensive industrial operation: four hundred buildings, six furnaces, a railroad from the furnaces to the mine, and nearly two thousand employees in 1865. Until the 1890s, mercury mining was the second-largest industry in California after gold production.[101]

Laborers at New Almaden, particularly those belowground, were largely Mexican-Americans. *Barateros* dug the dark red mercuric sulfide ore, called cinnabar; *tanateros* packed 200-pound loads of ore to the surface. The belowground work was dangerous. In February 1888 an underground explosion at New Almaden permanently blinded and crippled a miner, Marcelino Soto. A judge, ruling that such an accident "was one of the ordinary risks of the mining business," decided against Soto in his suit for damages.[102] Aboveground, where workers heated the cinnabar in furnaces to transform it into elemental mercury, what one observer called the "deplorable indifference to the health of the workmen" continued.[103] The odorless, colorless vapors escaping the furnace were highly toxic. According to William Wells, who visited New Almaden in 1863, the vapor from the chimneys "withers all green things around. Every tree on the mountain-side above the works is dead." Farther away, vegetation survived but was "shrunken and blanched." Cattle sickened if they grazed within a half-mile radius of the furnace. The furnace was likewise poisonous to the laborers at the mine. Employees worked at the furnace for only one week out of four. "Pale cadaverous faces and leaden eyes are the consequence of even these short spells," according to Wells. "To such a de-

New Almaden furnace. Vapor from the furnace has denuded the hill above it of vegetation.

gree is the air filled with the volatile poison," Wells concluded, "that gold coins and watches on the persons of those engaged about the furnaces become galvanized and turn white. In such an atmosphere, one would seem to inhale death with every respiration."[104]

Indeed, mercury vapor is quite poisonous. Between 75 and 85 percent of inhaled elemental mercury vapors are absorbed by the human body, and are rapidly distributed throughout. Short-term effects, likely familiar to the workers at the New Almaden furnace, range from tremors to fatigue to nausea and vomiting. In part because mercury easily transcends the blood-brain barrier, it is particularly toxic to the nervous system. Chronic nervous system effects include mental instability, personality changes, memory loss, and speech impairment.[105]

For the industrial laborers of the Coast Range, quicksilver production was debilitating, but for the hydraulic mining companies of the Sierra, the close availability of mercury was fortuitous. As the degradation of gold coins and watches by mercury vapors at New Almaden demonstrated, mercury's ability to amalgamate with gold allowed hydraulic miners to harvest greater amounts of gold from their sluices. Accordingly, the addition of copious amounts of quicksilver to the sluices quickly became an integral part of the hydraulic mining process. An 1885 treatise on hydraulic mining recommended that a "charge" of quicksilver consisting of three flasks, or 225 pounds, be put into the upper 200 to 300 feet of a sluice, with a further amount distributed farther down the sluice. The North Bloomfield mine put between fourteen and eighteen flasks, or between 1,050 and 1,350 pounds, of mercury into its main sluice every twelve days. The Blue Tent mine charged its sluice with two tons of quicksilver.[106] Miners recaptured some of the mercury but lost much of it. According to an 1869 estimate, the mines consumed over 14,400 flasks, or 1.1 million pounds, of mercury a year. An 1874 estimate put the yearly consumption at 19,000 flasks, or 1.4 million pounds.[107]

Cleanup crews could not recover all of the mercury-gold amalgam from the sluices. Much of it washed out of the sluices with the rest of the debris. The eighty feet of debris that the *Placer Herald* had reported in the Bear River in 1872 contained large amounts of both gold and mercury.[108] By 1881, some enterprising miners viewed the amalgam in the debris as a lucrative business opportunity. The Bear River Tunnel Company estimated that hydraulic miners lost between one and four flasks of mercury during large runs and that large hydraulic mines lost as much as twenty-five flasks or 1,875 pounds of mercury a year. Altogether, the company estimated that the canyons below the largest hydraulic mines contained twenty tons of mercury every mile. Each pound of mercury contained one dollar's worth of gold.[109]

Much of the mercury in the rivers downstream of the mines, together with mercury in vapors that returned to the earth's surface in rain and snow, was likely converted by bacterial microorganisms in rivers to methyl mercury, an organic compound. Methyl mercury moves readily through the food chain, from microorganisms, to the fish that consume them, to the larger fish that eat the smaller fish. As methyl mercury moves through the food chain, it concentrates at higher levels in the bodies of animals. This process, known as bioaccumulation or biomagnification, can result in predacious fish having concentrations of mercury 100,000 times higher than the water in which they swim. Human beings, when they consume such fish, absorb 100 percent of methyl mercury through the gastrointestinal tract. Methyl mercury poisoning produces the same ill effects as the inhalation of mercury vapors.[110]

By the early 1880s, hydraulic mining had transformed the river environments of the Sierra and the Sacramento Valley. Thirty years of hydraulic mining overturned the ecological order of these environments: it unearthed long-buried minerals; it washed away hilltops and flushed them to the bottom of San Francisco Bay; it raised riverbeds above the level of their banks. No less significant than the extent of these changes was their rapidity. Hydraulic mining left large mines as steeply eroded "badlands," not unlike the Badlands of South Dakota or Wyoming. The Badlands were created by a geologic process similar to hydraulic mining: as one geologist called it, the "cutting action" of water on a slope.[III] A process that in South Dakota took two million years was complete in California in a mere three decades.

Hydraulic mining had social as well as environmental costs. The industrialization of mining closed off opportunities for independent prospectors. Hydraulic mining diffused its pollution widely, endangering the health of Californians well downstream of the mines. In effect, the operators of hydraulic mines profited by extracting valuable commodities from nature while passing along the costs of extraction to less powerful members of the community in the form of industrial pollution. The transformation of nature to make possible the extraction of gold was extensive, invasive, and, when one considers the damages to riverlands, forests, fisheries, and human health, arguably as costly as the wealth extracted from the mines was valuable.

Nineteenth-century environmental history is often told as a story of the shortsighted plunder of natural resources. Hydraulic mining in California was, ironically, a legal and technological effort to impose order on the environment, to make the extraction of resources regular and predictable. In large part, the enormity of the transformation of the environment was the result of the larger economic, cultural, and ecological context of California industrialization. Faced with high costs of labor and a shortage of investment capital, California placer miners imposed the burdens of industrialization on the environment. Hydraulic mining in nineteenth-century California was emblematic of the industrialization of the nineteenth-century West in general. The effort to shift the burden of industrial development to the environment characterized not only the mining West but logging, industrial ranching, and "bonanza farming": not capital- or labor- but resource-intensive.

2

Banking on Sacramento: Urban Development, Flood Control, and Political Legitimization

━━◆━━

In 1849, Elisha Crosby staked out his claim to a fortune in California. Crosby was not a prospector, however, but a city builder. He and his two partners approached the cash-strapped Swiss-Mexican *empresario* Johann Sutter, who in 1838 had received a grant from the Mexican government of 48,000 acres in the Sacramento Valley. They purchased from him 1,800 acres on the east bank of the Sacramento River at its juncture with the Feather River. There, at what Crosby and his partners mistakenly thought to be the farthest point that steamboats could ascend the Sacramento River, they laid out the lots for a town that they named Vernon.[1]

Crosby and his partners were not the only city builders in the Central Valley. Farther south, Sutter's son John and his partners had begun to develop Sacramento City at the juncture of the Sacramento and American rivers on what John Sutter assumed was part of his father's grant. By the summer of 1850, the Sacramento City developers discovered that the elder Sutter's original grant had not included the lowlands where they had laid out Sacramento's lots. No one was aware of this oversight in 1849, however, as the developers of Sacramento, Vernon, and other towns scrambled to create a commercial center for the gold country.[2]

Before the discovery of gold, California's largest urban centers were little more than villages. Then as now, the most substantial settlements were on the coast—it was the discovery of gold that created the opportunity for substantial urban settlements in the interior. Like Vernon, which Crosby hoped would become a commercial capital of the gold country, the settlements of Mexican California served as collection points for natural resources. Most coastal towns served as ports and way stations for hunters who preyed on aquatic mammals. For example, when the whaling vessel upon which Charles Brown served docked at Yerba Buena, California, in 1829, the town—later San Francisco—"had no house on it. It was nothing but chaparral and scrub oak—rabbit, deer, wolves, and bear abounded—and also snakes." Between five and six thousand Indians lived at the nearby San Francisco mission; the missionaries sold their surplus of cattle, corn, and wheat to the Russian sea otter and seal hunters of the northern California coast.[3] Rus—or Fort Ross—the hunters' settlement north of Yerba Buena, had a population of only a few hundred. Yet even such a small settlement had a sizable impact on the environment: by midcentury, the Russians' Aleutian hunters had nearly exterminated the estimated 20,000 sea otters that once inhabited the waters of coastal California.[4]

When James Marshall, one of Johann Sutter's employees, discovered gold on the South Fork of the American River in January 1848, most of the California interior was without a trace of urban settlement. In 1852, Stockton city boosters described the Central Valley prior to 1833 as a "vast prairie" where "wild cattle, horses, elk, and antelope ranged in herds of thousands, in undisturbed tranquility."[5] Although the Central Valley was certainly less settled at midcentury than the coast, depicting it as an untouched wilderness before the gold rush was an exaggeration. The valley under Mexican rule, with a probable Indian population of 20,000, was hardly the "undisturbed" environment that the boosters imagined it to be. The feral cattle and horses of the valley were not native to the region. Rather, like some fortunate Indians, they had escaped from the Spanish missions on the coast. Together with a drought between 1828 and 1830, the livestock's overgrazing of Central Valley grasses initiated the transformation of the region's vegetation from native to exotic European species.[6]

Farther north, near the confluence of the Sacramento and American rivers, the Central Valley's closest approximation of an urban place was Sutter's seigneurial estate of New Helvetia, which had an Indian population of almost three thousand. New Helvetia caused significant changes to its environment. Sutter's Indian laborers simplified and domesticated the local environment by cultivating wheat and raising livestock; in 1841, Sutter possessed one thousand horses, one thousand sheep, and over two thousand cattle.[7]

Following the discovery of gold, Sutter's Indian laborers abandoned the fiefdom as prospectors swept over New Helvetia. By November 1850, Isaac

Owen, an itinerant Methodist minister, described Sutter's adobe fort as being in a "dilapidated state."[8] The collapse of Sutter's settlement opened the way for other sites to become the urban centers of the gold rush. Indeed, in mid-1849, Vernon "assumed quite a little importance as a trading point for the Feather River miner." By autumn, it had a population of over six hundred and seemed likely to become an urban center for the mining region. Yet Vernon's great natural advantage—its position at the meeting point of two major rivers, the Feather and the Sacramento—also doomed its chances. "When the winter rains came in," according to Crosby, "that whole country was flooded, and one vast sea of water surrounded the little Elevation where the town was situated."[9]

The next year, a competing town builder laid out the city of Marysville farther up the Feather River at its juncture with the Yuba. By the end of 1850, Marysville and Sacramento had emerged as the primary urban centers for the mines to the east. So complete was the triumph of Marysville and Sacramento that their residents cannibalized Vernon's abandoned buildings. Isaac Perkins, a Sacramento merchant, passed by the site of Vernon on his way to Marysville in 1852. He wrote, "The only living things I saw in the place was one man & a dog & tha ware leving as fast as legs could care them."[10] Within four years of its founding, Vernon had vanished.

Like the ill-fated Vernon, the cities that eventually emerged as the leading commercial centers of the Central Valley—Sacramento, Marysville, and Stockton—hardly existed as settlements as late as 1848. Like Crosby and his partners, the founders of Sacramento, Marysville, and Stockton imagined that their cities would become centers of commerce for the gold-mining territory of the foothills. The imperative of trade dictated their selection of town sites. They chose places at the confluence of major rivers: Sacramento at the meeting of the American and Sacramento rivers; Marysville at the confluence of the Feather and Yuba rivers; and Stockton near the point where the Calaveras joins the San Joaquin. At these places, merchants and miners disembarked from their watercraft and set out overland for the gold country.[11]

To contemporaries, nature, in the Sacramento–San Joaquin river system, seemed to provide the routes to commercial wealth. "Looking at a map of California," J. D. Borthwick observed in 1857, "the Sacramento river running parallel with the mines, the San Joaquin joining it from the southward and eastward, and the Feather river continuing a northward course from the

Sacramento—all of them being navigable—present the natural means of communication between San Francisco and the 'mines.'" In accordance with this geocommercial logic, Sacramento, Marysville, and Stockton "sprang up," each as a "depôt" for the mines in its vicinity, "with roads radiating from it across the plains to the various settlements in the mountains."[12] The three cities thus each created what urban historians and geographers call nodal regions: territories that funneled their natural resources through an urban center, just as the commerce in sea otter pelts had flowed through Fort Ross. Taken together, the areas around the three cities also constituted a so-called uniform region, dominated by the production of a primary commodity, gold.[13]

Yet the emergence of the Central Valley cities as economic nodes for the gold country was neither an automatic nor a natural phenomenon, however much the long-standing tradition of scholarship in urban studies that views cities as evolving "organisms" might make it seem.[14] The Central Valley cities had been founded as speculative enterprises, and for the rest of the nineteenth century their governments and their residents alike continued to promote commerce actively in order to expand. In an 1854 editorial the *Marysville Herald* explained the competitive venture of urban growth. Marysville, the editors wrote, was the third-largest city in the state and, they predicted ambitiously, "will soon be rivaled only by San Francisco. But how to promote its growth—to place its advancement beyond the possibility of a doubt? Why, simply, to increase our trade."[15] Cities such as Marysville and Sacramento were rather more like joint-stock companies than organisms. Merchants and speculators in real estate were the investors in these companies; municipal governments, made up largely of the most prominent land speculators and merchants, acted as boards of directors.[16]

For the cities to emerge as commercial centers of the gold country, municipal governments had to construct means of transportation both to the coast and to the Sierra foothills. For example, while the rivers that joined at Marysville were an important natural advantage for the city, the municipal government was determined to improve the commercial possibilities of the streams. Thus, the Marysville City Charter provided the municipal government with the power to "grade the banks of the Yuba and Feather Rivers, so as to facilitate the discharge of merchandize from steamers, vessels, and boats."[17] Likewise, in 1854 Marysville residents voted overwhelmingly to build a railroad to Benicia and a plank road to Nevada City.[18]

Sacramento's city government had even grander ambitions. In 1853 the city council sought to issue bonds to finance the construction of a railroad to the interior.[19] In 1855 the city granted a right-of-way to the Sacramento Valley Railroad Company. By 1856 the company had laid twenty-two miles of track along the American River as far as Folsom. The company hoped its line would become the western leg of a transcontinental railroad.[20] The economic growth of Sacramento Valley cities was not an inexorable process but the result of deliberate choices by the cities' inhabitants.

Yet the proximity of the rivers that made this growth possible was a curse as well as a blessing: just as Vernon flooded in the winter of 1849–50, Sacramento, Marysville, and Stockton flooded repeatedly in the nineteenth century. (Indeed, Marysville residents eventually rued the day they had graded the riverbank.) The ecological hazards of the Central Valley cities were not limited to floods. Like all urban centers of commerce, because they were characterized by relatively dense populations and frequent influxes of newcomers, the cities were magnets not only for capital and merchandise but for microbes that carried deadly diseases. The rudimentary public sanitation of the cities—not atypical in nineteenth-century North America—exacerbated the effect of the microbes. That Sacramento had an outbreak of cholera in 1850, for instance, was not surprising. Nearly every major city in North America suffered an outbreak of the disease in 1849–50. That the outbreak became an epidemic, however, was due in large part to a municipal government that kept public health expenditures to a minimum in order not to overtax or interfere with the operations of business enterprises.[21]

The urbanization of nineteenth-century California was thus not a simple story of cities rising from the wilderness, as nineteenth-century boosters imagined it to be. Rather, the rise of urban centers in the decades after the discovery of gold was a complex and often contradictory phenomenon: positioned to profit from the exploitation of nature, cities found themselves in the path of natural catastrophe. Commerce in natural resources built the Central Valley cities, but the ecology of commerce brought flood and disease. Urban Californians thus faced an ecological dilemma: to mitigate the threat to their urban environment by imposing taxes to create levees and public sanitation systems, they had to restrain the commerce that was the source of their prosperity. Yet municipal public works projects, particularly levees, despite their expense, imparted significant political benefits. Such projects conferred political legitimacy on city governments that had been initially conceived as little more than real estate development companies. Following a summer of political and public health crises in Sacramento in 1850, such legitimacy was a prized commodity.

If ever a city's birth was illegitimate, it was the founding of Sacramento. In December 1848, while Johann Sutter was hiding from his creditors, his son John, acting in his place, entered into an agreement with Peter Burnett, later a governor of California, to develop Sacramento City. The elder Sutter would not have approved of the scheme, if for no other reason than that he had already staked his urban development plans on Sutterville, the town he had founded in 1844 downstream from the juncture of the American and Sacramento rivers. In January 1849, Burnett and the younger Sutter lured the principal Sutterville merchants Sam Brannan, Barton Lee, and Albert Priest to Sacramento by offering them each five hundred city lots to move their operations to the new city. Leaving nothing to chance, Brannan and other Sacramento merchants later descended on the one large commercial establishment remaining in Sutterville and destroyed its stock of goods.[22]

Merchant-speculators dominated the Sacramento city government. Brannan and Lee had served on the committee to draft laws for the provisional government of California; both served on the board of commissioners to draft laws for Sacramento. Other members of the board included the merchants William Petit and William Carpenter; John Fowler, a sometime partner of Brannan who had a near-monopoly on freighting between Sacramento and the mines; and John McDougal, a real estate investor in Sacramento and later a governor of California. The first city government, elected in April 1850, included Lee as city treasurer; Hardin Bigelow, a merchant and real estate speculator, as mayor; and as members of the city council the merchant-speculators Demas Strong and James Hardenburgh. In short, a list of the most prominent businessmen in Sacramento in 1849 and 1850 was virtually indistinguishable from the roster of the city government.[23]

By October 1849, Sacramento had a population of over two thousand. The rapid growth of the city outpaced construction supplies: of the nearly 350 buildings in the fall of 1849, 85 percent were hastily assembled of wooden frames with canvas walls and roofs. Lumber was too expensive in 1849 for all

Sacramento, 1849. The watercraft are docked at the Sacramento River's natural levee.

but the most extravagant builders to consider constructing a house entirely of wood. Brick buildings did not become commonplace until 1853.[24]

The largest and most notable structure in Sacramento in 1849 was the "Round Tent," a gambling hall fifty feet in diameter. The Round Tent typified Sacramento commercial buildings in 1849 not only for its canvas walls but for the frenetic and all-consuming pursuit of wealth that went on within its confines. According to John Morse, a New England physician, its interior was characterized by card playing, music, alcohol, and "obscene pictures that lined this whirlpool of fortune," attractions that lured many prospectors into a "vortex of penury and disgrace."[25] Speculation dominated Sacramento outside the Round Tent as well. Merchants scrambled to acquire the best commercial spaces. Isaac Perkins, who migrated from Massachusetts to Sacramento, arriving in April 1850, quickly concluded that the success of his dry goods business depended on "getting a good location. It is here just as it is everywhere else some parts of the city you could not sell enough to pay your expenses wilst in others you can sell all the goods you can get."[26] In the scramble for space, some speculators made fortunes. Some lots sold for as much as $8,000 in 1849. When Sacramento assessed property taxes for the first time in 1850, Brannan's property in the city was valued at over $26,000 and Lee's at over $22,000.[27]

Gradually, Sacramento began to assume a more citified appearance, replacing canvas buildings with wooden structures. To supply Sacramento with lumber, loggers cut immense numbers of trees on the American, Sacramento, and Feather rivers. On the American River alone, loggers cut a million board feet of lumber in 1852 and four million board feet in 1853.[28] During this period both Isaac Perkins and Amos Catlin, one of the founders of the Natoma Water Company, invested in sawmills on the streams above Sacramento.[29] By May 1850 the price of lumber, which had stood as high as $1.50 per foot in Sacramento a year earlier, had fallen to three cents per foot. "Lumber is extremely plenty and there is great quantity in this market," wrote one observer in Sacramento.[30] Loggers' industriousness may have lowered the price of lumber in Sacramento, but it contributed to the destruction of the dense forests of the Central Valley riverbanks above Sacramento.[31] Below Sacramento, increasing steamboat travel deforested the riverbanks, as steamboats consumed trees for fuel and cut trees from the riverbanks to prevent snags.[32]

The consumption of the riverine forests for lumber exacerbated the lowlands' inherent tendency to flood. Deforestation removed trees that stabilized the natural levees flanking the rivers. The dense roots of the riverbank forests had helped to confine rivers to their channels during spring floods. When loggers cut the riverbank trees, they liberated currents to erode the levees. Loggers' practice of floating their timber downstream to urban markets furthered erosion. According to an 1854 report, when loggers pushed the logs they had cut into the flood-swollen rivers in the spring, the logs "thunder down the rapids, sometimes end over end, until they bring up on some rocky point or sand bar."[33] Such logging debris jams forced currents around obstructions in the river, scouring banks and levees in the process. Altogether, logging left the rivers in such a condition that floodwaters were more likely to transcend the streambed.[34]

Floods occur regularly in the dynamic environment of the Sacramento River and its thirteen largest tributaries. The system drains a watershed area of over 58,000 square miles. The volume of water in the rivers that flow from the Sierra is unpredictable. Fifty percent of the flow is snowmelt from the up-

Sacramento and vicinity, 1855. The shaded portion of the street map indicates the settled part of the town.

per Sierra. The amount of snowfall in the mountains and the rate at which it melts—factors that vary considerably from year to year—largely determine the amount and the timing of spring floods.

Snowfall in the Sierra generally occurs between November and March, a period in which winter low-pressure systems in the Pacific carry precipitation to California. At Soda Springs, at an elevation of 6,900 feet, an average of eighty inches of snow usually accumulates by the end of March. Much of the upper Sierra usually accumulates sixty inches of snow each winter. The amount of moisture in winter storms can increase greatly during El Niño years, when pulses of warm water extend from the western to the eastern Pacific. Wet winter storms produce heavy snowpacks in the Sierra. During El Niño years, Soda Springs amasses an average of 160 inches of snow. Even greater extremes are possible: Tamarack in Alpine County accumulated 884 inches of snow in 1906–07. If snowpacks melt gradually, their impact on streams dissipates. When heavy snowfalls are followed by warm midwinter rains in the upper Sierra, however, the snowpack melts rapidly.[35]

If the volume of water in the rivers that flow from the Sierra is unpredictable, so too is the course those rivers follow when they reach the floor of the Central Valley. Because rivers cross a variety of geological formations, their rate of flow is uneven. Narrow streams confined by rocky canyon walls have rapid currents; the currents of broader streams are slow. Currents change speed as they flow across riffles, or high points, in the streambed. Water accumulates in deep pools at bends in the river, where it increases in pressure and, accordingly, downstream speed. Riffles and pools create the meandering courses of the Central Valley rivers. Such meanders are not static: especially during spring floods, high waters create cutoffs between meanders, leaving the old streambeds as oxbows or sloughs.[36]

Snowmelt brought flood to Sacramento in January 1850, just as it had to Elisha Crosby's settlement of Vernon. The *Alta California* reported a "vast lake of waters" from Sacramento to Sutter's Fort, submerging all but the tops of trees for miles. The flood made a mockery of Sacramento's commercial aspirations: "Lumber, bales and cases of goods, boxes and barrels, tents and small houses were floating in every direction." The city's inhabitants clustered on a bluff above the town until the water receded some two weeks later. In its wake were left "many gullies in which was deposited all the filth of the surrounding neighborhood."[37]

The flood did more than expose the folly of Sacramento's location in the low-lying floodplain at the juncture of two major rivers. The flood also revealed the limits of Johann Sutter's Mexican land grant that was the legal basis for the development of Sacramento—and, thus, for the wealth that speculation in city lots had produced. While speculators such as Brannan built fortunes in real estate, other residents of Sacramento had not purchased lots but merely "squatted" on the land without title, particularly on the natural levee along the Sacramento River.

These squatters challenged the legitimacy of the land grant that the Mexican government had made to Sutter in 1838. The Mexican government had never formally deeded the land to Sutter; moreover, the grant specifically excluded the riverine land on which Sacramento City stood. John Plumbe, one of the leaders of the squatters, who formed themselves into a "Settlers Association," discovered the limited extent of Sutter's property in the spring of 1850, when he secured a copy of the grant.[38] In the absence of a clear title, squatters argued that the land was part of the public domain. They appealed to American custom and the legal tradition of preemption that generally accorded title to those who occupied and improved public land.

Speculators, who styled themselves as the Law and Order party, used the power of the city government they controlled to evict the squatters. The city removed most of them from the levee in December 1849—a few weeks before floodwaters would have removed them anyway. Shortly after the eviction, the Law and Order Party called a public meeting intending to endorse the legality of the Sutter grant; they quickly discovered that most of the attendees at the meeting were squatters or their sympathizers, who held the speculators' city government in open contempt. "The squatters," wrote the overland migrant Israel Lord, who arrived in the city in December 1849, "had as much right to the land where Sacramento City stands as anybody (certainly more than the swindling minions of Sutter)."[39] The Settlers Association complained of "threats of violence" and "brute force" by the city government. They derided the legitimacy of the "so-called legislature of California" which had certified Sacramento City's charter, and the city's "legislative regulations, by them called *laws*."[40]

Facing a hostile majority in the city, the Sacramento speculators prosecuted a suit against the squatters in the county court; in August 1850 a decision that favored the speculators prompted a riot in the city. During a day of violence on August 14, a dozen squatters and several city officials, including the sheriff and the city assessor, were killed. Burnett, by then governor of California, ordered the state militia to restore order. The city declared martial law; in a matter of days the rioting squatters had been subdued, and the city had established its authority—if not, in the eyes of many observers, its legitimacy.[41]

Within months, Sacramento faced a new and more deadly crisis: it was one of the cities struck by the nationwide cholera epidemic of 1849–50. The city government did little during the course of the epidemic to establish its validity. Months before its outbreak, during which time municipal authorities might have established an effective public health system, Sacramento had instead become "a receptacle of the sick, unfortunate, and destitute from every quarter."[42] Many migrants, entering by land and sea, arrived in Sacramento exhausted and suffering from a variety of illnesses. John Eagle, who traveled to California via Panama, reported of his ship, "The amount of sickness aboard is truly terrifying."[43]

Morse collectively diagnosed such illnesses as scurvy, but ill emigrants likely suffered from a range of sicknesses caused by dietary deficiencies. Many overland emigrants, according to Morse, were "so exhausted in strength and so worn out with the calamities of the journey as to be barely able to reach" Sacramento. Emigrants' insufficient funds compounded the problems. "Not one in a hundred," wrote Morse, "arrived in the country with money enough to buy a decent outfit for the mines." While Morse likely exaggerated most emigrants' predicament, his observations reflected his peculiar perspective on the gold rush. Unlike most contemporary observers, Morse's work as an urban physician focused his vision on the "penniless and destitute" of Sacramento, "the only place men could think of stopping at for recuperative purposes."[44]

Indeed, the sick flocked to Sacramento as the best place to seek care. In early October 1850, for instance, Samuel Nichols, an Amador County prospector, wrote to his wife that his friend Luther Cleaves was so ill that "I have been nearly all of the time attending to him." Nichols resolved to take his sick friend to Sacramento, where he would be more comfortable.[45] As the sick multiplied in the city, according to Morse, "Sacramento became a perfect lazar house of disease, suffering, and death months before anything like an effective city government was organized."[46] The sick congregated in small private hospitals constructed—usually of canvas—by physicians themselves.[47]

The city government, still dominated by merchants and real estate developers, was reluctant to commit resources for the benefit of the propertyless or the poor. Morse attributed the paucity of public services to a disdain for charity born of the pursuit of individual fortunes. He wrote in 1853 that "men came to California to make money, not to devote themselves to a useless waste of time in procuring bread and raiment for the dependent, in watching over and taking care of the sick, or in the burying of the dead. The common god of the day (gold!) taught no such feminine virtues."[48] Sacramento did not establish a city board of health until 1868.[49]

Newcomers to Sacramento, whether healthy or ill, discovered a crowded, dirty city. By the early summer of 1850, Sacramento's population had inflated to seven thousand. According to one municipal waste engineer, the average nineteenth-century urban American annually produced between 300 and 1,200 pounds of ashes, 100 to 180 pounds of organic garbage, and 50 pounds of inorganic rubbish.[50] In 1850, Sacramento's residents thus produced, at a minimum, 1,000 tons of ashes, 350 tons of organic waste, and 175 tons of inorganic waste. Most Sacramento residents simply dumped this refuse in city streets; the city government made no effort to clear the streets of waste. On October 20, 1850, Israel Lord wrote in his journal, "This evening the streets are as filthy as ever, and the heated city is a living, moving, tailing mass of men and animals, crawling like maggots in the filth, and breathing an atmosphere filled with poison and dust."[51] In Sacramento's first year, the standards of public health slipped to a dangerously careless level.

By the fall, "disease was rioting in the community," particularly an affliction that Morse could only describe as "miasmatic fever"—probably malaria, which had been introduced to California in the early 1830s. Because wooden coffins were prohibitively expensive, the bodies of the destitute who died after arrival in Sacramento were buried "in the filth of unattended sickness," sometimes even without being sewn up in a blanket before interment. The Sacramento city council made a half-hearted effort to provide effectively for the public health, voting to build a hospital and appropriating $14,000 for the purpose. The building blew down in a storm, however, before it was completed.[52]

Before the council could establish effective public health services, cholera struck the city. Cholera is caused by a bacterium, *Vibrio comma*, that until the early nineteenth century was largely localized in Southeast Asia. Increased commercial steamboat traffic transported the bacteria to North America in

1832, where it caused an outbreak in New York City and other eastern urban centers. In 1849, when trade networks brought the disease back to North America, the disease was not limited to the East but broke out in western cities as well: San Antonio, for example, lost 10 percent of its population. The bacteria, which survived in watering holes along the overland trail, also accompanied emigrants to California: two thousand overland emigrants died of cholera in the late 1840s and 1850s.[53]

Alas for Sacramento in 1850, cholera is a disease that thrives in conditions of urban filth. The bacterium can be transmitted from one host to another through unwashed hands or raw sewage. When raw sewage containing the bacteria finds its way into the public water supply, cholera spreads rapidly.[54] Its symptoms include severe abdominal pain, vomiting, and diarrhea. The disease strikes without warning. In the course of a single day, cholera can be fatal to a previously healthy person. Perkins wrote on October 27, "Some have been taken who were to all appearances in Good Health & have died in a few hours."[55] Likewise, on October 23, Lord noted in his journal, "A man walking down J street last evening, dropped suddenly, and lived only long enough to be carried into the nearest door."[56]

The first death from cholera occurred on October 20. The number of cases rapidly multiplied over the next few weeks, radiating into the city from the commercial riverside district: 7 deaths by October 22; between 15 and 20 more by October 24; and a further 30 to 40 by October 26. Public health measures proved to be worse than ineffective. A city ordinance passed on October 21 ordered residents to burn their garbage or face a $500 fine. Lord wrote that "the filth is burned in the middle of the streets—old shoes and boots and clothes by the ton, and cart loads of bones, and raw hides, and putrid meat, and spoiled bacon—so that the end of the matter is worse than the beginning." By the end of the month, half of the population of the city had either succumbed to the disease or fled the city. By the end of the first week of November, it was 80 percent. "In this pestilential reign of terror and dismay the most dreadful abandonments of relatives and friends took place," according to Morse.[57]

Not all Californians were so heartless: fifteen physicians in Sacramento died of cholera during the epidemic of 1850; many no doubt could have saved themselves by abandoning the sick and fleeing the city.[58] Charity was deadly to others as well. Samuel Nichols, who had brought his sick friend to Sacramento for care just before the outbreak of the cholera epidemic, died of cholera in the city that fall. Lord estimated that during the twenty days that the disease raged through Sacramento, eight hundred people died. The *Alta California* reported that at the height of the epidemic sixty people died every day.

The exodus included several members of the Sacramento city council. "There are a thousand things which call loudly for supervision, but in vain," complained the San Francisco *Alta California* on November 3. "No means have been taken to disinfect the atmosphere (at least by the city), no precautions against the accumulation of filth."[59]

Despite a general understanding that urban filth had contributed to the cholera epidemic of 1850, poor public sanitation and a municipal government unwilling or unable to address the problem continued to plague Sacramento and other Central Valley cities in the years after the epidemic. For decades, Sacramento lacked an effective sewage system. As with other matters of public health, the city government sought first to ignore the problem. When they could ignore the situation no longer, they dealt with it as cheaply as possible— a strategy that was typical of nineteenth-century municipal governments.[60] One of the earliest sewers in Sacramento had no outlet. When it was excavated during the construction of a new sewer in 1854, it was found to contain "water enough to fill a moderate reservoir." The *Daily Union*, which described the sewer as representative of a "style of engineering peculiar" to Sacramento's municipal government, opined acidly, "A receipt for building Sacramento sewers may be graphically written thus: Dig a trench—line it with plank—cover it up—all right—get your pay—let it rot—try another." Sewers constructed in succeeding years were little better. During the rainy winter seasons, they tended to overflow, causing "a discharge of offensive matter."[61]

Raw sewage was a major cause not only of cholera but of typhoid fever. The disease—fatal in about 10 percent of cases—is caused by the one hundred varieties of the *Salmonella typhi* bacterium. "Billious Congestion, Typhoid, and Typhoid Pneumonia," John Kincade wrote in 1857, were "truly a lamentable feature in California," particularly "everywhere in the Sacramento Valley between the Sierra Nevada and Coast Mountains."[62]

By the end of 1850, the municipal government of Sacramento faced a crisis of legitimacy. It had shot its way into power in August and displayed apathy and cowardice in the face of the cholera epidemic of October and November. For one project, however, the city government enjoyed surprising public support: its efforts to build a levee to protect the city from flood.

Such efforts were initially the work of business leaders seeking to protect their investments. In February 1850, in the wake of the flood of 1849–50, Barton Lee called the first meeting to discuss the raising of a levee. A fellow merchant and speculator, Hardin Bigelow, was appointed to head the levee committee. The city council, always wary of public expenses, delayed action on Bigelow's recommendations, however, so when ten inches of rain fell in March 1850, Bigelow hired a workforce at his own expense and supervised the construction of a makeshift levee. The hasty construction may have prevented a flood. Whether or not the structure had kept the river from flooding the city, the levee was an unquestioned success as a political symbol. Bigelow was acclaimed as a civic hero; when the city held its first municipal elections on April 1, he was elected mayor.[63]

Bigelow's promising political career was cut short, however. He was shot by squatters during the August riots; while recovering from his wounds, he died of cholera in November. Bigelow's astute use of flood control to build political popularity was taken up by James Hardenburgh, who became chair of the city's levee committee in September. Hardenburgh supervised the construction of a levee nine miles in length. A section that was three feet high, six feet broad at the crest, and twelve feet wide at the base ran along the American River; along the Sacramento River the embankment rose to six feet, was fourteen feet broad at its crest, and thirty feet wide at its base. The construction, completed at the end of 1850, cost $175,000 at a time when the city's expenses for all other purposes totaled only $100,000.[64]

Construction necessitated condemning some private property along the waterfront.[65] The transformation of this area, the center of the squatters' movement, to municipal property, was the city's final triumph over the Settlers Association. More than protection from flood (which the levee provided only imperfectly), the levee was a cordon along the city's boundary to solidify the city government's tenuous claim to authority; it was a bulwark against challenges from within and without.

Whatever the levee's symbolic value, its efficacy as protection against flooding was soon to be tested. The flood of January 1850 had merely presaged a more extensive flood in the spring of 1852, when Sacramento, Marysville, and Stockton were inundated. In Marysville, the floodwaters submerged the city's business district, the Plaza, just as they had during the prior flood.[66] The wave of floodwaters continued on to Sacramento: on March 7, the level of the American River as it passed Sacramento rose at a rate of one foot per hour, and the water breached the city levee on the Sacramento River at I Street. The waters of the American also poured into a slough southeast of the city. By March 11, the water in the slough was three feet higher than the city, and water poured steadily from it into Sacramento. Sacramento residents hastily built a levee along J Street to hold back the waters, but their construction collapsed overnight.[67]

The damage to property and business notwithstanding, the floods of the early 1850s were mere trickles compared to the flood of the winter and spring of 1861–62, when unusually heavy snowmelts encountered streambeds raised by hydraulic mining debris. Unaware of this alignment of forces, Sacramento residents welcomed the commercial potential of the first rains of the season in November 1861. The rain, the *Sacramento Daily Union* opined, would "enable farmers to commence plowing on lowland" and ensure a "plentiful supply of the element so essential to the prosperity of the miner." The newspaper was still joking about rising waters later in the month, noting that at a slaughterhouse south of Sacramento on the road to Stockton, 250 rats had been flushed out of their holes and drowned.[68]

Sacramento residents had reason to feel secure that the fate of the rats was not a portent. Nine years had passed since the last flood, "a time so long that many of our citizens had concluded that the city was safe from damage by water," wrote the *Daily Union*. And the government had taken constructive steps to protect Sacramento. Since the floods of 1852, the government, at considerable expense, had extended the 1850 structure so as to ring the city with a levee. The two principal parts of the levee were on the banks of the Sacramento and American rivers. The levee alongside the Sacramento ran south from the mouth of the American as far as Sutterville. The levee alongside the American extended from the American's mouth eastward for three miles. In addition, a levee ran eastward along R Street from the Sacramento River levee as far as Sixteenth Street. Here, the levee encountered the slough that had flooded in 1852. The levee continued along the banks of the slough until it joined the American River levee. For added security, the city spent $8,000 in 1860 to build a wing dam that jutted into the American River to direct the current away from the city levee and toward the opposite bank.[69]

R Street levee, 1854

Even as the levee around Sacramento was raised, however, other Californians were raising the riverbeds of the Sacramento and American rivers. By the end of the 1850s, hydraulic mining operations on the Feather, Bear, Yuba, and American rivers—all of which drained into the Sacramento—were extensive.[70] Against rivers transformed by mining debris, the Sacramento City levee was not impregnable.

In March 1861, spring freshets severely damaged the wing dam, and by autumn the damage had yet to be repaired. In late November, by which time the level of the Sacramento River had risen two feet, the Sacramento Board of Supervisors met to consider bids to repair the city's defenses against flood. Perhaps lulled by the nine-year hiatus since the last flood, they proceeded at a leisurely pace, waiting until the last day of the month to appropriate $18,000 to repair the levee on the American River. The board's slow deliberations wasted precious time: in the first two days of December, the level of the Sacramento rose suddenly by ten feet, bringing the level of the river to twelve feet above the low-water mark.

Yet Sacramento remained safely barricaded behind its levee while towns upriver were overwhelmed by floodwaters. In Auburn on December 8, floodwaters swept away a number of houses. The flood reached Marysville at eleven o'clock in the evening of December 9. By early the following morning, flood-waters there were so high that a steamboat made its way through the city streets rescuing citizens trapped in the upper stories of buildings or on roofs. An observer reported that the agricultural land south of Marysville was a "waste of muddy water, on which are floating houses, fences, lumber, hay, straw, and the dead and living bodies of hogs, cattle, and horses." Indeed, livestock were "constantly passing down stream, some alive and struggling, and bellowing and squealing for life."[71]

On the morning of December 9, the floodwaters breached Sacramento's levees not, as was feared, in the northwest corner of the city, below the dam-aged wing dam, where the swollen American River flowed into the equally swollen Sacramento, but in the southeast corner of the city. There, a railroad line designed to bring commercial traffic into the city unintentionally admit-ted floodwaters.

The American River had breached the levee on its southern bank upriver of Sacramento, and proceeded to pour into the slough on the east of the city. The rising waters abutted against an embankment constructed a few years earlier by the Sacramento Valley Railroad Company. The railroad's line ran across the slough and entered the city at the corner of R and Sixteenth Streets, the levee's southeast corner. The city ordinance granting the railroad its right-of-way had stipulated that the company was to build a bridge across the slough, allowing water to pass beneath it. The company had constructed a bridge in 1855, but in the two years before the flood the bridge had fallen into disrepair. To shore up the structure, the company had transformed the bridge into an embankment by filling in its spans with earth. By the time of the flood of December 1861, the embankment was higher than the levee on the south-east side of the city. Floodwater flowing into the slough from the American River abutted against the embankment and rose until it overtopped the levee and poured into the city.[72] In both Sacramento and Marysville, where the flood had poured into the city over a levee that had been graded to facilitate steamboat traffic, the flood followed the gates of commerce into the cities.

After entering Sacramento at the railroad embankment at six o'clock in the morning, the floodwaters gushed through the southern part of the city, submerging one-story houses to their rooftops. By nine o'clock, the city south of J Street was under water. The flood exposed the weakness of the city's vaunted system of levees: once the river breached or overtopped any part of the twelve miles of embankments encircling the city, the levees, rather than keeping floodwaters out, kept them in. To drain water from the southern part of the city, residents opened breaches. Water flowed with such force through the openings that it carried a number of houses through them.[73]

As the floodwater receded from Sacramento, it left devastation in its wake. According to one observer, "Scores of capsized houses lay where they had been lodged against trees or other capsized or toppling dwellings, great piles of stray lumber and wood were floating about, and carcasses of dead cattle, horses, and swine here and there disfigured the general wreck." The drowned animals soon presented a health problem: skinners hauled them to Seventeenth Street where they stripped them of their hides and left them to rot.[74]

By mid-December, however, it appeared that the crisis had passed. Water had largely, although not entirely, receded from the southern part of the city. North of L Street, the city had remained dry. Teams of workers set about to repair the damaged levee in early January 1862, and a barge loaded with 100,000 feet of lumber arrived to rebuild the Sacramento Valley Railroad at R Street. Sacramento's boosters remained optimistic. "When the weather clears up," the *Daily Union* confidently predicted on January 10, "the streets and bridges leading to and from the city will be repaired and built, and Sacramento will resume her trade and activity as if nothing unusual had happened."[75]

That very evening, however, the city was flooded again. The flood originated in this instance from the Sacramento rather than the American River; the level of the Sacramento was half a foot higher on January 10 than it had been on December 9. Unlike the deluge of December 9, the flood of January 10 began slowly, as water in the still-submerged southern parts of the city began rising and seeping northward. It then rose rapidly, drowning four residents and five inhabitants of a ranch outside the city. By the evening, the water within the city had reached the level of the Front Street levee and was lapping over it at places. Workers feverishly shored up the American River levee to prevent that from giving way as well. On January 21, the *Daily Union*, ever confident, reported that as a result of these labors, "the levee was considered by good judges to be entirely safe." Two days later the repaired levee collapsed, and a "strong current" of water began flowing through the eastern part of the city, from the break on the American River south to openings in the R Street levee.[76] The American River had, in effect, transformed the eastern side of Sacramento into a cutoff.

In the aftermath of the 1861–62 flood, the Sacramento municipal government raised the city's levees still higher. By 1863 the levees ringing the city were four feet higher than the flood stage of 1862. When the American River threatened to overwhelm the levee in 1867, the city added five more feet. The next year, the city borrowed a tactic from the river itself. If in 1862 the river had used city streets as a cutoff, the city council in 1868 determined to create a cutoff that would reroute the American River's current away from Sacramento. The city thus paid for the digging of a canal from the point where the Central Pacific Railroad crossed the American River upstream from the city, to a point one mile north of the American's juncture with the Sacramento.[77]

Yet in February 1878, the city flooded again. Hydraulic mining debris was a significant contributor: sediment had continued to raise the bed of the American River, diminishing the effectiveness of Sacramento's towering levee, which had itself been compromised by humbler means. Although the levee was artificial, the earthen structure was rapidly incorporated into the natural environment. Significant numbers of burrowing rodents made their homes in it by 1878; its collapse that February occurred in part because gophers had weakened the structure considerably. The break in the levee occurred south of the city, flooded the lowlands, and then seeped into Sacramento as far north as N Street and as far east as Sixth Street.[78]

The founders of Sacramento had placed their settlement at the confluence of the Sacramento and American rivers because of the natural advantages that the streams offered. Within a few years, however, proximity to the rivers had become a distinct disadvantage. Once confident that they would profit from their location, the city's residents came to believe that they would profit despite it. Yet the same belief had animated the residents of such cities as Vernon and Marysville: floods destroyed Vernon and handicapped Marysville's commercial prospects. Sacramento survived only by constructing levees and canals to protect it from the unpredictable American River. Speculators who had touted the natural advantages of the city's location in 1850 trumpeted the artificial advantages of the city's levees in the 1860s. Founded as a city that relied on nature for its commercial prospects, Sacramento in little over a decade became a city that relied on artificial constructions to protect it from nature.

Sacramento embarked upon its flood control projects not because it was the wealthiest of the Central Valley cities, not because it had the brightest prospects, but ironically because its government, lacking even a shadow of legitimacy, intuited that a flood control project might boost public support. The levee failed to protect the city during the flood of 1861–62, but it was nonetheless a legitimization of the municipal government and in a broader sense a validation of the artificial hydrology that an urban, industrial society had created in California.

3

Capitalizing on Nature: Innovation and Production in the Redwood Forests

~—◄—~

Isaac Branham's route to California was a typical one for an ambitious Euroamerican from the Upper South. Born in Kentucky in 1803, Branham, like other farmers from the region in search of cheap land, migrated to Missouri in 1824. Twenty-two years later, like many whose families had outgrown their Midwestern farms, or who simply hoped for greater opportunities in the Far West, Branham pulled up stakes again and migrated to California. Arriving before the discovery of gold, Branham anticipated a fortune in the exploitation of California's extensive forests. He built a sawmill in the Santa Cruz Mountains and hired men to work it. His employees included itinerant laborers such as Charles Brown, who came to San Francisco aboard a whaling vessel, jumped ship, and found work cutting shingles. Branham prospered in his first year, but was short of labor. Just as Brown had once left his whaling ship for the mill, Branham's employees abandoned him for the goldfields in 1848.[1]

Within a few years, however, as bad luck and hydraulic mining technology destroyed the hopes of many independent miners, onetime prospectors began to drift into logging to support themselves. By 1855, for instance, G. C. Taplin had failed as a prospector and sought work chopping wood. By the end of the summer he had found full-time employment at a sawmill.[2] For such loggers and mill workers, the lumber industry was hardly more remunerative than prospecting—many earned only enough to support themselves.[3] For entrepreneurs like Branham, however, the lumber industry proved to be lucrative. Richard Stanwood, for example, was invited to become a partner in a lumber business in Marysville in 1853, as urbanization and demand for lumber were reaching an early peak. Stanwood invested every penny of his savings. By 1857 he had amassed $3,000. By the 1860s he had parlayed his earnings from the lumber business into extensive landholdings.[4]

Little wonder that Stanwood's investment reaped a return: wood was both the primary fuel and the leading construction material for nineteenth-century Americans. As one observer noted in 1874, "Our houses are built of lumber, our streets are planked with lumber, our fields are fenced with lumber, and our flumes and sluices are made of lumber."[5] While farms and cities consumed their share of wood, industrial enterprises also depended on extensive supplies of lumber. In its 1872 report, the California State Agricultural Society listed industry's uses of wood in the state: for "railroads, bridges, warehouses, wharves, factories, bulkheads, and timbering mines."[6] If mining was the heart of California's emerging industrial economy and cities its nerve centers, then lumber made up the sinews that knit the system together.

Entrepreneurs believed that timber to construct California's industrial enterprises and connect them to urban markets existed in ample quantities. Like gold miners, loggers perceived not only a demand but in the California environment a largely untapped supply. The *Humboldt Times* of Eureka, in the heart of the redwood country, noted in 1858 that "our immense forests of timber, as a source of wealth, are as valuable as the best gold mines in the State, and they are equally inexhaustible."[7]

Within three decades, the newspaper's claims to the inexhaustibility of California's forests were disproved. In the early 1850s commercial loggers concentrated upon the sugar pines of the Sierra Nevada. Though slightly inferior to the white pine of northern New England and the Upper Midwest—one forester called sugar pine "not quite so soft, light, and white as the white pine itself"—California sugar pine compensated for its deficiencies by its abundance and its proximity to markets in the gold country, the Sacramento Valley, and San Francisco. Growing on both slopes of the Sierra between elevations of 3,000 and 8,000 feet, reaching heights over 150 feet and diameters of between ten and fifteen feet, sugar pine comprised 15 percent of the timber stand in California outside of the redwood region.[8]

By 1856, sugar pine had largely replaced Eastern white pine in the California lumber market—a testimony both to its value and to the maturity of the California lumber industry. By 1858, there were forty-two mills in

Nevada County on the northwestern side of Lake Tahoe alone, and the Sierra mills were supplying sugar pine not only to the California market but to Salt Lake City, Utah, and the silver mining community of Comstock, Nevada.[9]

The fortunes of California timber cutters—there were over three hundred sawmills in the state by the mid-1870s—came at a cost to the environment. By 1870 loggers had consumed one-third of the state's forests. Two decades later, one observer noted that in the Sierra where the loggers had passed through, "little but stumps can any longer be seen." As a consequence, by the mid-1890s the mills around Lake Tahoe were forced to close down. The industry journal *Pacific Coast Wood and Iron* editorialized: "For twenty years or more Lake Tahoe has furnished the bulk of the timber that has gone into the bowels of the Comstock, and the wood that has made the steam to hoist the thousands upon thousands of tons of ore." By 1894 all wood along the Truckee River and within two miles of the shore of Lake Tahoe had been consumed. Deforestation was so sudden and thorough that the California State Agricultural Society considered it "one of the first duties of the state to check this reckless destruction of the natural forests."[10]

Despite the deforestation of the pinelands of the Sierra, as late as 1882 observers of the California logging industry had faith that at least one species, the coast redwood, would survive industrial California's appetite for lumber. One forester wrote, "The continual timber supply capacity of a redwood forest, under judicious care, is so prodigious as to be simply incalculable; none but a suicidal and utterly abandoned infanticidal policy, wantonly and untiringly practical, can ever blot them out."[11] Yet two years later, an observer commented, "it is just this 'abandoned policy' at work in the redwoods, which has sealed their doom."[12] In 1850 the Pacific Coast redwood belt covered approximately two million acres. By the beginning of the twentieth century more than a third of the old-growth forest had been cut. By the middle of the twentieth century, old-growth redwood forest remained on only 4 percent of the original extent, although second- and third-growth redwood covered some of the rest of the former redwood belt.[13]

Most environmental historians who have studied the Pacific Coast timber industry have concentrated primarily on the Douglas fir forests of Oregon and Washington and only secondarily on redwoods. They date large-scale deforestation in both regions from the very end of the nineteenth century, contending that only after logging companies had consumed the white pines of the Upper Midwest, a deforestation largely complete by about 1900, did they turn their commercial attentions and technological expertise to the West Coast. Before 1900, they argue, Pacific Coast logging was technologically rudimentary and, if wasteful, nonetheless limited in extent. The infusion of capital from Midwestern logging companies beginning in the 1890s initiated the destruction of old-growth forests in the redwood belt and in the Douglas fir forests of the Pacific Northwest.[14] Other historians who have studied the Pacific Coast lumber industry before 1900 characterize it as chaotic; if the influx of Midwestern logging firms to the West at the end of the nineteenth and beginning of the twentieth century did not initiate the utilization of the forests, at least it rationalized the industry's consumption of them.[15]

While these generalizations may be apt for the Douglas firs of the Pacific Northwest, a closer look at logging in the California redwood belt before 1900 reveals a different history, one that aligns more closely with the gold country's emerging resource-intensive economic model. Like the gold country, the redwood belt was a region rich in natural resources but poor in capital. The timber companies in the redwood belt confronted the high cost of labor, as did hydraulic mining companies in the gold country. The redwood loggers as well as the hydraulic mining companies sought solutions to both of these problems by using technological advantage to shift the burden of their endeavor from capital investment and labor power to the natural environment. As in the gold country, their effort was not chaotic piracy but rather one that strove to impose order upon an unpredictable nature. As in the gold country, resource-intensive industry in the redwood belt exacted a heavy environmental toll.

Exploitation of the redwoods began in the 1850s and was well under way by the 1870s, long before the infusion of Midwestern capital into the redwood lumber industry in the late 1880s. Midwestern investors did not bring technological innovation to California lumbering; rather, just as hydraulic mining technology established itself in the gold country in order to attract capital investment, California redwood lumberers had by the early 1880s developed the technology to harvest the massive trees. Only after those innovations were in place and had proved themselves successful did Midwestern timber companies begin to invest in California. Indeed, redwood logging technology eventually proved so successful that it not only depleted the forests but overwhelmed the ability of the market to absorb the lumber it produced.

The California coast redwood (*Sequoia sempervirens*) is the tallest tree species in the world; the tallest recorded redwood was 385 feet high. To reach such a height takes centuries of growth. Redwoods are among the longest-lived tree species; the oldest documented redwoods have lived for more than two thousand years. To survive for so long, the redwood, over the course of its evolution, developed an enviable durability. Its thick and fibrous bark, for example, is highly resistant to fire. Conflagrations in mixed forests typically consume Douglas firs and Western hemlocks, but leave large redwoods un-scathed. Indeed, following catastrophic fires, redwood seeds thrive. The red-wood is also highly resistant to decay and to the insects—borers, aphids, beetles, and mites—that infest it.[16]

Redwoods possess a prodigious capacity to reproduce. The redwood is a monoecious species, meaning that male pollen and female seed cones de-velop on separate branches of the same tree. During the rainy season, an abundance of pollinated, mature seeds fall to the ground, but fittingly for a species whose life span is measured in centuries, in a single season few if any seeds may survive to take root. Yet redwoods reproduce not only by seed-rooting but by resprouting. After fire or logging, sprouts often emerge from underground lignotubers, encircling the burned or cut stump in what is sometimes called a "fairy ring." Sprouts can also emerge from fallen logs or develop from branches that fall to the ground and lodge in the soil.[17]

Although the redwood is massive, long-lived, and vigorously reproduc-tive, the species is wholly confined to a narrow belt of land only a few miles in width. The redwood belt extends between Monterey and the California-Oregon border, though most trees of the species are concentrated in the northern half of the belt; those to the south are scattered thinly along riverbeds. The scarcity of redwoods was not always the case. Millions of years ago, when the planet's climate was moderate and moist, redwood species grew throughout the Northern Hemisphere. The redwoods of coastal north-ern California, as well as the redwood's few relatives such as the giant se-quoias of the Sierra Nevada and the deciduous dawn redwood of China, are the last remnants of the genus.[18]

Redwood forest, Humboldt County

Redwoods are limited in extent because there are few places on the planet that meet their demands for climate and soil. They require consistently moderate temperatures where the summer daytime high is 70°F, the summer nighttime low 60°F, and the temperature in winter rarely drops far below freezing. Soil temperatures must be likewise moderate. Most importantly, redwoods grow only where precipitation is ample. In the northernmost part of the redwood belt, in Del Norte County, just south of the Oregon border, mean annual precipitation is seventy-eight inches. At the southernmost part, in San Mateo County, the mean annual precipitation is twenty-eight inches. At all points along the narrow redwood belt, during the relatively dry summers the massive trees harvest coastal fog and utilize its moisture. Coastal northern California is characterized by summer fog, particularly in the mornings as warm air meets cold ocean water. When coastal fog encounters the high canopy of a redwood forest, it condenses into water, then drips from the canopy to the soil. So-called fog drip adds moisture equivalent to two to four inches of precipitation per tree per day. Fog drip contributes 25 to 50 percent of redwoods' total water intake each year.[19] The drip benefits other plants in the redwood forest as well. According to an 1884 observer, W. G. Bonner, blackberries and salmonberries in the redwood forests "attain remarkable proportions" and "common ferns grow to monstrous size."[20]

Even as the California timber industry developed profitable markets for Sierra sugar pine, lumberers coveted the redwoods for their prodigious size. A single old-growth redwood tree yielded between 40,000 and 100,000 board feet of lumber (a board foot, the logging industry's standard unit of measure, is one foot square and one inch thick). One redwood tree could provide enough lumber for a large structure: a substantial church in Sonoma County, for example, was built entirely of a single redwood.[21] Moreover, redwood, unlike pine, did not shrink after seasoning. The lumber, like the living tree itself, resisted not only rot and decay but fire: city dwellers took note that buildings constructed of pine were quickly consumed in the event of fire, while buildings built of redwood often endured.[22] Like the living tree, redwood lumber resisted insect infestation.[23]

Federal and state authorities facilitated logging companies' access to the redwoods, nearly all of which were located on the public domain. Most early loggers simply cut timber without regard to property rights. As the northern coast became more crowded with mills, timber companies resorted to federal land laws to acquire property rights to the redwoods in the public domain; federal laws were sufficiently liberal to allow mills to acquire extensive timber holdings. Indeed, federal policy from the middle of the nineteenth until the beginning of the twentieth century was to spur economic development by funneling public lands into private hands. For instance, in the summer of 1858, President James Buchanan announced that over half a million acres of federal land in Humboldt County would be opened to sale.[24] Following the passage of the Homestead Act in 1862, mill owners encouraged their employees to register claims to 160 acres and then allow the company to log the land. Already by 1868, some observers in Humboldt County feared that timberlands had fallen into the hands of a few speculators.[25] Regardless of such fears, the federal government accelerated the privatization of forest lands with the passage of the Timber and Stone Act of 1878, which opened forests on the public domain to sale for a small fee.

Despite the accessibility of redwoods, in contrast to logging in the Sierra the lumber industry in the redwoods began fitfully. Transplanted lumbermen from Canada and the northeastern United States who had failed as gold prospectors—J. R. Duff, J. T. Ryan, John Dolbeer, William Carson, L. E. White, Isaac Minor, and D. R. Jones—were the first to establish mills in the redwood belt. The first mill in Humboldt County was built in the fall of 1850. It had a capacity of only 4,000 feet per day and was too small to cut the large trunks of redwoods. Its operators ignored the redwoods entirely and cut only spruce, pine, and fir. By 1854, there were nine mills in Humboldt County, employing 200 loggers and 130 men at the mills. These Humboldt mills produced a modest 200,000 feet of lumber in 1854. In 1855 schooners transported the first load of sawn redwood lumber from the Humboldt mills to San Francisco. But later that year, as California suffered a banking crisis, the Humboldt mills were running at one-half capacity; by the end of the year four of the nine mills had failed.[26]

The difficulties of the mills did not prevent the Scottish immigrant James Beith from describing Humboldt Bay in September 1854 as "one of the greatest lumbering points in the state." In fact, as a producer of lumber, Humboldt County in 1854 lagged far behind the sugar pine country of the Sierra. It was the great size of the redwoods, rather than the efficiency or profitability of the mills, that led Beith to his conclusion. He wrote in awe of a redwood felled in order to be exhibited in New York: the tree was twenty-one feet in diameter; it took a team of loggers nearly two months to fell the giant, and eighteen oxen to drag it to the nearest river. The men and animals struggled to haul the behemoth twenty miles until they learned that it was ten feet narrower than a trunk already on display in San Francisco.[27]

Beith's anecdote pointed to the central challenge of the redwood industry: the inadequacy of loggers and their tools in the face of the gigantic trees. The enormous size of the redwoods, which had drawn the logging industry to the northern coast, also impeded the development of the industry: redwoods were too large for ordinary saws to fell; if felled, too heavy to be transported to the mills; and if moved, too large for mills to process. In short, the redwood logging industry faced a dilemma similar to the one that had confronted gold miners in the early 1850s: natural resources so abundant that they overawed those who sought to exploit them.

To log the redwood belt, timber companies concluded, required capital to invest in industrial technology. In early 1868, the *Humboldt Times*, in an editorial addressed "to the Capitalists of California," called for more investment in the redwood country. "We are not cutting our timber as fast as it grows. We are making twenty millions of feet of lumber per annum. We might just as well make one or two hundred million, and never exhaust our supply," the editors wrote. All that lacked was investment. "We want capital, and comprehensive skill, to facilitate and cheapen our operations. We want iron railroads and locomotives to bring our logs to the tidewater." Just as the hydraulic miners had believed a decade earlier, the redwood boosters insisted that California's natural abundance ensured prosperity. "There can be no failure or falling off in this business. The timber is here in abundance."[28] What the redwood lumber industry required was significant technological innovation.

Like early placer mining, logging in the redwood country was, at first, highly seasonal and labor-intensive. Work began shortly after New Year's Day, when the ground was still wet and soft and thus less apt to cause the falling tree to shatter. Choppers and sawyers worked in pairs; in tightly organized crews, a head chopper selected trees to be cut and directed the fall. Ideally, choppers directed the fall onto a hillside, falling uphill, to lessen the impact of the fall and to facilitate removal of the tree: trees that fell into ravines were oftentimes impossible to transport and had to be abandoned. In the first years of redwood logging, two- or three-man crews took five or six days to fell a single tree. Choppers, using three-to-four-pound double-headed axes, made an undercut. They made their cut standing on a platform ten to twelve feet above ground because the so-called butt log at the bottom of the trunk was too dense to float downstream to the mill. Sawyers then went to work with a felling saw on the opposite side of the tree, starting their cut slightly above the bottom of the undercut. The felling saws had detachable ears, so that if the diameter of the tree was great, the ear on one side could be removed. The sawyers drove steel wedges into the tree as they cut to keep the trunk from pressing on their saw and to direct the fall toward the undercut.[29]

Once the tree had been felled, peelers removed the bark; redwood bark being so thick—in some cases a foot or more—and heavy that it had to be removed in order to transport the log. After peeling, sawyers with crosscut saws divided the trunk into sections to further reduce weight for transport. By spring and summer, logging camps had swollen to dozens of men, many of whom were employed not in cutting redwoods but in building so-called skid roads. In a skid road, poles were placed five or six feet apart, notched and greased. Teams of oxen dragged peeled sections of trunk along the greased skids until they reached dry creekbeds. Teamsters deposited the logs there to dry until late autumn.[30] Even the best ox teams worked slowly: a good team could transport thirty logs per day from the woods to a landing.[31]

The operation of mills was as seasonal and as labor-intensive as loggers' work in the forests. Peeled and dried logs stacked in dry creekbeds awaited winter freshets, when the rivers filled with water, to float downstream to the mills. Mills were located by the mouths of creeks, at or near tidewater, both to receive logs from upstream and load them onto ships for transport. By the late 1860s, mills dotted the northern California coast every ten or fifteen miles where creeks reached the ocean. Most mills in the early years depended on waterpower, meaning that during the dry summer months the mills could not run.[32] When the rivers flooded, the mills shut down entirely. The rains of late 1861 and early 1862 that inundated Sacramento and other Central Valley cities, for instance, also caused flooding on the northern coast. James Beith described Mad River in early November 1861 as a "vast lake." By January he wrote that "all the bridges, flumes, water crossings, whether suspension or wooden, grist mills, saw mills, quartz mills, have been swept away."[33]

Dependence on animals and waterpower to transport logs to the mills and process them there was the most significant technological bottleneck in the production of redwood lumber. Not only was the procedure slow, seasonal, and expensive (apart from the cost of the oxen, teamsters were the most highly paid employees of the lumber companies), but reliance on river transportation limited loggers to cutting only the redwoods that grew within about two thousand feet of a riverbank.[34] To more easily float logs to the mill, in 1854 loggers cut a half-mile canal connecting the Mad River with a slough that extended inland from Humboldt Bay.[35] In the same year, the lumber company Jones, Kentfield, & Buhne constructed one of the first railroads in California: a short line to transport logs from the forest to the mill.[36]

The railroad presaged the technology that would transform the redwood lumber industry in the late 1850s and 1860s. In contrast to the gold country, where hydraulic power cratered hillsides and flushed tailings through sluices, the lumber industry relied on steam power to increase productivity. It was both apt and ironic: using wood, usually Douglas fir, as fuel to power steam engines, loggers and mill workers increased their capacity to consume still more trees.

Technological innovations began at the mills. Most waterpowered saws were too weak to cut through large redwood trunks. By the end of the 1850s, many mills had replaced their waterwheels with steam engines. Steam freed mills from dependence on river flow, but just as importantly it increased the capacity of the mills.[37] By 1868, six of the seven mills in Mendocino County were steam-powered. "It is an astonishing sight," wrote one awed observer of the steam-powered mills, "to see the immense saws pass through these mammoth logs. Many of the latter are from ten to fifteen feet in diameter, from twelve to fifteen feet in length." Yet "in a few minutes they are ripped into hundreds of boards and scantling—ready for shipment."[38]

Not quite. Sawn logs were in early years placed in slides or chutes to reach the shore, where they were loaded onto waiting ships by hand one piece at a time. This system persisted in some mills until the mid-1870s. Irving Slade worked at one such mill for $40 a month in 1873 and 1874 "piling timber": loading sawed lumber from the mill into a flume through which it traveled to the coast.[39] By that time, however, most mills had installed a boom to load ships.

These technological innovations enabled significant production increases. By the late 1860s, mill owners had opened extensive operations in the redwood belt. In Mendocino County in 1868, sixteen mills, employing nearly half of the laboring population of the county, sawed and shipped 48 million feet of lumber. Ten mills in Humboldt County, employing one thousand men, produced nearly 10 million feet in 1859, nearly 13 million feet in 1865, and 25 million feet in 1868.[40] Six years later, Mendocino produced 70 million board feet annually while Humboldt produced 40 million. By that time Mendocino and Humboldt had become the two leading lumber-producing counties in California; combined, they produced over 40 percent of the lumber in the state.[41]

Such production increases came at a cost, however, notably a rise in accidents. Bonner wrote of the mills in 1884,

In these mills, as in the woods, one is quickly impressed with the fact that the work is not the easiest in the world, nor the most desirable to a "thin-skinned" person. The incessant din of machinery, the flying belts and pulleys, the endless chains, the rattle and jar, the escape of steam, not to mention the inclines and chutes and other contrivances

which seem to be ever waiting to swallow up the unwary, must make it
a perfect pandemonium and place of fear and dread.[42]

Indeed, technological innovations in the redwood mills significantly increased the prospect of gruesome on-the-job injuries. The local newspaper
in Eureka reported accidents in the mills with alarming frequency from the
1860s onward. At one mill an operator had his arm crushed while he was ad-
justing a belt: his thumb was snagged by a wheel and his arm was dragged into
the machine, breaking his arm so severely that the bone protruded from the
skin. At another mill a worker's foot was sawn in half when he slipped while
trying to push a block away from the saw. Injured workers had to rely on private charity; as a local newspaper in Humboldt County noted in the case of an
injured mill worker in 1859, "He has a wife and two children, and the loss of
his time for several months will be a serious drawback to him."[43]

The prevalence of injuries—logging was the most dangerous occupation
in nineteenth-century America—prompted redwood loggers and mill workers
to propose, in early 1868, the creation of a Lumbermen's Protective Union.
"Accidents that will ever occur where a complicated machinery is in motion,
or where heavy masses are moved," noted an anonymous writer to the *Humboldt Times*, endangered every laborer in the redwood industry. Any healthy
worker might "to-morrow be a cripple, having his hands cut by a circular saw
in its rapid revolutions, or himself caught by a belt flying through a pully
literally crushing his limbs." The proposal for a Lumbermen's Union was
modest—a half-dollar every month to create a fund to support disabled workers—but it presaged more concerted efforts to organize lumber workers in
later decades.[44]

Despite these dangers to workers, timber companies introduced further
steam technology to the redwood industry. Steam engines, first introduced in
the mills, drove increased productivity and efficiency in the forest as well. By
the early 1880s, the donkey engine—a steam engine mounted on wooden
skids—had replaced teams of oxen. The donkey engine, the invention of
James Dolbeer, a mill owner on Elk River, powered a winch attached to a long
cable. By drawing in the cable the engine could both drag itself into the forest
on its skids, and, once staked to the ground, drag felled logs to a gathering
point. The mechanical donkeys, according to one observer in 1884, "work
most advantageously in 'snaking' these massive logs from a deep gulch or

Cable dragging redwood log, Humboldt County

steep hillside to convenient points."[45] An officer of the Pacific Lumber Company added that the machines "handle a log six to ten feet in diameter by steam as easily as you would a stick of wood."[46]

As long as loggers had relied on oxen to drag logs to the mill, they had been confined to areas near rivers. The donkeys opened up remote parts of the redwood belt, just as flumes and pipes had extended the reach of hydraulic gold miners. Yet like improvements at the mills, the donkey engines increased the danger of accidents, particularly when a cable snapped. "The velocity of a broken chain," wrote the 1884 observer, "has a rebound that can only be equaled by the speed of a cannon ball."[47]

To transport logs from the gathering points to the mills, lumber companies began in the mid-1870s to abandon the practice of floating logs on rivers.[48] By the mid-1880s transportation of redwood by rail was commonplace. "Old ideas of supplying mills on large streams, or at tide-water, with logs, have largely passed away, and given place to new ones more in harmony with the spirit of enterprise of the times," wrote Bonner in 1884. "The old

Railroad and mill, Mendocino County

methods have generally been abandoned, and the steel rail and ponderous locomotive are now at the fore among redwood lumbermen who operate extensively."[49] By 1892, for instance, the Excelsior Redwood Company controlled a separate corporation, the Humboldt Logging Railway, whose fifteen miles of track, four locomotives, and one hundred cars were dedicated to delivering logs to the Excelsior Mill in Humboldt Bay.[50]

Railroads and mechanical donkeys liberated loggers from having to work near rivers, yet the technologies also compelled them to cut more trees in order to recoup their investment in the machines. One might expect that loggers would have husbanded timber resources carefully to squeeze as much value from the forests as possible. Yet, impelled to realize a return on investment, technological energies invested in producing more lumber for the market also produced more waste.

Carelessness began in the forests. Not only did loggers leave behind ten to twelve feet at the bottom of the trunk, but they also removed and left in the forest the leafy upper portions of the tree. Some trees went entirely to waste, primarily when improperly cut trees shattered upon falling—a fate that, according to one estimate, awaited 20 percent of felled redwoods.[51] Decades of practice increased efficiency somewhat: by 1880, for instance, loggers had reduced shattering by first felling Pacific yews or Douglas firs to create a cushion for the falling redwood, but this practice merely shifted the waste from one tree species to others. Yet by the end of the 1880s, significant amounts of the trees were still wasted. Industry leaders claimed that they made use of 70 to 75 percent of the trees—figures that variously excluded breakage, the loss of the leafy uppermost part of the tree, or the butt. The California State Board of Forestry, however, estimated that all but 28 percent of each tree was wasted, and that even the most efficient loggers used only 40 percent of each tree.[52]

In 1889, the industry journal, *Pacific Coast Wood and Iron*, lamented that in Mendocino County "large portions of the trees felled are often left to rot or burn, and sometimes large, fine trees are not used at all, because they did not fall right, or for some such trifling reason." The great amount of waste on the forest floor became fuel for destructive fires that burned intensely enough to kill even the fire-resistant redwoods, especially young trees that had sprouted up in cutover areas.[53]

Waste continued at the mill. Although the replacement of circular saws by band saws in the mid-1880s reduced waste in sawing, there was still "an immense amount of waste in Redwood logs," as Oscar Redfield wrote in 1887. At the Pacific Lumber Company mill, he wrote of a wide, U-shaped conveyor, kept constantly moving by a revolving chain. The conveyor carried waste lumber, including "pieces of boards and scantling, and some sawdust, slabs &c &c," out of the mill and deposited it "onto a pile which is constantly burning night and day." If the conveyor were only extended to reach the nearest town, Redfield mused, the waste would exceed the townspeople's entire demand for lumber.[54] The burning of substantial amounts of mill waste was standard practice by the 1880s. Bonner described slab and scrap taken to "a mild sort of Gehenna, which is ever kept burning, fifty or sixty yards beyond the mill."[55] Most mills by the middle of the decade had abandoned open fires in favor of furnaces. At large mills, the furnaces, kept constantly active, were 30 feet in diameter and 120 feet deep. At the Excelsior Mill in Eureka, the mill owner estimated in 1896 that nearly half of the logs that arrived at the mill went to waste.[56]

Despite such waste, the expansion of production in the redwood belt drew a significant number of workers to coastal northern California. Particularly those men with logging experience in the forests of northern New England, the Upper Midwest, Lower Canada, and northern Europe were attracted to the redwood belt by the promise of high wages. Ordinary sawyers, road builders, and mill workers earned from $25 to $55 a month, while teamsters and crew bosses earned as much as $75 a month.[57] Accordingly, the population of Humboldt and Mendocino counties rose from a combined 6,661 in 1860, to 13,685 in 1870, to 28,312 in 1880. Over 70 percent of the counties' inhabitants were native-born Americans, with most of the newcomers arriving from the Northeast and Midwest. Most of the foreign-born population came from Canada, Germany, the British Isles, or Scandinavia.[58]

The usual pattern was one of so-called chain migrations, in which migrants from one region of the United States or overseas, already arrived in the redwood belt, facilitated further migration of family and compatriots from their home region. The prevalence of chain migration helped to maintain ethnic and regional identities.[59] A. P. Alexanderson, for instance, migrated directly from Sweden to Eureka because a friend of his had already emigrated there and found work as a logger. Alexanderson stepped off a steamboat from San Francisco speaking only Swedish, was met by his friend at the wharf, and went directly to work in a logging camp.[60]

The camps were austere places, consisting of little more than cramped, poorly ventilated bunkhouses. Loggers worked nearly twelve hours a day. According to Bonner, a workday consisted of "breakfast at six; work; dinner at twelve; work; supper at six; smoke; go to bed."[61] Like laborers in the gold country, the loggers enjoyed Sundays off, but during the work week, according to one observer, "there is no desire to spend the evening in any sort of amusement. They are only too glad to occupy their bunks after supper and a smoke."[62] Though a relative improvement in wages for some migrants, labor in the redwood industry was uneven. Some companies paid their employees only in coupons redeemable at company stores. Many let wages accumulate for months; if a company went out of business, a worker might lose all of his back pay.[63] If a mill closed for the season, it laid off its employees. To support themselves, some workers accepted timber companies' offers to spend the off-season repairing flumes, with payment only at the end of the season.[64]

Humboldt and Mendocino counties typified the emerging migration and labor patterns of the late nineteenth-century West. The migration of farm families such as the Branhams to the Midwest and Far West in the 1840s had centered on their effort to acquire larger tracts of farmland—a family patrimony—that would enable their children and grandchildren to inherit land sufficient to support themselves. Such patrimonial families, as the historian Kathleen Neils Conzen has termed them, migrated as family units and sought long-term agrarian stability. As wage labor increasingly replaced farming in the American economy, however, a new type, the proletarian family, migrated to places such as the redwood belt that offered high wages. While some workers migrated to the redwood belt with their spouses, children, or parents, many proletarian families were far-flung; like Alexanderson, they dispersed in search of work and sent some of their earnings home if they could afford it.[65]

Relatively high wages attracted chain migrants not only from Europe but from East Asia, particularly from Guangzhou (Canton), China's leading port city. Whereas the lowest wage offered to Euroamerican mill workers was $25 a month, mill owners imposed on Chinese laborers a monthly wage of $15. An industry journal described Chinese laborers as deserving of little more: "They know none of the wants, amenities, or decencies of civilization, and live on the cheapest and coarsest fare. They have no Sundays, holidays, churches, schools, or similar institutions. They are in fact without families, domestic relations, or ties of any kind."[66] Though conditions for Euroamericans in some logging camps were equally spartan, Euroamerican loggers and mill workers in the redwood belt, like nineteenth-century Euroamericans generally, regarded the penuriousness of some Chinese laborers as a predisposition—indeed, as a strategy to undercut Euroamericans' wages.

In truth, like many European immigrants to the United States, most Chinese immigrants were young men who came in search of wage-paying jobs. Like European immigrants, their rate of return was high: among the Chinese between 1848 and 1882, roughly 322,000 arrived in the United States and 151,000 departed, a return rate of 47 percent.[67] That Chinese workers received less pay and lived more frugally than most workers was not by choice but a consequence of widespread discrimination in employment and housing opportunities.[68] Ethnic discrimination, in short, made Chinese laborers into extremes of the proletarian family: overseas migration, wage labor, and racism imposed upon them a social alienation even more exacting than that imposed upon Euroamerican wage workers, despite mitigating benevolent societies and other forms of ethnic cooperation.

Chinese workers were never particularly numerous in the redwood belt. Of the 15,512 inhabitants of Humboldt County in 1880, only 242 were Chinese immigrants. Of those, 66 were miners, 62 were laborers, 37 were cooks, and 23 were launderers. Only 6 worked in the lumber business.[69] Yet to some Euroamerican workers they offered a powerful symbolic threat. Euroamerican wage laborers in the redwood belt, as elsewhere in California, tended not to see Chinese workers as suffering from persistent discrimination, but rather viewed themselves as victims of the low wages paid to Chinese workers. By driving down all wages, Euroamerican workers feared, Chinese labor "may be the means of degrading many white men to be fit associates for Chinamen only," editorialized the *Humboldt Times*. Accordingly, in early 1862, Euroamerican workers in Humboldt County founded an Anti-Coolie Association. Such nativist clubs were widespread in California in the 1860s. The group proposed a tax on Chinese labor that would make it cheaper to employ Euroamericans.[70]

The group's frustrations were misplaced: Chinese laborers in the timber industry were rare. It was not Chinese labor that drove down wages in California, but rather the introduction of production technologies that replaced skilled workers such as teamsters with low-wage, unskilled labor. Leaders of groups such as the Anti-Coolie Association cultivated what the historian Carlos Schwantes has called an "ideology of disinheritance." Members of such groups were resentful that unskilled labor was increasingly replacing skilled labor, and that their status as wage laborers was not a temporary stage on a path to some sort of proprietorship but was rather in all likelihood to be lifelong.[71]

Euroamerican laborers in the West expressed their resentment in sometimes violent protests. In the redwood belt, the loggers' and mill workers' scapegoating of the Chinese culminated in Eureka, a town whose population of 2,700 in 1880 included 101 Chinese immigrants. In February 1885, one thousand Euroamericans delivered an ultimatum to the Chinese, whose homes were concentrated in one block in Eureka: they must leave town within twenty-four hours. To demonstrate their determination, the vigilantes erected a gallows at one end of the Chinese neighborhood. Over the next year, expulsions of the Chinese followed in thirty-five California communities, as well as in Seattle and Tacoma in Washington Territory, and, most violently, in Rock Springs, Wyoming Territory, where vigilantes killed twenty-eight Chinese workers.[72]

By the late 1870s, the combined fears of on-the-job injury and declining wages—the latter often infused with anti-Chinese prejudice—emboldened loggers to organize. Initially, workers sought to join not in labor unions but in political parties. Their efforts drew on the ideological traditions of the "dignity of labor" espoused by both the Democratic and Republican parties at midcentury. By the 1870s, many wage workers believed that both parties had abandoned their interests.[73] In the late 1870s and early 1880s, Humboldt County voters strongly endorsed the candidates of two ephemeral parties that, in the course of their brief existences, advocated the old ideology of the dignity of labor: the Workingmen's Party in 1878–79 and the Greenback-Labor Party in 1880.[74] Neither party had much electoral success, however, and both folded quickly.

In the summer of 1884, Humboldt loggers organized themselves as a chapter of the Knights of Labor, an organization that, like the Workingmen's and Greenback-Labor parties, looked backward to the ideals of the dignity of free labor. However nostalgic, the ideology of the Knights was attractive: by 1886, the national organization had 800,000 members, including 2,000 in Humboldt County.

In Eureka, the Knights of Labor began to publish a journal, the *Western Watchman*, under the editorship of William Ayers, a former Greenback-Labor Party organizer. The publication was, like the Knights of Labor in the West generally, virulently anti-Chinese. It was also in favor of temperance—a leftover of earlier Republican social reform ideology, when the party had deplored alcohol because it besotted and degraded workingmen. Essentially backward-looking in its vision, the *Western Watchman* viewed labor as the moral equivalent of capital. Although the Knights' nostalgic rhetoric attracted thousands of laborers to its ranks, moral suasion alone was a weak weapon with which to confront capital. In 1887, when one of the mills discharged a large number of its workers, Ayers was powerless to do more than protest the layoff as a breach of an unwritten social contract between employees and employers.[75]

Editorial protest and scapegoating of Chinese workers did little to improve the working lives of Humboldt Knights. By the end of the 1880s, the Knights had lost their grip on Humboldt County loggers. The Knights—a complex and diffuse organization about which it is difficult to generalize—were an uneasy and unlikely combination of labor union and conservative fraternal order. In Humboldt County, they were too much of the latter to effectively advocate for workers: the Knights' leadership balked at endorsing Humboldt lumber workers' call for a strike to achieve a ten-hour day, yet steadfastly urged temperance on union members.[76]

Although mill workers staged a strike in Eureka in May 1892, by the end of the 1880s labor organizations in the redwood region were in disarray. In several guises—Workingmen, Greenback-Labor, Knights—they proved themselves unfocused, or, worse still, focused on trivia and cul-de-sacs: nativist resentment of the Chinese, temperance, and a nostalgia for the bygone heyday of free-labor ideology.

Given the expense of cutting and processing redwood, the high quality of the lumber, and the limited range of the species, one might reasonably expect that demand for the product would exceed the supply, and that redwood lumber would command a high price on the market. Indeed, some environmental economists have proposed that capitalism, through technological ingenuity and the discipline of the free market, automatically conserves scarce natural resources by first imposing high prices on them and then developing cheaper alternatives. Technology and the market in an economy left to regulate itself, according to this argument, act as efficient forms of resource conservation.[77] Yet until the end of the nineteenth century the redwood industry was plagued by chronic overproduction and a consequent depression of prices. Technological innovation did not create alternatives to redwood lumber, but rather more efficient production of lumber for the market. As Oscar Redfield of the Pacific Lumber Company reported in 1887, his company's mill processed 40,000 feet of lumber every day. Yet he added ruefully, "Of course, sales do not begin to cover the outgo, and it will be a consummation devoutly to be wished, when the income will exceed the expense."[78] Despite a glutted market, technologically sophisticated mills such as Redfield's continued to produce large amounts of redwood lumber, both driving down their profits and depleting the resource. Why should this have been so?

Two decades of technological innovation—donkey engines, railroads, band saws, steam-driven mills—increased the capacity to produce redwood lumber beyond the capacity of the market to consume it. The market for redwood lumber was chronically overstocked through the 1870s. Excess capacity drove down prices. In 1879, it cost approximately $11 per one thousand feet to mill lumber, and between $3.50 and $4.50 to transport it to San Francisco, where it sold for $18.00, at best.[79]

Faced with the instability of the market and the low profit margin in the best of circumstances, as early as 1871 redwood lumber producers organized themselves into a cartel, the Redwood Lumber Association. The purpose of the cartel, according to its by-laws, was both to "regulate the sale of sawn Redwood lumber entering the Bay of San Francisco by way of the sea" and "to prevent Strip and waste of Redwood timber."[80] To accomplish these aims, the association agreed to fix yearly the minimum price of redwood lumber on the San Francisco market, and to maintain that price by fixing yearly the maximum amount of redwood lumber each mill could ship. Each mill's share of the market was to be determined by its proportion of milling capacity. The cartel thus sought to function exactly as environmental economists who advocate market solutions to problems of resource depletion suggest that producers ought to function. Had the cartel succeeded, the mills might have earned greater profits by cutting fewer trees and selling less lumber, both increasing their profitability and conserving the resource upon which their enterprise depended.

Yet the Redwood Lumber Association failed. D. J. Flanigan, who emigrated from Northern Ireland to California by way of Massachusetts and became a partner in a redwood mill in 1871, explained that the producers were not able to control the San Francisco lumber market, which fluctuated considerably in response to larger economic changes. Indeed, the San Francisco market's consumption of lumber was 10 million feet in 1860, over 80 million in 1870, 116 million in 1875, but only 80 million in 1880.[81] "From time to time," Flanigan wrote, redwood producers "have organized combinations among themselves to maintain prices. These combinations have been a source of profit when the market was strong and healthy but have almost invariably gone to pieces in a depressed market."[82]

The national economic depression of 1873 broke the cohesion of the redwood cartel. In the wake of the financial collapse, the price for one thousand feet of redwood lumber on the San Francisco market fell from $18 to as low as $11. Several mills went out of business; those that remained cut wages from an average of $40 a month to $15.[83] As demand and sales plummeted, redwood manufacturers cut production not to maintain prices but because the market was soft. The Dolbeer and Carson Lumber Company, for instance, had processed nearly 10 million board feet in 1871 and over 12 million in 1872, but dropped to 6.5 million in 1873 and just over 5 million in 1874.[84] In the overstocked market, prices for redwood lumber remained low throughout the decade of the 1870s.

By the early 1880s, the market had rebounded—San Francisco's consumption of redwood lumber rose from 80 million feet in 1880 to 115 million in 1885.[85] The redwood industry reorganized its cartel as the Redwood Lumber Manufacturers Association and joined with the Pine Manufacturers Company in 1882 to create the California Lumber Exchange, whose plainly stated purpose, in its article of agreement, was "to fix the prices and terms at which Pine and Redwood lumber shall be sold at retail."[86] Stung by the depression of the mid-1870s, redwood lumber producers acquiesced to the Redwood Lumber Manufacturers Association's enforcement of production discipline, reducing shipments to San Francisco from 115,900,000 feet in 1886 to 93,546,000 in 1888. The reduced supply had the desired effect: prices began to rise. As prices began to inch up again, however, individual mills broke from the cartel and rushed to increase production to take advantage of the market.[87] Indeed, a profitable market was more dangerous to the cartel than a depressed one, as mill owners found irresistible the temptation to increase production and realize a short-term profit.[88] By the end of the 1880s, the Redwood Lumber Manufacturers Association no longer carried any authority to force mill owners to rein in production, and consumption of the redwoods proceeded apace.

Despite waste and the unreliability of the market, by the end of the 1880s the introduction of steam technology had sufficiently stabilized the redwood logging industry to make it attractive to Midwestern logging companies. Midwestern capital did not revolutionize the production of redwood lumber; rather, it was technological innovations developed in the redwood belt that made redwood logging an attractive investment. "The value of redwood timber lands as a safe investment for capital," one observer wrote in 1887, "is now conceded by all," and "redwood timber land is now being bought up by the big timber men of Michigan and Wisconsin."[89] Indeed, the Midwestern timber magnate Frederick Weyerhaeuser told the *San Francisco Examiner* in 1887 that redwoods were "mighty giants" and "a revelation to me." He added, "The man who owns a quarter section of redwoods and holds on to it, even though it may be fifty miles away in the wilderness, will soon make a good thing out of it."[90]

Far from rationalizing the production of redwood lumber, however, the infusion of Midwestern capital destabilized it further. Midwestern investors transformed small mills into large ones, "with double and triple their former output," according to *Pacific Coast Wood and Iron*. "This forced upon the market large quantities of lumber, which had to supply a market hardly able to consume the amount formerly bought here. In fact, the mills can now cut in one year enough to last three years." To combat overproduction and the depressed market, the editors of *Pacific Coast Wood and Iron* urged a reinvigorated cartel, "a great trust as strong as American Sugar or Standard Oil."[91]

Yet cartelization never imposed complete control on the production of redwood, and the standing timber in the redwood belt declined accordingly. In 1850 the redwood belt had contained about 33 billion board feet of timber. By the mid-1880s, at least 10 billion board feet had been consumed. By the end of the 1880s, no less than 12 billion board feet—36 percent of the original stand—had been converted to lumber. An unknown further amount had been converted to sawdust, or fuel for mills' scrap furnaces, or rotting logs on the forest floor. The lower reaches of the redwood belt, from the southern part of Mendocino County south to Santa Cruz, had been reduced to a few remote stands. The only commercially viable redwood forest remaining extended from the northern half of Mendocino County through Humboldt County to Del Norte County on the Oregon border.[92]

The decimation of the old-growth redwood forests cannot be measured simply in board feet. Redwoods are part of an interconnected ecological community. The removal of large numbers of trees created ecological disturbances throughout the community. In logged-off areas, grasses, shrubs, forbs, and hardwood trees invaded. Redwood seedlings in cutover areas have a window of only a few years to establish themselves before such grasses and brush crowd them out.[93] Shrubs and forbs attracted browsing animals such as deer and elk. The browsers in turn prevented some redwood forests from re-growth by consuming redwood seedlings as quickly as they appeared. While inviting in ungulates such as deer and elk, logging destroyed the redwood forest as a habitat for other mammals. Martens and fishers, endemic to the redwood belt, depended on established old-growth forests, with closed canopies and dense, woody snags and debris, for their sustenance. The simplified, even-aged redwood tree farms that replaced some old-growth forests lacked the complexity and woody debris upon which these animals depended. Other carnivores once common to the redwood forests such as grizzlies and wolverines disappeared entirely.[94]

Some of the most significant disturbances resulting from redwood deforestation were of riverine environments. Redwoods, like most trees, stabilized
riverbanks and prevented erosion. Deforestation increased runoff into
streams, raising the level of sediment in the rivers and reducing stream depth
while increasing their width. The removal of the canopy increased solar radi-
ation and thus both soil and stream temperature. All of these changes to the
riverine environment worked to the detriment of migrating fish such as
salmon, which depend on cold, clear, gravely streams to spawn.[95]

Pro-market environmental economists generally regard such environmental degradation as an acceptable cost. (Just as other economists might
dismiss the social costs of low wages and on-the-job accidents that resulted
from steam technology.) What does it matter, they might argue, that the habitat for a few fish and mammals was destroyed, when measured against the
wealth that the redwood lumber industry produced? Yet overproduction not
only deforested the redwood belt, it undercut the profitability of the industry.
Both the redwood forest and the redwood lumber industry faced a shared
problem: too much lumber in the market and too few trees in the forest.
Greater technological restraint might have not only conserved the redwood
forest but increased the profitability of the industry.

To argue the case against overproduction on such terms implies an ac-
ceptance of the basic premise of pro-market environmental economists: that
the value of nature is measured in monetary terms. Yet martens, salmon, and
redwoods are worth more than just their price on the market. They are part of
an interconnected and interdependent natural environment. The loss of the
value of a commodity is but the most trivial cost of these species' depletion.
The destruction of these most vulnerable species is the mark of an environment whose viability is in decline. In an environment shared by all, the costs
of such ruination are ultimately shared by all.

PART II

THE INDUSTRIAL FRONTIER

The transformation of the California environment was entangled in California's complex multiethnic society. Industrial societies in the West emerged at the expense of Indians and, as elsewhere in the southwestern borderlands, Mexicans. By contrast, a half-century earlier, on the coasts of the Atlantic and the Great Lakes and along the rivers that flowed into them, manufacturing succeeded Euroamerican agricultural societies that to varying degrees were already integrated into the market economy.[1] In California after 1850, in direct contravention to the historian Frederick Jackson Turner's notion of a tidy linear progression from wilderness to subsistence farming to commercial agriculture to urbanism and industrialism, an industrial society arose on the frontier of Anglo-American settlement.

The social costs of industrialization fell disproportionately on those societies on the opposite side of the frontier: the Mexican rancheros of southern California and the fishing-hunting-gathering Indians of the interior. These societies encountered a more powerful Euroamerican presence than indigenous groups in eastern North America had encountered in the seventeenth and eighteenth centuries. In particular, the industrial society of the nineteenth century possessed a greater ability to transform the natural environment and thus undermine indigenous resource strategies. Indians and Mexicans made extensive adaptations to the new order in an effort to survive the transformation to an industrial society with a remnant of their environments and their resource strategies intact. Mexican elites in southern California tried to draw Anglo settlers into their cultural web. Indians in northeastern California and elsewhere intermarried with Anglo settlers and sought to find a niche as wage laborers. Their efforts at accommodation were only partly successful.

Indians and Mexicans on the periphery of California's industrial transformation were most profoundly affected by the expansion of commercial ranching.[2] California in the second half of the nineteenth century was not only an emerging industrial place but also one of the most productive agricultural regions in the United States. In 1870 the value of livestock in California exceeded that of Texas. Most California cattle were raised on large ranches, some a legacy of extensive Mexican land grants and some allotted from United States public lands.

The simultaneous rise of industry and commercial agriculture was far from antithetical. From the emergence of enclosed estates in early modern England to the commercialization of agriculture in the early nineteenth-century United States, the rise of manufacturing often has been accompanied by a rise in the production of agricultural commodities on relatively large estates. Such agricultural enterprises complemented the rise of industry not only by specializing in the large-scale production of foodstuffs for urban and wage-earning consumers. By enclosing large estates, they also transformed the inhabitants of the industrial periphery into a wage-earning proletariat. By the mid-1880s, California produced the bulk of its cattle not on family farms but on vast estates staffed by wage laborers.[3]

The picture that emerges in nineteenth-century California is thus the inverse of the popular understanding of the transformation of the American West. That understanding posits an initial encounter between Anglo-American settlers on one side and Indians and Mexicans on the other. In this encounter, the groups are generally, if imperfectly, understood to be more or less evenly matched in population and technology. After the triumph of Anglo-Americans on this frontier, the settlers transformed the wilderness to civilization. Industry and urbanism eventually followed. Rather, in California, industry and urbanism developed rapidly after the discovery of gold. Few Anglo-Americans who came to California immediately after the discovery of gold were interested in farming; those who were co-opted (or perhaps were co-opted by) Mexican agrarian elites. By the end of the 1850s, Indians and Mexicans in California faced not a handful of Anglo-American pioneers but a populous industrial society impelled by the full weight of such a society's demand for land and natural resources.

4

Gambling on the Grassland: Kinship, Capital, and Ecology in Southern California

In October 1873, a year before his death, the San Diego cattle rancher Cave Johnson Couts wrote to his sons that he was selling his horses and getting out of the cattle business. "I have sold and delivered all my caballada, bronco, throwing in the colts, at $8 per head. It was almost giving them away, but there was no help—costing one about $10 per day," he wrote, adding resignedly, "Have bought a lot of sheep, and if nothing better turns up you must prepare to be shepherds."[1] Raising sheep was a viable economic alternative to cattle, but for Couts as for other large landowners in southern California, sheep raising lacked the seigneurial allure of cattle ranching; the shift from cattle to sheep dashed the aristocratic pretensions that he had nurtured for over two decades.

Couts had entered into cattle ranching in the early 1850s, as California livestock production mushroomed. As the non-Indian population of California rose from 14,000 in 1848 to 380,000 in 1860, ranchers such as Couts exponentially increased their livestock holdings. According to the California Agricultural Society, the population of cattle rose from 448,796 in 1852 to 1,116,261 in 1859.[2] By the end of the 1850s, not only were there more cattle in California than any other single domesticated species, there were nearly three times as many cattle as people.

The Californians seemingly best situated to profit from the demand for beef were the large estate owners of coastal southern California. Possessed of hundreds of thousands of acres of land and tens of thousands of cattle, these Californios—who included many Britons and Americans such as Couts who had married into established Mexican families—were southern California's rural elite. Beyond their dominance in land and cattle, the Californios possessed a powerful and practical tradition of commercial cooperation. The elite families were extensively intermarried; as with other large landholders in the Americas in the nineteenth century, bonds of kinship encouraged families to cooperate in business matters.[3]

Yet the Californios' dominance was short-lived. The sudden rise of the cattle population in the 1850s presaged an equally abrupt decline in the mid-1860s. Two opposing interpretations, which dominate the historiography of Mexican California, have offered explanations.

The older of the two interpretations, associated primarily with the historian Leonard Pitt, characterized Californio society as colorful yet backward. According to Pitt, the decrepit and indolent Californio society was unable to adapt to the changes that followed the Mexican-American War and the gold rush. Pitt was critical of the racism and brutality of the Anglo-Americans, but he credited the newcomers' superior economic vigor with sweeping away the Californios.[4]

The opposing interpretation, advanced by historians including Albert Camarillo, Richard Griswold del Castillo, Tomás Almaguer, and Lisbeth Haas, contradicts most of Pitt's postulates, particularly his sweeping caricature of Californio culture: according to the newer interpretation, Mexican society and culture in Alta California was vigorous and creative—so much so that while some large landowners lost much of their wealth as a result of the American conquest, Mexican-American culture and society persisted. Indeed, these historians contest Pitt's central premise that Mexican-American culture and society suffered a dramatic decline. Instead, like recent historians of Native American and African-American cultures who have argued for cultural persistence in the face of conquest and slavery, they argue that while conquest reduced Mexican-Americans to a segregated proletariat, Mexican-Americans offered resistance through persistence.[5]

In its rejection of ethnic stereotype and its attention to the strength of Mexican-American culture, the recent scholarship is an important contribution to American social and cultural history. Yet neither it nor the interpretation it sought to replace offers much understanding of the subject of Couts's letter to his sons: the decline of southern California cattle ranchers. Couts hardly exemplified Pitt's caricature of the indolent Californio; he was an energetic entrepreneur, despite shortfalls of capital and unreliable markets for his agricultural products. Yet the sense of loss that Couts expressed in 1873 is at odds with the cultural persistence that the newer school of historians has sought to demonstrate. Indeed, because of their mutual focus on the cultural and racial clash between Anglo- and Mexican-Americans, neither interpretation offers much understanding of Couts at all: a Tennessean who emigrated to southern California in the 1840s, married into a prominent Californio family, and thus inhabited two cultural worlds. Both schools of interpretation insist on viewing Anglo-American rancheros such as Couts as transitional figures who helped to shift California from Mexican to United States control.[6]

Both interpretations also emphasize cultural conflict over cultural interpenetration and borrowing. Pitt softens the edges of Frederick Jackson Turner's frontier analysis by casting Mexican-Americans as static rather than savage, and by lamenting the excessive cruelties of the Anglo-American conquest, yet like all classical frontier studies, it suggests a zero-sum game: the rise of the Anglo-Americans must come at the expense of the Californios. The work of Camarillo and others argues that Mexican-American culture transcended Mexico's military defeat by the United States in 1848, the influx of millions of Anglo-Americans to what had been Mexico's northern provinces, and the artificial border between Mexico and the U.S. Southwest. This kind of borderland study is also a sort of zero-sum game, with Mexican culture persisting in the face of the Anglo-American conquest.

The decline of southern California's landed elite has fallen hostage to this historiographical standoff. Yet there is another kind of borderland study that suggests a way out of the current impasse. This definition of borderland emphasizes not only the permeability of the U.S.-Mexican border and the endurance of Mexican cultural integrity, but cultural interaction and borrowing.[7] Mid-nineteenth-century southern California was characterized by the blurring of cultural borders. Couts and other Anglo-American ranchers epitomized this process.

How, then, to explain the decline of the Californios? Historians who emphasize Mexican cultural persistence, well aware of the hostility of U.S. authorities to Mexican-Americans, largely attribute the decline of the large ranching estates of Mexican California to the efforts of the U.S. Land Commission. Between 1852 and 1856 the commission reviewed the legitimacy of all Mexican land grants. Yet of the 813 claims that it reviewed, 612 (75 percent), totaling over eight million acres, were confirmed. Confirmation was

Cave Johnson Couts

virtually universal in southern California—indeed, in deference to the southern California estate owners the commission traveled to Los Angeles to hear
their claims, rather than require them to come to San Francisco like all other
claimants. By the end of the 1850s, when the commission had largely completed its work, most southern California estates remained intact.[8] Some historians argue that even where the commission confirmed Mexican titles,
Anglo-American squatters nonetheless ignored the Mexicans' property rights
and simply settled on estates. Squatters were less common in southern California than to the north, but some ranchos, such as the 326,000-acre de la
Guerra estate in Santa Barbara, attracted numerous squatters. Yet not all
squatters were an unwanted and unremunerative presence: many landowners, including the de la Guerras, transformed squatters into tenants.[9]

The focus on differences of race and culture and on the economic conquest that followed the discovery of gold in 1848 has fueled the argument (now
largely one-sided) between observers of cultural decline and proponents of
cultural persistence. That focus has crowded out other subjects, particularly

the concern that was central to Couts's declining fortunes: the unpredictable southern California environment. In the southern California ranchlands, the changeable environment was a crucial historical agent. Despite the racist brutality of Anglo-Americans—and here Couts was no exception—and despite squatters and the work of the land commission, rancheros had for decades proven adept at incorporating wealthy Anglo immigrants into their midst. It was not simply the influx of large numbers of Anglo-Americans into California that destroyed the large estate owners of southern California and led to the barrioization and proletarianization of Mexican-Americans. Rather, the leading cause was the drought-prone southern California environment.

To give primacy to the agency of the environment is not to argue for environmental determinism. The reasons for the Californios' downfall are complex. The impact of drought was exacerbated by the production techniques of Couts and other large landholders. Like the hydraulic mining companies of the gold country and the timber companies of the redwood belt, the southern California rancheros had little capital to invest to improve their acreage, or to hire laborers. Because of these shortfalls, southern California ranchers neither constructed fences nor cultivated hay, practices that are the hallmarks of *intensive* stockraising. Although such practices are both costly and laborious, intensive stockraisers lose few animals to drought or predators and are, moreover, able to send heavy and thus valuable animals to market. The Californios found such expensive strategies unnecessary. Rather, like most ranchers in the Americas who possessed significant pasturelands, southern California ranchers were *extensive* stockraisers; they let their herds forage over an immense area, relying on the vast grasslands of the southern coast to support them.[10]

In Los Angeles, San Diego, San Luis Obispo, and Santa Barbara counties, over 250,000 cattle, excluding milch cows and working oxen, grazed in 1860. These four southern counties contained nearly one-quarter of the cattle in the state, yet together they mowed less than five thousand tons of hay, or less than 2 percent of the hay mowed in California.[11] In short, like hydraulic miners and redwood loggers, southern California ranchers compensated for their shortages of capital and labor by shifting the burden of their enterprise to the natural environment.

The grasses of California were an unpredictable resource, however, particularly in the southern counties. In the largely bygone environment of the coastal grasslands, as in other steppe or prairie environments of North America, precipitation was highly variable: unusually wet seasons were as likely as not to be followed by drought. While precipitation in coastal southern California averages between ten and fifteen inches per year, the actual annual precipitation is rarely within 25 percent of the average. Instead, drought years are interspersed with flood years.[12] Extensive stockraisers bound the fate of their cattle to this unpredictable climate. When a two-year-long drought struck southern California in 1863–64 (punctuated by a plague of grasshoppers which consumed any grasses that had survived), the region's extensive ranching system collapsed.

Aridity usually characterizes southern California because an atmospheric anomaly known as the Pacific High, a seasonal ridge of high pressure west of the Los Angeles Bight, deflects most oceanic atmospheric moisture away from the southern coast. As a result, while coastal northern California receives about 20 inches or more of average annual precipitation, increasing to almost 80 inches at the northernmost point of the redwood belt, Los Angeles receives only 15 inches. San Diego is drier still; it receives only 10 inches of average annual precipitation. Such meager precipitation supports only smaller plant species such as grasses and shrubs. Accordingly, native California species such as needlegrasses and bluegrasses predominated along the southern coast. Lightning fires frequently smoldered in the dry region. Chaparral and scrub plants of the southern California hillsides were well adapted to fire; indeed, low-temperature fires were an integral part of the ecology of the region. They initiated new growth in chaparral and opened niches for grasses.[13]

Like other North American grasslands, those of southern California were prone to drought. Almost every fall, hot, dry air from the desert interior flows toward the southern California coast, bringing high winds, the so-called Santa Anas, that can transform smoldering grassfires into conflagrations. Such Santa Ana fires are ordinarily extinguished during the late fall and winter, when the Pacific High weakens, allowing cooler, wetter air currents to bring rain to coastal southern California. Sometimes, however, the Pacific High persists. Without the cool-season rains, the grasses upon which grazing animals depend wither and die.[14] Southern California experienced such droughts with grim regularity in 1809–10, 1820–21, 1828–30 (when an estimated 40,000 cattle died), and 1840–41.[15]

The native grasses of southern California were adapted to these intermittent drought conditions, but Spanish settlement beginning in 1769 radically altered the coastal grasslands. By 1773, the five missions of California had introduced 205 head of cattle. In Spanish-Mexican California, pasturelands were vast: grasses covered one-quarter of Alta California. Domesticated livestock thus had few natural constraints on their numbers. Like invading Old World animal and plant species throughout the New World, their populations erupted.[16] By 1805, the missions held 95,000 cattle. Many of these cattle were concentrated in southern California. In 1833, when Mexico secularized the missions, two-thirds of the cattle in the province belonged to the herds of just three missions: San Gabriel, just north of Los Angeles, and San Luis Rey and San Juan Capistrano, on the coast between Los Angeles and San Diego.[17]

In broad terms, the rise of cattle ranching in southern California was one of three ecological eruptions of domesticated grazing animals on New Spain's eighteenth-century northern frontier; the other two were horse nomadism in the Great Plains and sheep pastoralism in New Mexico.[18] Population biologists have repeatedly demonstrated that such eruptions, often the result of an exotic species entering a rich new ecological niche, are typically followed by abrupt crashes.[19] Indeed, by the middle of the nineteenth century, nomadism in the plains, pastoralism in New Mexico, and ranching in southern California were in sharp decline—with significant consequences for the societies that had organized their subsistence around these exotic grazing animals.

In southern California, the cattle transformed the vegetation of the coastal grasslands. California bunchgrasses, though highly nutritious, cling to the soil by slender and shallow roots, and thus cannot withstand heavy trampling and grazing.[20] The pressure of cattle destroyed native grasses, while Old World grasses, whose seeds the missionaries had accidentally transported to California along with seeds for domesticated plants, flourished in the disturbed environment. These European plant species, which had evolved alongside large ruminants, were better adapted to trampling and heavy grazing. By the beginning of the nineteenth century, the coastal grasslands consisted primarily of such Old World species as soft chess and wild oats.[21]

The only significant environmental limitation on the burgeoning cattle population of California was the semiarid climate. Rainfall in southern California is both scarce and seasonal. Ninety percent of the precipitation in Los Angeles and San Diego falls between November and April. San Diego rainfall records indicate that between 1850 and 1869, an average of 8.42 inches of rain fell during the rainy months between November and April. An average of only 0.83 inches fell during the dry season between May and October.[22] In an 1873 letter to his brother assessing the prospects for commercial ranching in California, the settler John Kincade explained how the seasonal rainfall imposed limits on stockraising. Kincade wrote that "here there is only the grass of the winter and spring growth. After about the middle of May grass not only ceases to grow, but dries up, and when once grazed off does not appear again until the next winter or rainy season."[23] The missions' large landholdings— 100,000 acres were typical—were thus essential to their stockraising operations; they needed the extensive acreage to absorb the grazing pressure of their herds in the dry summer and fall seasons.

By the time of the discovery of gold, the livestock in southern California belonged not to the missions but to the ranchos, the great agricultural estates of Mexican California. Generations of historians, beginning with Hubert Howe Bancroft in the 1880s and continuing with Pitt in the 1960s, have thoroughly romanticized the rancheros in a style similar to the traditional caricature of Old South planter families: proud yet carefree inhabitants of a sunny clime who loved luxury, despised toil, and happily (for them) commanded the labor of others. A fuller understanding of the rancheros is more complex. While they were provincial elites, the rancheros were nonetheless ambitious and innovative participants in the international market economy and speculators in land and cattle.[24]

These were not the ranchos of central or northern Mexico, where the term referred to modest landholdings of middling, commercially oriented farmers and ranchers. In the terms of Mexican historiography, the southern California ranchos are better described as haciendas, grand estates whose owners constituted the rural elite.[25] The California ranchos emerged following Mexico's independence from Spain in 1821, as part of the effort to spur the economic development and bolster the population of the northern provinces. The Colonization Act of 1824 provided for governors of frontier provinces such as California to grant large tracts of land of up to eleven leagues, or over 48,000 acres, to private entrepreneurs. Because the missions, which were concentrated along the California coast, continued to control the best coastal pasturelands, however, between 1824 and 1832 California governors granted only twenty-one petitions under the Colonization Act. After Mexico confiscated the mission lands in the Secularization Act of 1833, the number of land grants rose quickly: California governors made 452 grants between 1833 and 1846.[26] By 1840, Los Angeles County had forty ranchos; Santa Barbara twenty; and San Diego seventeen.[27]

One of the most prominent proponents—and beneficiaries—of secularization was the California politician Juan Bandini. The son of a Spanish merchant, Bandini was born in Lima, Peru, in 1800, and came to California in 1819. He subsequently served variously as a legislator and tax official in the province. In 1831 he was a participant in the overthrow of the conservative, pro-clerical governor, Manuel Victorio, and his replacement by José María Echeandía, a governor more favorable to secularization and economic development. Bandini's reward for his political intrigues was to become California's representative to Mexico City in 1833. There, he actively lobbied for secularization and land distribution. Upon his return to California in 1834, as an officer of a colonization and land speculation company, he received his first grant, the five-league Tecate rancho in San Diego. By 1839 he had received four more grants in Los Angeles, bringing his total landholdings to nearly thirty leagues. He received further grants at San Juan Capistrano in 1841 and at Guadalupe in Baja California in 1846.[28]

Yet Bandini's colonization enterprise failed, and like most other California rancheros, he remained land-rich but cash-poor. His ranchos teemed with cattle that had once belonged to the missions, but there was only a limited market for the beef. Don Juan's predicament typified Mexican California. Largely because of its remoteness, secularization neither enriched nor populated the province. Unlike New Mexico, which carried on an extensive trade with Missouri, or Texas, where the offer of land grants attracted tens of thousands of foreign settlers, relatively few settlers came to California in the 1830s and 1840s.[29] The economy of the province languished. When the overland emigrant Joseph Pownall arrived in Los Angeles in August 1849, the town had only two thousand inhabitants.[30]

In provincial California's sluggish economy, rancheros such as Bandini sustained themselves by selling cattle hide and tallow to British and American merchant vessels that docked at Santa Barbara, San Pedro, and San Diego. The work of tending to the cattle and producing hides fell to vaqueros, principally the descendants of Indians Christianized and Hispanicized at the missions. Twice a year, in the fall and the spring, the vaqueros conducted the rodeo, or roundup, of the cattle on the various estates. One observer, Charles Nordhoff, wrote that the cattle "roam at will over large districts, and those of a dozen or twenty owners feed together on the pastures of all." The vaqueros drove the cattle to an agreed-upon point, where representatives of the rancheros "parted out" the herds according to their owners; the vaqueros then branded or "ironed" the calves.

The work required extraordinary skill. Nordhoff marveled at "the certainty with which the lasso or riata is flung, and the admirable training of the horses, which co-operate with their riders and turn like a flash," and at how the vaqueros "rode into the mass of cattle and singled out one by its mark, . . . turned its head out of the circle, [and] drove it adroitly aside." Herding, parting out, and ironing calves lasted for weeks; it required the labor of one vaquero for roughly every four hundred cattle. Vaqueros held spring rodeos not primarily to brand but to slaughter cattle for the hide and tallow market. They staked the animals' skins to dry in the sun; when ready, they transported the stiff and heavy hides to warehouses on the coast. The industry was technologically rudimentary but was nonetheless provincial California's largest economic sector. Between 1826 and 1848, California exported an estimated six million hides.[31]

The hide trade supported the rancheros in what might be described as genteel poverty. They maintained comfortable villas staffed by large numbers of Indians from the former missions. The household staff showed elaborate deference to the ranchero, whom they referred to as Padrone, and his family. Nordhoff noted that "no vacquero addressed the master without either touching or taking off his hat."[32] Yet the aristocratic edifice of the ranchero system rested on an unstable economic foundation. The rancheros were chronically indebted to the merchants who bought their hides and tallow. The rancheros were so cash-poor that they relied heavily on barter to conduct their commerce with other rancheros and with the townspeople of the pueblos.[33]

The stagnant economy of southern California reflected the general pattern of Mexican agricultural estates in the eighteenth and nineteenth centuries. While haciendas varied greatly across Mexico, from those remote and semi-feudal to those closely tied to the agricultural export economy, some generalizations are possible. According to the historian David Brading, Mexican

Rancheros

haciendas, especially those engaged in raising cattle, were stately but leaky economic vessels. Merchant families like the Bandinis acquired higher social status when they purchased such estates, but the hacienda was a drain on their resources. Brading wrote that in Mexico, "the fortunes created in mining and commerce were invested in land, there to be slowly dissipated."[34]

Brading's characterization, slightly modified, aptly describes the California rancheros. For them, the acquisition of a large estate was an expensive assertion of social privilege, but it was also a gamble on future prosperity. Like Bandini, many rancheros had originally secured their ranchos from the government as get-rich-quick colonization schemes. After they had shifted their hopes of fortune from colonization to cattle, they neither fenced their lands nor sowed hay; rather, they borrowed against the day when they would reap a large profit.[35]

Such an approach left the rancheros vulnerable to better-financed competitors, such as the Massachusetts-born merchant Abel Stearns, who arrived in the cattle country in 1829. Within two decades he had become "Don Abel," the wealthiest and most powerful ranchero in southern California. Stearns's

Abel Stearns

rise to the status of ranchero was hard won. He had gone to sea in 1810 as an impoverished twelve-year-old orphan. He served aboard merchant vessels, primarily in the Pacific Ocean, eventually rising to the position of super-cargo—the officer in charge of the ship's cargo and commercial dealings. He returned in success to Massachusetts, married, fathered two children, and joined a Masonic Lodge in Roxbury. Yet Stearns did not settle into a perma-nent home in Massachusetts. His daughter died in 1818 three days after being born; after 1819 records of his wife and son disappear; by 1822 Stearns had re-turned to sea, having purchased a schooner that engaged in trade in Latin America.[36]

Stearns's fortunes improved markedly over the next decade as he assimi-lated into the Latin American commercial world. In 1826 he established him-self as a merchant in Mexico; two years later he became a Mexican citizen. By the time he made his way to California in 1829, he had amassed enough capi-tal to establish a large warehouse in San Pedro, which became a center of the hide and tallow trade. Stearns, a shrewd dealer, both bought hides at the most advantageous terms and advanced loans at extortionate interest rates to the chronically underfunded rancheros.[37]

Had Stearns been content to remain a merchant on the periphery of ranchero society, he might have successfully preyed on the rancheros' financial weaknesses for years to come. Yet to be a merchant, even a successful one, fell far short of his social ambitions. When he had first come to California he had spent two years fruitlessly petitioning Governor Victorio for a land grant. The pro-clerical Victorio was skeptical of the Yankee trader, whose Casa de San Pedro was somewhat disreputable: it was an open secret that Stearns ran an extensive smuggling operation out of the store. It was also occasionally dangerous: an 1835 knife fight with a customer who quarreled over the price of liquor left Stearns permanently disfigured. Four years after that altercation, Stearns once again petitioned the governor of California for a rancho, imploring that he wanted to be "a farmer instead of a Marchant." Once more he was rejected.

Rather than receiving a government grant, the route to ranchero status taken by Californio insiders such as Bandini, Stearns's rise to respectability culminated in two other legal proceedings. In one of those proceedings, in 1842, Stearns became a landowner, purchasing the Rancho Los Alamitos for $6,000 from a ranchero, Francisco Figueroa, heavily indebted to him. Using the same technique over the next decade, he acquired several more parcels of land, including the ranchos La Laguna, Las Bolsas, La Bolsa Chica, Los Coyotes, and parts of the ranchos Temescal and Santiago de Santa Ana. By the early 1850s he controlled all or part of seventeen ranchos. He amassed a huge swath of land stretching from the Santa Ana Mountains to the Pacific Ocean, embracing most of the territory between the Santa Ana and San Gabriel rivers—an empire of over 450,000 acres.[38] How many cattle he owned is impossible to know, but in 1853 Stearns estimated that four of his seventeen ranchos altogether held 20,000 cattle.[39]

The first United States Census of California, in 1850, showed Stearns to be the wealthiest person in Los Angeles County. His real estate holdings were valued at $80,000. The figure, in all likelihood a vast underestimate, was nonetheless 60 percent higher than the next-richest landowner in the county. While the other wealthy landholders in 1850 described themselves to the census taker as "merchants" or "graziers," Stearns alone styled himself a

TABLE I.
WEALTHIEST LANDHOLDERS IN LOS ANGELES COUNTY, 1850

Rank	Name	Value of Real Estate	Age	Occupation	Place of Birth
1	Abel Stearns	$80,000	59	Gentleman	Massachusetts
2	John Temple	50,000	56	Merchant	Massachusetts
	Juan Luis Vignes	50,000	71	Farmer	France
	Benjamin D. Wilson	50,000	39	Merchant	Tennessee
5	Henry Dalton	30,000	46	Grazier	England
6	Eulogio Celis	20,000	42	Agriculturist	Spain
	John Foster	20,000	36	Grazier	England
	Antonio Maria Lugo	20,000	76	Grazier	California
	Bernardo Yava	20,000	49	Grazier	California
10	Francisco Figueroa	15,000	46	Merchant	Mexico
	William Woolfskill	15,000	52	Farmer	Kentucky
12	Manuel Requena	14,500	50	None	Mexico
13	Alexander Bell	13,000	51	Merchant	Pennsylvania
14	Hugo Reid	12,500	39	Merchant	Scotland
15	José Sepulveda	12,000	58	Grazier	California
16	Narcisso Botella	10,000	40	Agriculturist	Mexico
	José Anto. Carillo	10,000	56	Farmer	California
	Augustin Oliverez	10,000	30	County Judge	Mexico
	Isaac Williams	10,000	51	Grazier	Pennsylvania

Source: United States Census Office, Census of the City and County of Los Angeles, California, for the Year 1850 (Los Angeles: Times-Mirror Press, 1929).

"gentleman."[40] Like the Bandinis a generation earlier and the merchants-turned-hacendados of Mexico, Stearns plowed the profits of his commercial enterprise into prestigious but unremunerative ranching estates.

In another legal proceeding, in 1841, the forty-two-year-old Stearns joined one of the most socially prominent families in southern California when he married thirteen-year-old Arcadia Bandini, one of Juan Bandini's five daughters. In many respects, the union was an unlikely one, even in a society in which it was common for a woman in her early teens to marry a much older man. California authorities questioned Stearns closely about the legitimacy of his Mexican citizenship and his Catholicism. For his part, Stearns never mentioned to authorities his previous marriage in Massachusetts.

Some Californio observers were skeptical of the union, or more likely envious of Stearns's emerging place in southern California elite society. One

Juan Bandini and one of his daughters

contemporary, José Anaz, remarked that while Arcadia "had the reputation of being the most beautiful woman in California," Stearns, disfigured by the 1835 knife fight, was widely known as Cara de Caballo ("Horse-Face").[41] Yet as Anaz knew, marriages in elite Californio society were rarely love matches and more often the formalization of financial and cultural alliances between families.[42] While Stearns's marriage lent him social respectability, for the Bandini family, Stearns brought a welcome infusion of capital. El Palacio, the elaborate Los Angeles house Stearns had built for his child bride, was a demonstration of both his wealth and his newfound social prominence.[43]

As Anglo-American trade came to dominate the southern California economy, Juan Bandini shrewdly secured both Yankee capital and sons-in-law who knew how to navigate the American economic and legal systems. Four of his five daughters wed Anglo-Americans: Arcadia married Stearns; Ysidora married the Tennessee Army officer Cave Johnson Couts; Dolores married Charles B. Johnson, the nephew of Alfred Robinson, an Anglo-American merchant who had married into the de la Guerra ranchero family of

Santa Barbara; and Margarita married the physician James B. Winston. Such a strategy was also common in Texas, where wealthy Tejano estate owners often married their daughters to Anglo immigrants, thus acquiring both capital and better standing in Anglo courtrooms.[44] In California, the marriages literally wedded American capital to Californio land.

The marriages were not loveless acts of pure calculation.[45] The letters of Couts and Stearns to the Bandinis are replete with expressions of genuine affection; Stearns was particularly fond of his sister-in-law Ysidora, who lived at El Palacio for several years before her marriage to Couts. Nor were these unions anomalies.[46] In Los Angeles, seven of the nine wealthiest landowners in 1850 had been born not in California but in the United States or Western Europe, and the wealthiest two dozen Anglo-Americans owned half of the developed real estate in Los Angeles.[47] There was no stark opposition between elite Anglos and Californios in Los Angeles and elsewhere in southern California in the 1850s; rather, a complex genealogy of land and cattle ownership blurred the lines between Mexican and American proprietorship.

The American bridegrooms found themselves enmeshed in a precariously financed ranchero political economy that relied on kinship for protection from outside creditors. In 1851, Stearns rescued his father-in-law from financial ruin, paying Bandini's creditors nearly $13,000. During the rest of the decade of the 1850s Stearns advanced Bandini more funds until his father-in-law owed him $24,000. Bandini eventually repaid his son-in-law in the only currency he possessed—land—deeding him part of Rancho La Jurupa in 1859.[48]

When Bandini died later that year, his will left most of his estate to his wife and ten children. Yet his heirs could inherit only what was left after Bandini's creditors took their share. Bandini still owed Stearns $2,000. He owed a further $1,800 to merchants and other creditors. His will instructed his three executors (his two eldest sons and Stearns) "to arrange the payments to my creditors so that they are satisfied in the best harmony with my family, begging them to avoid any kind of trouble or breach which may take to poverty my wife and older and younger children."[49] As both Bandini's executor and his largest creditor, Stearns must have understood the meaning of Bandini's plea: that he would be expected to support Bandini's widow and children.

In 1852 it appeared to Stearns that his new brother-in-law, Couts, might be as much a financial liability as Bandini. While Stearns had risen to the status of ranchero from humble origins, Couts had been born to an influential

Springfield, Tennessee, family. Political connections ensured his admittance to West Point, from which he graduated in 1843, and he came to California as a lieutenant in the First Dragoons during the Mexican-American War.

Whether in Springfield or at West Point, by adulthood Couts had acquired two characteristic traits of the antebellum planter officer class: a pretension to aristocracy and a penchant for gambling, for which in 1850 he faced a court martial. His gambling continued after he resigned from the Army and married Ysidora Bandini; just a year after the wedding, Couts lost between eight and ten thousand dollars. Stearns, mindful of his obligation to his sister-in-law, resolved to support her while watching over Couts. In 1853, Stearns made a wedding gift to Ysidora of half of Rancho Guajome near San Diego. Stearns allowed Couts to graze cattle on the other half so long as Couts paid the taxes on it, and he extended to Couts the option to buy the land. To further help Couts get started as a ranchero, Stearns reached an agreement with his brother-in-law to graze one thousand head of Stearns's cattle on the rancho for three years. At the end of that period, Stearns and Couts would divide evenly the number of calves in the herd. The arrangement worked so well that at the end of the three-year period Stearns and Couts agreed to extend it.[50]

Such cooperation among kin was a hallmark of the ranchero system. Stearns, his brothers-in-law, and, until his death in 1859, his father-in-law cooperated in the production and marketing of their cattle. They looked after the others' interests, loaning each other cash, cattle, and the use of pastures and vaqueros. Cooperation limited the rancheros' vulnerability to outside creditors—exactly the sort of vulnerability that Stearns had once capitalized upon to acquire his landholdings. The rancheros trusted kin over nonrelations; after 1856 Stearns employed his nephew Oliver as a sort of floating troubleshooter on his properties; Couts employed his brother-in-law Juan de la Cruz Bandini as his majordomo.[51] Charles Johnson summed up the business benefits of the cooperative system in a letter to Stearns in 1853: "As long as we keep our liabilities amongst ourselves, we understand each other, and always know how we stand."[52]

The rancheros' cooperation resembled the informal system in the plantation South, where planters and some yeomen who aspired to become planters loaned each other funds and the use of slaves and cotton gins in a complex system of cooperation based on kinship. It likewise resembled cooperation among elite, interrelated families in parts of rural Mexico such as Yucatán, where the production of henequen for export, like the production of cattle in southern California, concentrated land in the hands of a few families but left those families acutely liable to shifts in the market.[53] In southern California, such cooperation among rancheros linked by kinship ties helped them to compensate for chronic shortages of capital. Yet at the same time, the burdens of cooperation clearly fell more heavily on Stearns than on his family; propping up the weak finances of his kin slowly drained his capital.

Kinship and cooperation partially compensated not only for a lack of capital, but for southern California's chronic shortage of affordable labor. Couts and his in-laws shared laborers as they did other resources. In the spring of 1853, for instance, Stearns complained to Couts that "I am short of Baqueros for ironing calves" and requested that his brother-in-law send him "eight or ten of them for a fortnight or so."[54]

To exchange laborers so readily, the rancheros needed to be able to compel the vaqueros' labor. Unfree labor regimes varied greatly among agricultural export economies in the Americas in the nineteenth century. In ranching economies in which ranchers and political leaders were not closely allied, such as in early nineteenth-century Argentina, wage labor came to replace peonage and slavery as the most feasible labor system. Where ranchers and the state were close, slavery endured: the authoritarian governments of Paraguay between 1814 and 1870 confiscated church lands and transformed them into state ranches; they similarly transformed free blacks to government slaves. By 1860, half of the slaves in Paraguay labored on government ranches.[55]

In California, where following secularization the ranchers inherited from the missions both political control of the province and paternal control of Indian laborers, the status of vaqueros fell somewhere between the extremes of slavery and wage labor. The California rancheros tied most Indians to their estates by advancing them goods that had to be repaid by the labor of a year or longer. The responsibility of enforcing such a system fell on the rancheros and required only the passive cooperation of the state.

In the years after 1850, the American rancheros increasingly complained of the scarcity and independence of vaqueros, prompting them to greater reliance on state power to enforce their control over labor. They had access to such power in the person of Benjamin D. Wilson, the federal Indian agent for southern California. Like Stearns and Couts, Wilson was an American immigrant

who had acquired land (he bought part of Rancho La Jurupa from Juan Bandini in 1843) and married into Californio society (he wed Ramona Yorba, the
daughter of Don Bernard Yorba, in 1844). By 1850 the value of his landholdings in Los Angeles County was second only to that of Stearns.[56] In an 1852
report on the condition of the Indians in southern California, Wilson envisioned the former mission Indians of southern California continuing as com-
pulsory laborers on the ranchos. In 1853 he appointed his fellow Tennessean
Couts to be the Indian subagent for San Diego County. In appointing Couts,
he instructed him to "encourage them [the Indians] to labor."[57]

Because of their dominance of southern California government, Couts
and other rancheros found it easy to have "vagrant" Indians bound to their
service according to the provisions of the 1850 California Act for the Government and Protection of the Indians. The law allowed Indians convicted of
crimes from theft to loitering to be indentured to rancheros for extended pe-
riods by justices of the peace or county judges. The law borrowed directly
from the tradition of Mexican California, and was also common in nineteenth-
century southern Texas, northern Mexico, and Venezuela.[58] Altogether, the
rancheros compensated for shortages of labor, and for their own shortages of
capital to employ wage laborers, by using the powers of the state to extort labor from local Indians. In assessing the system in 1852, Wilson frankly characterized the Indians of the ranchos as "practically slaves."[59]

One of the most important grounds for cooperation among the rancheros
was sharing pastureland. To maintain their cattle in the drought-prone coastal
grasslands, Stearns and Couts regularly exchanged precise reports on the condition of the pasturage. More importantly, they shifted cattle among their landholdings to ease pressure on drought-stricken areas. The scramble to find
sufficient pasturage for their herds was virtually a yearly rite of spring.[60] The
search for pasturage, like the borrowing of capital and the extortion of Indians'
labor, exemplified the rancheros' political economy: they lived in a borrowed
opulence, beset by shortages of markets, labor, and rainfall.

The fortunes of the rancheros improved significantly, however, following
the discovery of gold in the Sierra foothills. The gold rush created a large
market for commercial food. Both Couts and Johnson, during visits to San
Francisco in the early and mid-1850s, reported on the high price of beef.
Johnson intimated that prices might rise higher still, as "there is not Stock
enough here to support the demand."[61]

The demand for beef in the gold country gave the rancheros what the hide and tallow market had only minimally provided: a market for their cattle. After 1850, rancheros reoriented their production from hide and tallow to beef, transforming their enterprise from one that merely financed their social position in a rural province to one designed to turn a significant profit. The market in the gold country fueled the rancheros' speculative impulses. In early 1852, Couts reported to Stearns that cattle were selling in San Francisco for anywhere between $40 and $75 a head. To reach that market, however, the rancheros had to drive their cattle nearly four hundred miles to the north. The California legislature facilitated such drives, enacting a law in March 1851 giving cattle free range throughout the state.[62]

In 1852, a year before he deeded him Rancho Guajome, Stearns relied on Couts, a former cavalry officer, to drive cattle to the gold country. Couts departed for the north in mid-May with about a thousand head of Stearns's cattle. When he reached his destination in mid-August, he settled for a price of $20 a head, far below his initial expectations. Within six months of that sale, however, Couts, ever the gambler, proposed to Stearns to drive more of his cattle to the north, with the two men sharing in the profits. "I think they can be brought up *fat*," he wrote. "My word for it they will pay handsomely."[63]

Prices for cattle continued to drop for most of the 1850s, however, as Arizona and New Mexico ranchers drove both cattle and sheep to California to join the competition. Couts sold a herd in April 1856 for only $18 a head.[64] The cool-headed Johnson, however, waited until later in the season, and sold his herd for between $23 and $25 a head. He explained to Stearns that "as soon as the buyers are convinced there is no more on the road, those that are here will bring a good price."[65] Indeed, clever rancheros began to hold back some of their cattle from the market in order to drive up their price. In 1858, Stearns reported to Couts, "Owners are not inclined to sell many this year and hold large cattle at 20$ and upwards." Stearns executed this gambit more shrewdly than other rancheros, holding out until everyone else had disposed of their stock. By then he was able to tell Couts, "As my Steers are from 3 to 5 years old, I ask 25$ and probably shall get it, as there are none left except mine."[66]

Stearns's manipulation of the market had its limits, however. Driving large numbers of cattle to the north not only earned the rancheros much-needed cash, but it also relieved the intense pressure on their pastures in southern California. In dry years such as 1856, drought at least as much as the lure of profits motivated Couts to drive eight thousand head to the north.[67] The long trek north caused the cattle to lose weight, however, significantly reducing their value. In 1852, when the market was at its early peak, Stearns had briefly considered buying a ranch in northern California "to drive cattle to, to be near and ready for market." On a ranch in the north, Stearns's cattle could fatten while he waited for the price he wanted. Yet he eventually abandoned the idea as too costly and difficult to manage.[68] Instead, he came to prefer to sell his cattle to dealers in Los Angeles.[69] Indeed, by the end of the 1850s he had decided to consolidate his ranching operations in Los Angeles County; he moved all his cattle there from his Rancho San Rafael in Baja California.[70]

By the beginning of the 1860s, the apex of the ranchos' extensive system had passed. Between 1852 and 1859 the number of cattle in California had more than doubled. According to one estimate, by the early 1860s the annual increase of cattle in California was 600,000 head, while the annual consumption was only 400,000.[71] In the glutted markets of the early 1860s, Stearns ruefully reflected that prices were low and purchasers few. Johnson reported to Stearns in 1862 that rancheros in Santa Barbara were desperate to sell cattle in the coming season to pay off their debts. Prices were as high as $15 a head in rare cases, but hovered generally between $12 and $13. In some cases, cattle sold for as little as $8 a head.[72]

The inability to dispose of cattle increased pressure on the available range. The 52 million acres of grazing land in California might have reasonably supported 1.8 million livestock. By the early 1860s, 3.5 million cattle, horses, and sheep overgrazed the range.[73] Even in northern California, close to consumers in cities and the gold country, pastures were overstocked and cattle died without their owners finding buyers for them.[74]

In an effort to drive up prices, Stearns revisited business tactics he had once rejected: he not only ordered over one thousand head driven to within one hundred miles of San Francisco, but he rented a 5,000-acre ranch there to fatten his cattle before sale. Stearns thus belatedly and partially adopted the techniques of intensive stockraising in the effort to raise the value of his cattle.[75] Stearns's adjustments to the changes in the market came too late, however, for him to improve his finances and so survive the environmental catastrophes that beset southern California in the early and mid-1860s: flood, pestilence, and most disastrously, drought.

Southern California's series of pharaonic disasters began with the floods of 1861–62—the same flood that overtopped Sacramento's levee and flooded the redwood mills. San Diego received three inches of rain in December 1861 and over five inches in January 1862—as much rain as had fallen in the previous twelve months. Altogether, over thirteen inches fell between November 1861 and April 1862.[76] Southern Californians initially welcomed the heavy winter rains. "The clouds let down their favors in a most acceptable manner," reported the *Los Angeles Star* in late November 1861. "We are rejoiced thereat, knowing that the seasonal rain will soon bring forth the bright green grass." By early 1862, despite reports that the San Gabriel and Santa Ana rivers had both overflowed their banks, the journal continued to celebrate the rain, proclaiming that "the prospects of the stock-owners are better than for many years before."[77]

By late January, however, the Los Angeles River flooded and the city embankment was washed away. Likewise, in San Diego and Santa Barbara, the floods washed away houses, farms, and, ironically, the grasses that the *Star* had proclaimed the rains would nurture.[78] The cold and wet winter left the southern California cattle weak. Johnson, overseeing Stearns's estates in Los Angeles while Stearns spent several months in San Francisco battling legal challenges to his title to several ranchos, reported that in the wake of the flood "there is absolutely no feed" on Stearns's main estate, the Rancho Los Alamitos. The poor condition of the grass had left Stearns's cattle *delgado* (thin).[79] Accordingly, Stearns dispatched two herds of cattle to the north, one to be driven by his nephew Oliver and the other by Cave Couts's younger brother William. Arriving in Monterey County in June, Oliver refused an offer of $15 a head, then watched prices plummet to $10 a head by October.[80]

While the winter of 1861–62 had been unusually wet, the rancheros endured an especially dry winter in 1862–63. Less than three inches of precipitation fell in San Diego during the rainy season of 1862–63—one of the driest winters in southern California's history. The rancheros knew as a consequence that there would not be enough forage to support their herds during the summer of 1863. Johnson wrote to Stearns in January 1863 that "the stock is all poor. . . . Grass is very backward, though your Majordomos say very few cattle die as yet." By February, Johnson could not be as hopeful: "There is no grass and the Cattle are very poor, and your Rancho men report a great many dying."[81] By the end of March, Johnson estimated that half of the cattle in southern California would perish.[82]

The cattle that survived the drought of 1863 were in such poor condition that they could not be sold. Stearns sold twenty head to a Los Angeles butcher in June, but, after inspecting the herd, the butcher could find only nine animals worth slaughtering.[83] As the drought progressed, Johnson suggested to Stearns that the best way to avoid catastrophe was to drive the herds from the desiccated coastal grasslands to the interior hillsides of the coastal mountain ranges, where in the cooler elevations the animals might find enough forage to survive the dry season. Johnson urged Stearns to approve the removal of at least five thousand head to the interior. By shifting cattle from the coast, Johnson hoped, "the grass on the low lands may come up again." Moreover, "if the Cattle are not moved," Johnson warned, "you will lose at least one half."[84]

Stearns, however, was opposed. The southern California rancheros had faced drought before, most recently in 1856, and the extensive system of ranching had seen them through. Earlier in 1863 he had explicitly advised Couts to let his herds remain on the coast rather than drive them to the mountains, maintaining that "you would lose more Stock by moving them to a place like that, two to one than would die. Let them take their chances where they are is my opinion." By June, however, Stearns had at least partially accepted the truth of the reports of the devastation in southern California, and he authorized Johnson to drive a thousand head to the interior.[85]

Cattle were not the only animals that consumed the coastal grasses. As Stearns, Johnson, and Couts debated moving their herds to the interior, grasshoppers overswept the grasslands and devastated its already thin forage. The grasshoppers belonged to one or more species of North American insects that inhabit nearly all grassland environments. They thrive on cereals such as wild oats. Ecological changes—such as the heavy rains of 1861–62—can cause a sudden eruption of grasshopper populations by temporarily expanding the areas in which the insects lay their eggs.[86] Outbreaks of grasshoppers had bedeviled farmers and ranchers throughout the state since the late 1850s.[87] In the summer of 1863 they swept into the coastal grasslands, concentrating in the San Fernando Valley and at Anaheim.[88] "The grasshoppers have absolutely swept everything clean, and the cattle have commenced dying," Johnson wrote to Stearns in June 1863.[89]

Rain might have restored the forage of the southern grasslands, but the winter of 1863–64 was as dry as the previous season. While 1862–63 was the driest rainy season in San Diego between 1850 and 1869, the 1863–64 season was the second-driest: only three and a half inches of rain fell between November 1863 and April 1864.[90] Between the beginning of November and the end of January, an average of seven inches of rain ought to have fallen in Los Angeles. By the end of January 1864, only an inch and a half had fallen. The *Star* reported that the lack of rain and unseasonably warm weather had left "not a green spot on the whole plain. The hills are now as red and arid as we ever saw them."[91] With the prospect of another drought, Stearns reversed his previous advice to Couts and urged him to drive cattle to the mountains.[92] His advice came too late, however. As Johnson told Couts, such a move had become impossible, because the cattle were too weak to drive. Nor could they be sold. "It is impossible to sell anything in the shape of stock. There is no place to keep them."[93]

The drought of the summer of 1864 devastated the already severely weakened cattle population of southern California. Throughout the state on the eve of the drought, there were approximately three million horses, cattle, and sheep. Of those, an estimated 800,000 died. Most of the losses were in southern California, where some counties, such as Los Angeles, lost between two-thirds and three-quarters of their cattle. Of the approximately 1.1 million cattle in California in 1860, only 820,000 remained by the early 1870s.[94] In Los Angeles County, the decline was even more severe: there had been 71,078 cattle excluding milch cows and working oxen in Los Angeles County in 1860; by 1870, there were only 19,178.[95]

TABLE 2.

LIVESTOCK IN LOS ANGELES COUNTY, 1850–70

Year	Horses	Milch Cows	Working Oxen	Other Cattle	Sheep
1850	5,487	338	1,185	88,454	6,541
1860	14,035	3,397	733	71,078	94,639
1870	9,652	2,468	48	19,178	247,603

Sources: United States Census Office, *The Seventh Census of the United States: 1850* (Washington, D.C.: Robert Armstrong, 1853), 976–77; United States Census Office, *Census of the City and County of Los Angeles, California, for the Year 1850* (Los Angeles: Times-Mirror Press, 1929), 120; United States Census Office, *Agriculture of the United States in 1860* (Washington, D.C.: Government Printing Office, 1864), 10–11; United States Census Office, *The Statistics of the Wealth and Industry of the United States, Ninth Census*, vol. 3 (Washington, D.C.: Government Printing Office, 1872), 104–5.

The loss of cattle devastated the rancheros' fragile finances. In the wake of the drought, many ranchers were forced to sell both their stock and their land to cover their debts.[96] Stearns had been flush with cash when he had bought his first rancho, Los Alamitos, in 1841, for $6,000. Two decades as a ranchero had drained his reserves, however, and in 1861 he had mortgaged Los Alamitos for $20,000 to Michael Reese.[97]

By the summer of 1864, when Stearns finally returned to Los Angeles from San Francisco after having spent almost two years securing the titles to his Mexican estates before the land commission, his finances were in a bleak condition.[98] In a gambit typical of the rancheros, he sought to hide his remaining assets among his kin. In November, in an evident attempt to evade having his cattle seized by another creditor, John Parrott of San Francisco, from whom he had borrowed $35,000, Stearns transferred the ownership of his cattle in San Diego County to Juan Bautista Bandini, Don Juan's son. The scheme failed to fool Parrott, one of the leading moneylenders and land speculators in San Francisco. A few months after the transaction, Couts informed the younger Bandini that the sheriff of San Diego County "has laid various attachments" on the herd "on account of the debts of Don Abel," and had ordered that the cattle be gathered up. Desperately short of cash, in December 1864 Stearns borrowed $150,000, at 18 percent annual interest, from a St. Louis, Missouri, creditor.[99]

Stearns put his hopes for recovery on the assumption that the decimation of the cattle population in the state had driven up the price for surviving livestock. In early 1866, he wrote to Couts that "here in this county there will be hardly enough left for our own consumption." He urged Couts to adhere to their earlier practice of holding back their stock to force buyers to accept their price. Yet cattle had been so overstocked in the seasons before the drought that the market for beef did not improve much in the late 1860s. In early 1866, the price stood at $10 per head.[100]

Unable to raise cash, Stearns lost Los Alamitos to Reese in February 1866. In April, Stearns put two of his remaining ranchos, Los Coyotes and La Jurupa, up for sale, asking $2 per acre.[101] The collapse of stockraising had depressed land prices, however. Stearns only extricated himself from his crushing debts by abandoning stock and entering into a real estate partnership with his creditors. In return for forgiving the loan on one of his ranchos, and for advancing sufficient sums to cover his debts, Stearns turned over his remaining lands—70,000 acres—to a trust. Stearns's three primary creditors each held quarter-shares; Stearns held a one-eighth share. The trust sold tracts of land to settlers, many of whom were migrants from the depressed postwar South, in lots that ranged in size from 20 to 640 acres, at prices between $5 and $13 an acre. A year before his death in 1871, the trust sales had enabled Stearns to reestablish a small part of his former fortune.[102]

Couts avoided Stearns's fate by shifting his interests increasingly into sheep raising. Couts had diversified his ranchos in the mid-1850s, raising sheep alongside his cattle as an ancillary enterprise.[103] Other rancheros followed Couts's example: the population of sheep in Los Angeles County rose from 6,541 in 1850 to 94,639 in 1860.[104] Because most buyers judged southern California wool to be inferior, Couts's sheep venture long remained subordinate to the production of cattle.[105] Yet sheep had several advantages over cattle in southern California; these advantages became crucial after the drought of the mid-1860s. Most importantly, they survived on a broader variety of forage than cattle. As one observer wrote in 1874, "sheep thrive in lands where cattle and horses would starve, and are well adapted to the dry hills and plains, where little rain ever falls."[106] Moreover, the production of sheep required less labor than the production of cattle. A single shepherd could easily oversee thousands of sheep.[107] Finally, the disruption of southern cotton production during the Civil War created a lucrative market for wool.[108] These factors encouraged increasing numbers of rancheros to shift from cattle to sheep. By 1873, California had a population of four million sheep, up from just over 600,000 in 1859. The production of wool in California rose from 18 million pounds in 1860 to 30 million pounds in 1874.[109]

Couts's shift from cattle to sheep spared his family from financial ruin but merely changed the terms of the rancheros' effect on the California environment. Overgrazing by sheep in late nineteenth-century California created a host of ancillary ecological consequences: defoliation led to erosion and gullying in riparian environments; runoff from overgrazed meadows fouled streams and therefore decreased fish populations; the very presence of domesticated sheep in the mountains likely transmitted ovine disease to wild mountain sheep; and trampling and overgrazing inhibited nutrient recycling.[110] John Muir wrote in 1882 that the trampling of domesticated sheep "has uprooted and buried many of the tender plants from year to year, without allowing the time to mature their seeds."[111] Seconding Muir, one observer in

1892 reported that there were no trees in the Kings River watershed in the Sierra Nevada younger than thirty years, a date that coincided with the "invasion of the mountains by numerous bands of sheep."[112]

In the years after the drought, cattle ranchers abandoned the old extensive system. "The old system of letting the animals take care of themselves," editorialized the *Placer Herald* in 1873, "is proving inadequate." The remedy, according to the newspaper, "will be found in the growing of root crops, of Mesquite grass, Alfalfa, etc., and providing shelter for the stock during the rainy season." In 1872 the California legislature effectively outlawed extensive stockraising by enacting a law requiring ranchers to enclose their livestock to prevent damage to neighboring croplands.[113] Ranchers also increasingly shifted their stock from the southern California Spanish cattle to "American cows" from the Midwest. The Midwestern cattle were less efficient grazers in the desiccated grasslands, but their owners did not rely on turning them loose to forage for themselves. Rather, they found that the cattle fattened well under the program of intensive stockraising.[114]

Similarly, by the end of the 1860s, the old rancheros had been replaced by a new breed of California rancher, whom the historian David Igler has called "industrial cowboys." Typified by the San Francisco-based partners Henry Miller and Charles Lux, the new ranchers raised the techniques of intensive stockraising to unprecedented levels. Far better capitalized than rancheros such as Stearns, they enjoyed a cooperative rather than confrontational relationship with financiers such as John Parrott. Unwilling to be victim to the unpredictability of retailers, they controlled many of the butcher shops in San Francisco. Unwilling as well to be victim to the unpredictable environment, they constructed vast irrigation networks that watered their fields of alfalfa and hay. Yet they too ultimately had to reckon with the ecological costs of their enterprise and the competition of better-capitalized stockraisers. By the end of the century, Miller and Lux lands were overstocked. Decades of irrigation salinated the soil, reducing productivity. Finally, just as the better-financed Stearns had overtaken the lands and cattle of the Mexican rancheros and the better-financed industrial cowboys had triumphed over Stearns, by the early twentieth century a better-capitalized consortium of Chicago meatpackers replaced Miller and Lux.[115]

Yet capital alone did not ensure the triumph of the industrial cowboys over the Californios. For three decades, the Californio kinship system had proved adaptable enough to weather secularization, Anglo-American immigration, the gold rush, and the land commission. The shift in ranching regimes occurred only on the heels of an ecological catastrophe. Drought had beset the missions in the early nineteenth century, of course, but the missions were neither as ambitiously scaled nor as overstocked as the ranchos. In the 1860s the impact of drought proved decisive. This does not mean that environmental change dictates history. Yet to marginalize the agency of the environment can prove highly misleading. Rather, as the decline of the ranchos demonstrates, the environment was and remains a presence in the California borderlands as important as and inextricably connected to economic and cultural change.

5

The Enclosure of the Plateau:
Land and Labor in the High Lake Country

S hortly before noon on Good Friday, April 11, 1873, just south of Tule
Lake in northeastern California, a United States Indian Peace Commission prepared to parley with the leaders of a group of Modocs. The
members of the peace commission—Brigadier General Edward Canby, commander of the Department of the Columbia; the Reverend Eleazar Thomas, a
Methodist minister from Petaluma, California; and Alfred B. Meacham and
Leroy S. Dyar of the U.S. Indian Service—hoped to end the hostilities that had
persisted since late November of the previous year between the Modocs and
the U.S. Army.

The violence of 1872–73 was the last stage of a conflict over the control of
land and natural resources that had begun two decades earlier. The incur-
sions of Euroamerican hunters, miners, and ranchers into the high lake country of the Modocs in the 1850s and 1860s had crowded the Indians into ever
smaller territories, and the consequent degradation of habitats for fish and
game left the Indians increasingly unable to subsist by gathering, fishing, and
hunting. "In the case of the Modocs, the subject of the dispute may be cor-
rectly termed *geographical*," wrote one visitor to the plateau in 1874, William
Simpson. "Every day sees the area of cultivation enlarged, and the hunting-
grounds of the Indians reduced in extent."[1] Hemmed in by Euroamerican settlers, most Modocs had assented in 1864 to a treaty that ceded their homeland
in California in return for a reservation in Oregon.

But not all. A few Modoc bands remained, combining their traditional resource strategies with occasional labor on ranches or in the largest Euroamerican town, Yreka. Indeed, the utility of the Modocs as ranch hands led

many ranchers to oppose removal of the Modocs to Oregon, and to support the creation of a small reservation for the Indians near Tule Lake. Modoc leaders likewise sought a political accommodation that would allow them to remain in California, and as late as New Year's Day 1873, Newton Booth, the governor of California, wrote to the War Department urging the Army to reconsider its decision to remove the Indians and rather to grant them a small reserve of three thousand acres on Lost River. Such a policy, the governor argued, would be popular with Euroamerican ranchers.[2]

By the time the governor wrote, however, violence had already erupted. In November 1872 the Army had tried to force a Modoc band, which had settled into its winter camp on the bank of the Lost River near Tule Lake, to return to Oregon. The Indians fled to the barren volcanic tableland south of Tule Lake, where they were eventually joined by two other Modoc bands. In the rugged tableland, pitted with twisting rock walls and crevasses, roughly 150 Modocs barricaded themselves in a natural fortification of shallow caves and intricate lava flows. On the banks of Tule Lake, the stronghold was provided with fresh water, and with stray cattle rounded up from the grasslands south and east of the lava beds and corralled in the largest crevasse, the Indians were prepared to endure a long siege.

Between November 1872 and April 1873, the Army failed to dislodge the Modocs from their stronghold. The Modocs, for their part, had confounded their attackers, but had proved unable to break the siege. Both parties knew that the resolution of the conflict—not just the recent violence but the long-standing struggle for control over the resources of northeastern California—depended on the outcome of the April 11 meeting.[3]

The peace commissioners came to negotiate with the young Modoc tyee, or band chief, Keintpoos. He had emerged as the most influential off-reservation tyee because of his long-standing opposition to the treaty of 1864. Partly because of that notoriety, the Euroamericans assumed that Keintpoos wielded considerable authority, a perception reflected in their name for the Modoc leader. Keintpoos, whose name in the Modoc language means "Man of Few Words," was known to the Euroamericans by the wry nickname given to him by an Indian agent in Yreka, California: Captain Jack.

Yet the Euroamerican perception of Jack as a "captain" was a misapprehension: Modoc tyees led their bands not by compulsion but through persuasion and consensus. Leaders relied on oratory to sway listeners; thus, Jack's

The Modoc band chief
Keintpoos, or Captain Jack

Modoc name was an unlikely one for a tyee. Indeed, Jack's career was a struggle to establish himself as a legitimate leader. His weak authority was complicated by the presence of other tyees in the stronghold. Jack's band was but one of three barricaded in the lava beds stronghold. Accompanying Jack to the negotiations were other tyees and prominent men with influence equal to his own.[4]

While Jack had long urged the other Modocs to pursue negotiation, the other tyees at the parley had counseled violent resistance. Most skeptical of negotiation was "Hooker Jim," the tyee of one of the three off-reservation bands. When the soldiers had attacked Jack's camp in November 1872, Hooker Jim's band, camped on the opposite side of the Lost River, had fled to the lava beds, killing over a dozen Euroamerican settlers along the way. Also favoring battle was Skietteteko ("Left-Handed Man"), tyee of a third Modoc division, the Hot Creeks. Skietteteko was known to the Euroamericans as "Shacknasty Jim" because his house was notoriously untidy. When the violence had started in November, the Hot Creeks had sought the safety of the

Oregon reservation. A Euroamerican lynch mob had prevented them from fleeing the Tule Lake region, however, so the Hot Creeks, angered by their confrontation with the mob, had joined Jack in the lava beds stronghold. The Hot Creek faction included Shacknasty Jim's brother, "Ellen's Man George" (the Modocs' best military strategist, so known to the Euroamericans because his Modoc wife was nicknamed Ellen); "Bogus Charley" (so called because he frequented the Bogus River); and "Boston Charley" (so named because of his fluency in English).[5]

Although the conflict with the Modocs centered on their right to remain in their homeland, they were neither cultural traditionalists nor irreconcilable enemies of Euroamerican settlers, as the Indians' English nicknames testified. The Modocs at the meeting were indeed highly acculturated to Euroamerican mores. According to Alfred Meacham, Jack was "not a wild Indian, but rather in the habits of civilized men, in dress and manner, having learned many of the common arts of civil life from his white neighbors."[6] Of the Modocs in the stronghold, Meacham likewise wrote, "They were not wild, uncivilized men. They had associated much with white people, and had adopted many of the customs of the white race."[7] The Modocs had found a niche in the Euroamerican economy, the women in household service (or prostitution) and the men driving teams or working as ranch hands. Shacknasty Jim and his brothers earned not only wages but their colorful English nicknames working for Euroamerican ranchers. Most of the Modocs, including Jack, spoke English.

The Modocs were frequent visitors to the town of Yreka, the largest Euroamerican settlement in the region. They enjoyed good relations with the townspeople. Meacham wrote, "There was not one [of the Modocs] whose credit among white men would not have obtained for him any reasonable amount of goods. Not one of them had ever been arrested for crime."[8] Many of the men's female relatives were married to Yreka settlers; indeed, Jack's sister, Mary, was a companion to a Yreka miner, and Jack's niece, Toby Riddle, was the wife of a Yreka hunter, Frank Riddle. The Modocs had become so bound by economic and personal ties to Yreka and its inhabitants that they identified their fate with that of the town. On the Fourth of July 1871, for instance, Jack and some other Modocs were in Yreka to attend the holiday celebrations when a major fire broke out. Like any concerned citizens, the Modocs joined the Euroamerican townspeople in extinguishing it.[9]

If the commissioners hoped on the morning of April 11 that the existence of such economic and personal bonds might make a negotiated peace easier to achieve, they were to be disappointed. Shortly after the negotiations began, it became clear that the meeting would yield no diplomatic progress. The Modocs reiterated their established bargaining positions. The commissioners, in turn, replied with well-worn responses. Jack called for Canby to withdraw his soldiers and lift the siege. Canby replied that he would allow the Modoc women and children to leave—under guard—while the men negotiated a settlement. Canby's offer must have been particularly galling to the Indians: when the Army had come to Jack's camp in November, a Modoc man and his wife en route to the Lost River had stumbled upon the soldiers, who put the man in custody and raped his wife. During the attack on Jack's camp, the soldiers had put to the torch a lodge housing an ailing Modoc woman who, too ill to flee, was consumed in the flames.[10]

Without warning, as the commissioners' interpreters, Frank and Toby Riddle, were translating a Modoc's demand for a new reservation, Jack rose and excused himself. Returning, he shouted an order and a number of armed Modocs burst from hiding. Jack drew a hidden pistol and shot the unarmed Canby, who rose and took a few steps before collapsing. While Jack slit Canby's throat to make sure of his death, the other Modoc negotiators drew concealed weapons and unleashed a volley of shots. One bullet killed Rev. Thomas; another ricocheted off a rock and struck Meacham in the head, rendering him unconscious. Dyar and Frank Riddle bolted to safety. Toby Riddle remained behind; her kinspeople did not harm her. The Modocs stripped the bodies of Canby, Thomas, and the unconscious Meacham, whom they took for dead, and returned to their stronghold.[11]

The killing of the peace commissioners briefly brought the Modoc War national notoriety. Yet the Modoc War, which ended later in 1873 with Jack's capture and execution, was soon eclipsed by the other incidents of Indian-Euroamerican violence in the West, including the Sioux wars in the northern Great Plains (which led to the death of Lieutenant Colonel George Armstrong Custer at the Battle of the Little Bighorn in 1876) and conflicts with the Nez Perce in Idaho (culminating in the Nez Perce flight across the Pacific Northwest in 1877). On the surface, the predicaments of the Sioux and the Nez Perce bore striking similarities to the situation of the Modocs. Like the Modocs, the primary aim of the Sioux and the Nez Perce was to return to or

"The Modocs-Murder of General Canby" (*Harper's Weekly*, June 28, 1873). Captain Jack is at the center. Seated in the foreground are Jack's niece, Toby, and her husband, Frank Riddle. Canby, Meacham, and Thomas are standing. Dyar is on horseback in the background.

retain control over their homeland, rather than surrender to the reservation system. Like the Modocs, the Sioux and Nez Perce had resorted to violence only after long and unsuccessful attempts at negotiation. Like the Modocs, the resort to violence by the Sioux and Nez Perce was driven, in part, by factional divisions within their societies.[12]

Despite these similarities, while the Sioux and Nez Perce have been the subject of several excellent studies, American Indian and western historians have barely reflected upon the Modoc War. The handful of studies of the conflict provide little clue to its underlying social, economic, and ecological causes.[13]

The tangled economic and cultural interactions between the Modocs and Euroamerican settlers occurred within the context of the extraordinary economic and ecological changes that swept over California in the quarter-century following the discovery of gold. Those changes began with the discovery of gold in Yreka in 1851 and in Jacksonville, Oregon, in 1852. Mining exerted the same economic pressures on Indian land and labor as in the Sierra foothills. Ecological change continued with the extension of ranches and farms into Modoc territory in the 1860s, further marginalizing the Indians. In the high lake country, those changes resulted in the decline of the Indians' resource base, their consequent shift into the wage labor market, and the decline of the population owing to epidemic disease and the migration of Modoc women into Euroamerican households as wives, prostitutes, or domestic laborers.

The Indians' ecological and economic predicament—fundamentally a consequence of the transformation of the California environment—was the underlying cause of the Modoc War.[14] That transformation was part of a transnational process of change. The appropriation of the Modocs' lands and the proletarianization of Modoc labor were remote extensions of the process known as enclosure that began in late medieval and early modern England and occurred elsewhere in northern Europe. In England between the fifteenth and early nineteenth centuries, the gentry coerced peasants into ceding their strips of land and grazing rights in common pastures. The gentry reduced many of these newly landless peasants to tenants or day laborers. Most of the rest drifted into cities to become wage earners. The gentry enclosed their estates and turned their land to the systematic production of agricultural commodities such as beef, mutton, and wool. Enclosure played an important role in northern European industrialization by creating both landless wage laborers and the large estates that produced agricultural commodities for manufacture, export, and burgeoning urban populations.[15]

Both Adam Smith and Karl Marx devoted considerable attention to the phenomenon of English enclosure, as have generations of subsequent scholars.[16] These studies, focusing on the spatial and macroeconomic dimensions of the process, have expanded the understanding of the geography, periodization, and types of enclosure. Yet enclosure was not simply an economic problem. Following on the earlier insights of others, the eminent English historian E. P. Thompson analyzed enclosure as a problem of social order, dismissing those who would seek to understand the process merely in terms of acreages and average wages. One of the fundamental reasons for elites to enclose lands was to impose what Thompson called "social discipline" on the rural poor. Its enforcement ensured the relative docility of former peasants as the new economic regime transformed them into tenants and wage laborers.[17]

What happened in a remote corner of California in the last third of the nineteenth century was a form of enclosure. Such an interpretation continues scholars' efforts to understand enclosure not merely as a phenomenon of England or the eighteenth century but as a transnational process extending over many centuries. At the same time, Thompson's identification of "social discipline" as a critical component of enclosure helps make sense of the Modoc War: the Indians not only once possessed extensive lands that ranchers regarded as underutilized, they were also a racially and culturally distinct minority whose continued occupation of even a small portion of those lands constituted a resistance to the emerging economic order in California. Although the Modocs had made extensive accommodations to the ranching economy, in the eyes of state and federal authorities they were merely Indians. The Modocs' defiance, authorities feared, might embolden other Indians to resist enclosure as well.

Historians usually exclude the United States from the history of enclosure. Indeed, historians of early America juxtapose the tenancy and landlessness of many western Europeans with the relatively widespread competency in eighteenth-century America: 70 percent of heads of households in the villages and small towns of Massachusetts owned land in 1771, as did 90 percent of men over the age of forty in Connecticut and 80 percent of East New Jersey's men over the age of twenty-seven.[18] After independence, the United States government, according to this interpretation, encouraged widespread land ownership. A series of preemption acts in the early nineteenth century permitted squatters on western public lands to purchase from the federal government the lands they had improved for the minimum government price. Government policy to encourage competency culminated in the Homestead Act of 1862, which transferred title to 160-acre tracts of public land to settlers who improved their claims and remained upon them for five years.

Despite the popular renown of the Homestead Act, much of federal land settlement policy favored the creation of large agricultural estates. In the late eighteenth and early nineteenth century, the federal government acquiesced to wealthy speculators' dubious acquisition of large tracts of land west of the Appalachians.[19] Moreover, the series of land acts that governed the sale of public lands in the first half of the nineteenth century contained stipulations including a minimum size of lots, minimum purchase prices, and a requirement for cash payment that effectively excluded the poor. Instead, speculators acquired extensive landholdings. As a result, tenancy was widespread. In ten counties in East Tennessee between 1783 and 1809, the percentage of households owning land varied between 32 and 72 percent, but altogether only 55 percent of households actually owned their land.[20] In Sugar Creek, Illinois, in 1850, 10 percent of farm households were tenants—not surprisingly, inasmuch as speculators had locked up some 40 percent of the state's lands.[21]

Little changed after the passage of the Homestead Act. By the time of that landmark legislation, the federal government had already embarked upon a policy of granting millions of acres of land to railroad companies; the companies sold the land to finance their construction. Congress distributed 30 million acres to railroad companies in the 1850s. Between 1862 and 1871 the federal government awarded 174 million acres to four transcontinental railroad companies. Corporate lands dwarfed homesteads in the settlement of the West. In California in the second half of the nineteenth century, homesteaders claimed 11.4 million acres of public land, while 20.2 million acres went to railroads and cash sales.[22] By 1900, 62 percent of the farmland in California was in farms that exceeded one thousand acres in size.[23] Twenty-six percent of farmers in the nation were tenants in 1880; that percentage had risen to 35 percent by the end of the century—with rates of tenancy as high in parts of the wheat-producing West as in the cotton South.

Before public lands could be enclosed by such bonanza farms, the federal government had to alienate them from Indians, who supplemented their agriculture by using large territories as hunting and gathering commons.[24] Beginning in the late eighteenth century, Indians ceded about 450 million acres of land to the United States by treaty—the Modoc treaty of 1864 was one of 245 ratified by the U.S. Senate. Far distant in time and space from the Midlands estates where enclosure began, the Modocs, like those English peasants, nonetheless faced the dual process of the appropriation of their lands and the proletarianization of their labor. Jack, in his failed efforts to negotiate a settlement over an eight-year period that preceded the war, knew full well that Euroamerican settlement was a fait accompli and that wage labor had become a permanent part of the Modocs' lives. Yet he hoped to mitigate enclosure by securing a reserve in their homeland where they could continue to fish, hunt, and gather on what remained of the Modoc commons. He turned to violence only when these efforts seemed futile.[25]

The Modoc Plateau in the northeastern corner of California is a forbidding geological formation. One nineteenth-century observer described the landscape as consisting of "irregular broken ridges" interspersed with grassland.[26] The landscape of plateau was created by the same geological process that created the Sierra Nevada: the abutment of the North American and Pacific tectonic plates. In the plateau, the power of the collision forced upward along fault lines ridges that run in a regular north–south pattern. Yet the tectonic plates sometimes recoiled from their collision, pulling apart and creating depressions between the ridges. One such depression filled with water to become Tule Lake.

Before farmers drained the lake for irrigation in the early twentieth century, reducing it to 15 percent of its original size, Tule Lake covered 100,000 acres. The lake once had an outlet to the Pit River, but volcanic activity created by the collision of the tectonic plates caused lava to flow to the surface, cutting off the lake's outlet. Similar lava flows created the rugged black lava beds in which the Modocs took refuge.[27] The roiling activity beneath the plateau continues. Shastina, a volcano near Mount Shasta on the western edge of the plateau, erupted in 1786; Lassen Peak, on the southern edge of the plateau, experienced a series of eruptions in 1914–15. Hot springs, mud pots, and steam vents also abound, a testimony to the continuing underground turbulence.

The Pit River divides the plateau, flowing from its headwaters in the Warner Mountains on the plateau's eastern edge southwestward between Lassen Peak and Mount Shasta before ultimately depositing its flow into the Sacramento River. Standing on the banks of Tule Lake, in the center of the Modoc country, the upland appears nearly isolated. To the east, the Warner Mountains, whose Eagle Peak reaches nearly 10,000 feet, stand on the California-Nevada border. To the south is the Medicine Lake Highlands, an eastern outcropping of the Southern Cascade Mountains. To the east looms the 14,162-foot Mount Shasta, the highest peak of the Southern Cascades.[28] To stand on the banks of Tule Lake, seemingly encircled by the mountains, is to understand the Modoc folktale that the world is a disk with the eastern bank of Tule Lake at its center.[29]

Apart from the Pit River Valley, the lake region, the center of the Modoc Indians' territory, is the only arable part of the Modoc Plateau. Long, cold, snowy winters characterize the plateau: 65 percent of the region's annual pre-

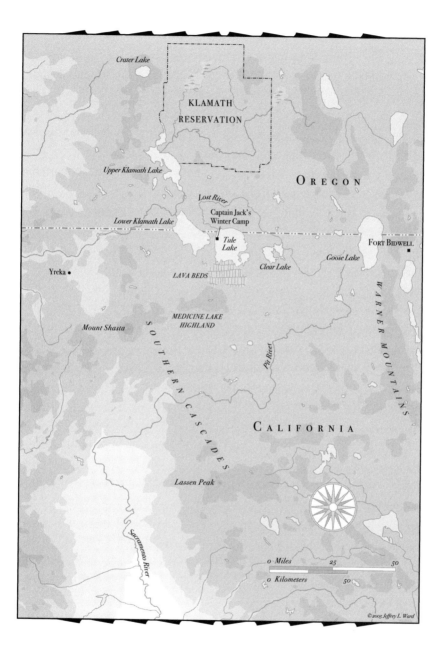

Crater Lake

KLAMATH
RESERVATION

Upper Klamath Lake

OREGON

Lost River

Captain Jack's
Winter Camp

Lower Klamath Lake

Tule
Lake

FORT BIDWELL

Yreka

LAVA BEDS

Clear Lake

Goose Lake

MEDICINE LAKE
HIGHLAND

Mount Shasta

Pit River

WARNER MOUNTAINS

SOUTHERN CASCADES

CALIFORNIA

Lassen Peak

Sacramento River

0 Miles   25   50

0 Kilometers   50

© 2005 Jeffrey L. Ward

cipitation falls as snow between November and May. Yet the Cascades trap most of the eastward-moving, moisture-bearing air currents in the region; precipitation on the western side of the Cascades is six times higher than on the plateau side.[30] The Cascades rain shadow leaves the Modoc Plateau relatively dry during the summer. The flora of the tableland are accordingly primarily sagebrush shrubs and several varieties of long-stemmed bunchgrass adapted to the short, dry growing season. Coniferous forests consisting largely of Western yellow pine and white fir cover the lower elevations of the mountains on the edges of the plateau, but deciduous trees are rare. Only a few quaking aspen are found on mountain slopes, and an equally few cottonwoods along streams.[31]

Although the Modoc Plateau seems isolated, it is in fact a busy ecological borderland between the Sacramento Valley to the southwest and the Great Basin of Nevada, southeastern Oregon, southern Idaho, and western Wyoming. The Pit River Valley is the main thoroughfare between the two regions; fauna have traversed this route for centuries. As a result of this traffic, the wildlife of the Modoc Plateau has characteristics of both the Sacramento Valley and the Great Basin. In the nineteenth century, the plateau was inhabited by elk and antelope from the Sacramento Valley and bighorn sheep from the Great Basin and the interior mountains.[32]

The resource strategies of the Modocs reflected their borderland environment. Lacking salmon and acorns, the two staple resources of the Indians of the Sacramento Valley and Sierra foothills, the Modocs relied instead on a diversity of resources, combining the subsistence strategies of both the Great Basin and the Sacramento Valley. Their seasonal subsistence cycle began in the spring when they gathered on the banks of the Lost River, the largest stream in the lake region, which flowed in a long arc from Clear Lake north into Oregon before turning south to Tule Lake. They strung nets across the stream and harvested suckers on their spawning run upstream. After nearly a month of fishing, the Modocs shifted to gathering. Their staples were camas, a root that grows in moist soils near wetlands, and wocas, a yellow water lily from which the Modocs gathered the seeds. When camas and wocas were in short supply, the Modocs harvested tule grass, the stems of which are (barely) edible, but under ordinary circumstances they harvested tules from the marshes not to eat but to weave baskets and house mats.[33] They also gathered nettles, which yielded a more supple fiber than tule, to weave snares and nets for hunting and fishing.[34] The Modocs harvested many of their food resources—fish, camas, and wocas—on the banks of rivers and lakes. These areas were thus central to their subsistence.[35]

In the late summer the Modocs hunted antelope in the grasslands and bighorn sheep in the rocky lava beds, before returning to the banks of the Lost River for the fall sucker run and to hunt the waterfowl that passed by the lake region during their seasonal migrations. In the fall, the Modocs moved to their camps in the higher elevations, where the men hunted deer and elk and the women gathered huckleberries. The winter camps were dispersed among the lakes and creeks on the northern edge of the Modoc Plateau: at Hot Creek, on Lower Klamath Lake, on the Lost River, and by Tule Lake. While the Modocs' resource strategies usually provided for their subsistence, they could occasionally be proved inadequate by the volatile environment. During one winter in the early 1830s, for instance, heavy snows buried the Modocs' caches of camas and wocas and made hunting impossible. As many as half of the Modocs starved. By the middle of the nineteenth century, the Modocs had not yet recovered from this demographic disaster and numbered only about four hundred.[36]

The Modoc economy was multifaceted. The Modocs were not only fisher-hunter-gatherers who exploited the variety of resources of their transitional environment. By the early nineteenth century they had become borderlands traders who profited from their dominance of the major avenue between the Sacramento Valley and the Great Basin. Trade had exploded in the Pacific Northwest in the eighteenth century, largely as a result of the introduction, via intertribal trade, of New Mexican horses into the region.[37] In the Northwest, the profitable and prestigious trade was centered at the Dalles, the narrow rapids on the Columbia River. Because it was relatively easy to catch migrating salmon where the Columbia narrowed at the Dalles, the area had been an exchange center for centuries, where neighboring groups traveled to trade for dried fish. By the early nineteenth century, the Dalles had become a major trade emporium. Commodities from across North America found their way there via extended intertribal trade routes.[38]

Indeed, the rise of trade may have been the factor that induced the Modocs, in the interest of having better access to valuable trade commodities, to separate from the Klamaths in the late eighteenth century and migrate from Oregon south to the plateau. The name Modoc likely derives from the Klamath word *Moaktokni*, meaning "southerners." By the early nineteenth century,

Modoc traders trafficked in two principal commodities: obsidian, which other native groups coveted for hatchets and arrowheads; and slaves. They harvested sharp-edged flakes of mahogany obsidian from the Warner Mountains on the eastern side of the plateau and Glass Mountain in the Medicine Lake region.[39]

They captured slaves from neighboring Indian groups, primarily the more numerous Achomawis and Atsugewis of the southern Modoc Plateau and the Paiutes to the southeast. During the summer, the Modocs broke off from their subsistence cycle to visit the Klamaths, their former kinspeople in Oregon, where they exchanged their obsidian and captives for horses and other trade goods. Captive boys could be exchanged for one horse; girls, who were valuable as household laborers and producers of trade commodities, for as many as five horses.[40] Particularly commercially ambitious Modocs bypassed the Klamaths and traveled directly to the Dalles, returning with rare trade goods such as seashells and bison robes whose possession—and redistribution—meant prestige in Modoc culture.[41] Thus, long before enclosure brought wage labor to the Modocs, intertribal exchange had commercialized Indian labor and expanded the ultimate form of labor exploitation, slavery.[42]

Slave raiding and the attendant intertribal competition for territory and trade advantages exacted its costs on the Modocs. Some time in the early 1840s, Keintpoos's father, an influential tyee, was killed in a battle with Oregon Indians. Leadership was not automatically hereditary among the Modocs, but the members of a few well-regarded families usually occupied the tyeeships. Keintpoos, still a boy, was too young to succeed his father, however, and the leadership of the band passed to another family. For the rest of his life, Keintpoos struggled to establish his place as his father's heir, an ambition that helped lead the Modocs to the violence of 1872–73.[43]

On the eve of the discovery of gold in California, the Modocs had a tenuous dominance of the plateau, drawing on its diversity of resources and jostling with other native groups for territory and captives. Their dominance began to erode in the 1840s. By 1846, over seven thousand Euroamericans had settled in Oregon, disrupting the trade in horses, obsidian, and slaves.[44] Still more disastrously, in 1847, emigrants on the Oregon Trail transmitted a disease, probably smallpox but perhaps measles, to numerous native groups in the Great Basin. The disease or diseases diffused through the Great Basin and Sacramento Valley. When the epidemic had run its course, between one-quarter and one-half of those afflicted had died.[45] According to one contemporary estimate, 150 Modocs—40 percent of the population—died in 1847.[46]

The Euroamerican settlement of Oregon disrupted the Modocs' trade patterns, and the California gold rush dealt a severe blow to their subsistence strategies. Still reeling from the effects of the epidemic, the Modocs confronted a massive influx of Euroamericans into California following the discovery of gold. In the early years of the gold rush, many emigrants followed a route explored by John Frémont and Kit Carson in 1846 (an expedition characterized by the explorers' casual brutality against Indians in their path).[47] The emigrants reached California by following the Oregon Trail to a point north of the Modoc Plateau, then cut southwest through the plateau along the Pit River to reach the Sacramento Valley.

The ecological consequences of the Euroamerican invasion disrupted the Modocs' seasonal subsistence cycle. Euroamerican emigrants passing through the Modoc Plateau, like overland emigrants elsewhere in North America, degraded environments for wildlife. They drove large numbers of livestock through the plateau. In 1853 alone, travelers herded 12,000 head of cattle through Beckwourth's Pass in the southern plateau.[48] Livestock consumed grasses and fouled water sources, while the settlers shot any unwary wildlife that strayed too close.[49]

Emigrants also visited violence upon the Indians. J. H. Holeman, an Indian agent on the California-Nevada border, wrote in 1852 that Euroamerican emigrants "have been in the habit of persuading Indians into their camps, under the most solemn assurances of friendship—and then, without any cause on the part of the Indians, they would shoot them down." Such settlers, Holeman continued, "frequently take excursions through the country, in search of Indians, robbing and plundering them of everything they possess."[50]

As elsewhere in North America where Euroamerican emigration degraded wildlife environments in native territory and some emigrants killed Indians, the Modocs resorted to violence to deter them from passing through their homeland. "The flooding of the country with strangers," the emigrant James Beith wrote in 1858, roused "the whole Northern Indians to an active spirit of hostility."[51] General Joel Palmer, the superintendent of Indian affairs in Oregon, wrote in 1857 that the "Siskiyou mountains"—referring to the Southern Cascades—were "infested by Indians who seldom allow an opportunity to pass without steeling [sic], plundering, and killing emigrants."[52] The

Modocs were not alone: the Paiutes, Achomawis, Atsugewis, and other groups participated as well. In the aftermath of the Modoc War, however, chroniclers retroactively attributed most of the Indian violence of the late 1840s and early 1850s to the Modocs. For instance, Governor Lafayette Grover of Oregon fulminated in 1874, "The Modoc tribe of Indians have been known since the earliest emigration to Oregon and Northern California as a band of murderers and robbers." He characterized them as "fiends," "the most treacherous and bloodthirsty savages west of the Rocky Mountains," who had "attacked and butchered indiscriminately" over three hundred "innocent and unoffending emigrants."[53]

If Grover's calculations were accurate, then the Modocs would have been responsible for most of the attacks on emigrants in the history of the American West. According to the precise research of the historian John Unruh, only 362 overland emigrants died at the hands of Indians between 1840 and 1860.[54] Rather, according to Elisha Steele, a Yreka judge and Indian agent, the troubles between Euroamericans and Modocs were generally nonviolent. The most common problem was stolen livestock. Equally common was for Modocs to return stray stock to emigrants in return for a small reward.[55]

Modoc violence against Euroamerican travelers was largely confined to the summer of 1852, when, in contradiction to Grover's wild exaggerations, the Modocs killed fewer than twenty emigrants. Typically, the Modocs set ambushes in the rocky areas near Tule Lake, where emigrants often stopped to water their stock. The victim of one such attack in 1852 survived and escaped to Yreka, however, where a group of volunteers undertook to punish the Modocs. The volunteers were under the command of Ben Wright, who had emigrated from Indiana to California in 1847 and, modeling himself on Kit Carson, quickly established a reputation as an Indian fighter. Wright's campaign began in late August, when his forces attacked a Modoc camp on Tule Lake. The Modocs took flight in their dugout canoes; in the chaos and under fire from Wright's volunteers some women and children drowned. The brief war ended in November 1852, when Wright entered a Modoc camp ostensibly to negotiate the return of some emigrants' stolen property. On a signal, Wright's confederates fell on the camp. Of the forty-six Modocs in the camp, only five, including John Schonchin, who later became one of Captain Jack's advisers, survived. In 1873 the Modocs argued that their killing of Canby and Thomas was revenge for Wright's treachery.[56]

The violence between Modocs and Euroamericans was typical of encounters between Indians and Euroamericans in 1850s California. During the decade, the Indian population of the state fell from approximately 150,000 to 30,000. Violence was probably the second-leading cause of Indian mortality after epidemic disease. Although Indians killed their share of Euroamericans, the anthropologist Theodora Kroeber has estimated that in the case of the Yana Indians just southwest of the Plateau, who like the Modocs were renowned for their violent resistance to Euroamerican conquest, Euroamericans killed between thirty and fifty Indians for every Euroamerican killed by an Indian. The Yana case was sadly representative of the disproportionate consequences of violence between Indians and Euroamericans in interior California.[57]

Disease, war, and emigrants' degradation of the environment decimated the Modocs in the 1850s. In the next decade, the Modocs faced a renewed invasion of their lands by Euroamerican settlers. At first, emigrants and their livestock had passed southwestward through the plateau on their journey to California. In the 1860s, that flow reversed. Mineral discoveries in Idaho prompted California miners to remove to the northeast. In early 1864, the California settler John Kincade commented on the exodus of Californians, writing that "our people are leaving by the thousands for Washoe, Reese River, Washington, and Idaho Territory."[58] Traffic through the plateau was so great that in 1866 the U.S. Army established Fort Bidwell at the base of the Warner Mountains at the midway point between Sacramento and the Idaho mines, to protect travelers en route.

The ecological impact of emigration paled in comparison to the effect of commercial farming and ranching. After the drought years of 1863–64, many California ranchers moved their stock out of the overcrowded Sacramento Valley and into the cooler, wetter upcountry. Major G. G. Kimball drove 3,000 sheep out of California through the Modoc Plateau in 1865; the rancher Peter French drove 1,200 head of cattle from the Sacramento Valley through the plateau to southern Oregon in 1872.[59] By the time of French's cattle drive, ranchers had already begun to select lands in the plateau rather than press on to Oregon. The first cattle in Modoc territory were one hundred head that summered there on their way north in 1865.[60]

Settlement quickly ensued. Surveying of what would become Modoc County began in 1866 and was complete by 1872.[61] In July 1864 the *Sacramento Daily Union* promoted Surprise Valley, just east of the Warner Mountains on the California-Nevada border, as "the original Garden of Eden." The valley, "the most beautiful in the state," was reportedly "rapidly filling up with permanent settlers."[62] By 1868, Surprise Valley had between three and four hundred settlers, mostly farmers, who had enclosed thousands of acres of land to produce foodstuffs for the mining populations of California and Nevada.[63]

Yet relative to the rest of the state, especially the urbanized coast and Central Valley, the population of northeastern California was sparse. Many of the residents of Siskiyou County, which encompassed all of northeastern California until the state legislature created Modoc County in 1874, resided in the town of Yreka, which had a population of five thousand when it was incorporated in 1857. In 1860, the county's other two thousand inhabitants were dispersed among three hundred farms and ranches, of which nearly two hundred were greater than one hundred acres in size, and only two were greater than one thousand acres. By 1870, the number of farms had increased to nearly four hundred. When Modoc County was created out of Siskiyou County in 1874, it contained only 4,000 of the original county's 12,000 inhabitants, but almost five hundred of its eight hundred farms.[64]

The ranches were spartan places, rich in cattle but poor in comforts. William Simpson, who traveled through the Modoc Plateau in 1874, described the ranching region as "a great many miles of land with thousands of cattle on it." Of the inhabitants and their dwellings, Simpson wrote of the ranchers' "tendency to backwardation," and concluded that the ranchlands were "where our civilization ends and the condition of the primitive race begins." Ranch houses were built of logs with earthen floors. "If a sort of missionary society were to be formed to send out soap, brushes, combs, needles, and thread," Simpson observed, "I should at once subscribe to it as one having the most charitable of purposes." Yet the ranchers' wealth in cattle was extensive. Simpson wrote that they "were very wealthy, and the number of dollars they were worth was often mentioned to me."[65]

Euroamerican settlers imposed a new seasonal round of economic activities on the land, displacing the Modocs' cycle of fishing, gathering, and hunting. The Euroamerican economic cycle began in the spring, when they planted a variety of crops for their own subsistence. The Euroamericans' gardens combined plants that had originated in the Old World, including cabbage, parsnips, carrots, turnips, and onions, with those that had originated in the New World, including squash, beans, and potatoes. They planted as early as they dared in order to harvest before the short summer growing season passed and their crops were destroyed by frost. In the spring settlers planted two grain crops, barley and wheat, departing from the practice of wheat growers in the Central Valley, who planted in the fall to take advantage of the mild winter rainy season. By 1874 Modoc County had 18,200 acres planted with wheat, barley, and oats. If they could, wheat growers channeled water from the Warner Mountains to irrigate their crops. Despite such intensive labors, yields of barley and wheat in the plateau were modest; ten bushels per acre was the average. Some grain crops failed altogether. As a result, farmers not only were obliged to forgo the profits of commercial wheat production but were forced to make a journey of up to two hundred miles to obtain flour for their own consumption. Until 1876, the residents of Modoc County purchased two-thirds of their flour from outside the county.[66]

The primary commercial agricultural enterprise in the high lake country, as in the Central Valley and the southern grasslands, was cattle production. The floods of 1861–62 and the droughts of 1862–64 had devastated cattle herds in central and southern California: between 1862 and 1866, cattle declined over 80 percent in Santa Barbara, San Luis Obispo, and Monterey counties; over 70 percent in the San Joaquin Valley; and approximately 40 percent in the Sacramento Valley and the southern California counties of Los Angeles, San Bernardino, and San Diego. By contrast, northeastern California was spared the worst effects of both flood and drought. Ranchers observed that cattle in northeastern California survived the scourges, and accordingly began to shift their livestock there. Siskiyou and Shasta were the only counties in California to increase their cattle populations between 1862 and 1866. The number of cattle in Siskiyou County rose from 11,845 in 1862, to 16,574 in 1866, to 22,426 in 1870.[67] By 1876, 21,580 cattle grazed in Modoc County, which had been hived off from Siskiyou County two years earlier.[68]

Unlike the rancheros of southern California, the ranchers of the Modoc Plateau practiced intensive stockraising—or, rather, a less expensive version of it. Rather than cultivating forage they harvested and stored wild grasses. In midsummer they brought their mowing machines to the plateau's grasslands to cut wild hay, clover, and tule grass. They dried the forage to feed to their stock over the winter; in an average year, they had to collect enough winter feed for three months.

Like the rancheros, the stockraisers of the plateau faced the temptation to overstock the range. By the middle of the 1870s the effects of overgrazing were apparent in the river valleys and along the shores of lakes. "Already has the remorseless process of depasturing and extirpation been begun," wrote Powers in 1874, owing to "the rapacity of our countrymen, by crowding the herds too thick." As a result, according to Powers, "one of the earliest settlers informed me that, each succeeding spring, the grass comes up thinner and weaker."[69] By the end of the nineteenth century, 60,000 sheep and 40,000 cattle inhabited the valleys on either side of the Warner Mountains, causing severe overgrazing.[70] While the Modocs had sustained their resource strategy in the plateau for decades—disasters such as the starvation winter of the early 1830s notwithstanding—within a few years the Euroamericans had noticeably degraded the environment.

The Euroamerican economic and ecological conquest of the plateau reoriented the Modocs' economy from the Dalles to the town of Yreka. By the early 1860s, wildlife populations had declined so dramatically that the Modocs could no longer rely on hunting. Even Euroamerican hunters were alarmed by the rapid disappearance of game. In 1877, 116 inhabitants of Siskiyou County, complaining that market hunters had already exhausted deer and other wildlife, petitioned the state government for stronger game laws.[71] The Modocs, still more dependent on game supplies, had no such recourse, so in large numbers they shifted from hunting and gathering to wage work. By the early 1860s, many Modocs had found employment in Yreka. Men and boys worked occasional odd jobs; women worked as household servants or as prostitutes.

Both forms of employment were common for Indian women throughout California in the 1850s and 1860s, according to the historian Albert Hurtado. Euroamerican demands for the labor of Indian women sprang from the unusual gender imbalance of the initial Euroamerican migration to California. Most forty-niners were men: in 1850, there were twelve Euroamerican men for every Euroamerican woman in California. By 1860, the ratio was still two to one.[72] In parts of the sparsely populated plateau, the gender imbalance was still more skewed. At Dorris Bridge, a ranching settlement in the lake country, a local newspaper reported a population of fifty-eight unmarried men and just one unmarried woman in 1875.[73] The gender imbalance created a social and sexual demand for the labor of Indian women: Simpson noted that "in none of the ranches in this out-of-the-way quarter did I see a European woman." Rather, "there was generally at these ranches a *wikieup*, or rude tent of mats and branches, inhabited by Modoc women."[74]

Just as slave raiding had exacted its social costs on the Modocs, prostitution and household labor took its toll. Both forms of labor furthered the decline of the Modoc population. The effects of sexually transmitted diseases left some Modoc prostitutes sterile. Not only disease but the out-migration of Indian women stifled Indian population growth. Household servants, or those Indian women who married Euroamerican settlers, were in most cases more fortunate than prostitutes. Yet as Indian women were siphoned off to become wives or servants in Euroamerican households, Indian populations began to mirror the gender imbalances of the Euroamerican population. Hurtado has noted that according to the 1860 census, in every county in California in every age cohort Indian men outnumbered Indian women.[75]

The absorption of Indian laborers by the expanding Euroamerican economy quietly decimated native populations. Wage labor was thus a factor that must be considered alongside disease, war, and the constriction of territory in accounting for Indian population decline. Recognizing the significance of Indian labor in California also sheds light on the roots of the Modoc War: by 1872, Captain Jack and his followers were no longer fighting to preserve a purely precontact culture and resource strategy. So profound were the effects of enclosure that they fought to preserve their status as wage laborers.

Despite the adaptability of some Modocs to the Euroamerican presence in northeastern California, in the early 1860s the federal government undertook to force the Modocs to move from California to Oregon. Since the death of Jack's father in the early 1840s, the most influential Modoc tyee was Schonchin ("The Rock"), the elder brother of John Schonchin. He had pronounced himself amenable to removal to Oregon.

Seeking to avoid removal, or to mitigate its effects, Jack embarked for Yreka in February 1864 to meet with the former Indian agent Elisha Steele. Steele and Jack drafted an unofficial treaty according to which Jack's Modocs would have permission to leave their reservation (the location of which had not yet been determined) to trade, act as guides, and otherwise labor for Euroamericans. Jack promised to halt the traffic in Modoc women as prostitutes—a ban that Jack likely wanted to stem Modoc population decline, yet would have forced the Modocs to surrender a major source of income. Steele promised to lobby for a reservation for Jack's Modocs on Lost River, where they would be able to obtain their most important resources: fish, camas, and wocas.[76]

In October 1864 the U.S. Indian Service presented the Modocs with a treaty that largely superseded the agreement between Steele and Jack. It compelled the Modocs to remove to Oregon to share a reservation on the north side of Klamath Lake with the more numerous Klamaths. A sizable minority of Modocs—those most adapted to the Euroamerican economy—resisted, wishing to remain in the Tule Lake region as laborers. By virtue of his negotiations with Steele, Jack emerged as their advocate. The unpopular treaty thus presented Jack with a political issue with which he could solidify his claim to leadership, transforming him from a minor tyee into a leader with broad recognition in Modoc society. Yet despite his new celebrity, Jack had little authority to dissuade others from acquiescing to the treaty. Sensing that other prominent tyees, including Schonchin, were resigned to it, Jack added his consent in return for recognition from the U.S. Indian Service that his claim to leadership of the Modocs was equal to that of Schonchin's.[77] Not for the last time, Jack's desire to bolster his claim to leadership drove him, against his better judgment, to shortsighted compromise with other Modoc leaders.

Jack visited the Klamath-Modoc reservation only briefly. By early 1865, he and his band had returned to the Lost River. Yet Jack's Modocs were not simply traditionalists determined to adhere to their trusted resource strategies in the face of the Euroamerican conquest. Between early 1865 and late 1869, Jack and his band, which numbered about forty, alternated between foraging on the banks of Lost River and laboring on the margins of the Euroamerican economy. Yreka employers welcomed the illegal migrant Modoc workers. Influential Euroamericans in Yreka, who appreciated the importance of Modoc workers to the local economy, supported Jack. In August 1865, Steele and A. M. Rosborough, a Siskiyou County judge, petitioned the commanding officer at Fort Klamath to allow the Modocs to remain in northeastern California. "These Indians have been always disposed [to] peace and friendly intercourse with the whites," Steele and Rosborough wrote. "They now wish to care for themselves and say with fish and fowl with which their country abounds they can provide for themselves better than can be done by the Government."[78]

In truth, the Modoc Plateau no longer abounded with fish or fowl. The ecological changes in the plateau during the previous two decades had made subsistence by fishing, hunting, and gathering impossible even for a small band. As Steele and Rosborough were well aware, the Modocs combined their foraging with wage labor. The labor market was a perilous place for off-reservation Indians, however. Fearing that they might at any moment be apprehended and returned to the reservation in Oregon, Jack and his followers secured written passes from Steele or Rosborough attesting to their identities and occupations. In April 1868, for instance, Rosborough wrote the following pass for Bogus Charley:

> Charlie, the Indian to whom I give this paper, makes a living for himself and his family by farming, driving team, &c&c. and wants me to give him this paper to certify that he is a civilized Indian & not a wild Indian—that he is an independent freeman entitled to the protection of life, liberty, and pursuit of happiness, by the laws of civilization.[79]

What is most immediately striking about Charley's pass is how in just a few words, Rosborough synthesized nearly all of the permutations of nineteenth-century rights language, asserting not only Charley's universal rights according to the Declaration of Independence ("life, liberty, and pursuit of happiness"), but his constitutional rights according to the Thirteenth and only recently ratified Fourteenth Amendments ("freeman entitled to protection"), his economic rights according to the doctrine of free labor ("makes a living for himself"), and his social rights as an assimilated Indian ("he is a civilized Indian and not a wild Indian"). Less immediately apparent but just as significant is how the pass reflected the proletarianization of Indian labor by the process of enclosure. The pass makes no assertion of Charley's traditional right to inhabit the Modocs' customary territory—indeed, Rosborough distances Charley from such an assertion by noting that he is not a "wild Indian." Rather, the pass asserts only his right to sell his labor. It subtly and eloquently articulates the transformation that enclosure brought to the Modocs.

Yet as E. P. Thompson noted in his analysis of English enclosure, the process was meant not simply to alienate people from their traditional commons and transform them, like Bogus Charley, into wage laborers. It was also an imposition of social discipline by a new economic regime upon the remnant population of an older system. The very presence of Modocs in California, and thus out of the bounds of the Oregon reservation, challenged that regime. The U.S. government therefore embarked upon an effort to rationalize its Indian affairs in the late 1860s and 1870s. At the center of that effort was a renewed campaign to cajole or coerce off-reservation Indians to submit to the reservation system.[80] The policy applied even to those Indians such as Bogus Charley and the many members of Jack's faction who had assimilated into the ranching and mining economy as wage laborers. Accordingly, stragglers from Old Schonchin's band were induced to settle on the Klamath-Modoc reservation in 1867. After nearly five years at Lost River, in late 1869 Jack allowed himself to be persuaded by Meacham, the newly appointed superintendent of Indian affairs for Oregon, to go to the reservation as well. In return for his acquiescence, according to the custom of Indian-Euroamerican diplomacy, Jack received a large supply of goods.

On the Oregon reservation, Jack's Modocs were as industrious as they had been in the Tule Lake region. The 1864 treaty, anticipating the integration of the Modocs into the Euroamerican economy as agricultural laborers, had provided for the construction of a blacksmithy, carpenter's shop, wagon and plow maker's shop, sawmill, flour mill, and a manual labor school.[81] Jack's band, long accustomed to laboring for Euroamericans, needed no such instruction. Immediately upon arriving in December 1869, Jack asked the reservation agent to provide his band with axes, saws, wedges, and maul rings. According to Jeff Riddle, the son of Frank and Toby Riddle, the interpreters at the 1873 parley, Jack told the agent "he wanted to put his men to work making rails." While perhaps Jack intended to enclose a pasture for stock on the reservation, in all likelihood he planned to transport the rails south and sell them to ranchers in California. Jack's endeavor was obstructed by the Klamaths, however, who confiscated 1,200 pine rails from the Modocs. "This is my land. You have got no business to cut my trees down. This is not your country," one of the Klamaths reportedly told Jack. "The grass, water, fish, fowl, deer, and everything else belongs to me."[82] The Modocs, having ceded their homeland to the Euroamericans, and living as a minority alongside the more numerous Klamaths in Oregon, found themselves effectively landless.

The Klamaths' husbanding of the resources on the reservation was not without reason. Simpson characterized the Klamath-Modoc reservation as "so high, cold, and poor, that nothing but sagebrush is to be found; and it is a current saying that where you find sagebrush nothing else will grow: even the poorest crops of rye are produced with difficulty from such a soil."[83] Major C. G. Huntt, the assistant adjutant-general of the Department of the Columbia, candidly admitted that the Klamath reservation's "sources of subsistence are not sufficient for a large Indian population. Game is not very abundant." Moreover, the supply of salmon ascending the Snake River "sometimes nearly fails."[84] In early 1872, an anonymous soldier at Fort Klamath wrote to the editor of the *Portland Oregonian* that the Indians on the Klamath Reservation were "at the point of starvation."[85]

The Modocs did not tarry on the reservation long enough to reach that point. In December 1869 Jack had come to the reservation at the head of a band of forty-three people. In April 1870 he led 371 people—nearly all of the Modocs—back to their homeland in northeastern California. Even Old Schonchin followed.[86] The moment marked the height of Jack's influence.

Yet the plateau to which the Modocs returned in the spring of 1870 was a place transformed. The Modocs found that in their absence between late 1869 and early 1870 the process of enclosure had proceeded apace. Ivan Applegate, an Oregon Indian agent, wrote to Thomas Odeneal, who at the time of the Modoc War was the superintendent of Indian affairs in Oregon, that most of the Modoc territory "has been located as state land and nearly every foot of it fit for cultivation has been taken up by settlers, whose thousands of cattle, horses, and sheep are ranging over it."[87] Euroamericans' livestock were concentrated principally near the creeks and lakes where the Modocs gathered their camas and wocas, fished for suckers, and hunted waterfowl.

Federal officials were unsympathetic to the Modocs' dilemma. Odeneal believed that the "whole matter may be summed up in a few words: These Indians made a treaty, agreed to go to Klamath Reservation, which they accepted in lieu of all other lands to which they had ever before set up any claim," Odeneal wrote. "The country they thus relinquished all right to was settled by whites under the homestead and pre-emption laws of the U.S."[88] Gradually, some Modocs, under the leadership of Old Schonchin, submitted to the enclosure of the Tule Lake region and began to drift back to the Oregon reservation.

To subsist, the Modocs who chose to remain in California needed more than ever before to combine their traditional hunting-gathering-fishing economy with wage labor on the margins of the Euroamerican economy. Some Tule Lake ranchers welcomed the Modocs back; in the sparsely populated plateau, the Modocs were among the few people the ranchers could hire to mow hay, ride fences, and retrieve strays. In the spring of 1872, the rancher Henry Miller told two Indian agents, J. H. High and Jesse Applegate, "I have Indians in my house, and at present, while I am here, they have the key of my house and are herding my stock."[89]

Determined to build a case for forcing the return of the Modocs to Oregon, High and Applegate scoured the ranches for accusations against the Indians. The best they could muster were modest complaints. One rancher stated that he agreed to pay two Modocs $2.50 to catch his stray horse. The Modocs drove the horse, the rancher claimed, but he himself caught the animal, and thus he paid the Modocs only $1. The Modocs, the rancher complained, then "followed me to the house and acted as though they wanted the rest of the money." More troublesome to some ranchers were Modoc claims to ownership of grasslands. The Modocs allowed the ranchers to mow hay, but charged a fee. Some ranchers, in the interest of pacifying the Modocs, paid willingly. John Fairchild, for instance, negotiated a private treaty with the Modocs according to which he paid them a nominal rent. Others refused.

As an extortion racket, the Modoc scheme operated on a curiously voluntary basis only: those who refused to pay rent suffered no violence.[90] Nonetheless, in 1872, ranchers submitted two petitions to Meacham and Canby complaining of the Modocs' bullying. Canby, wary of allowing his small force to be drawn into violence, dismissed the ranchers' claims as exaggerated. So far as Canby could tell in mid-1872, while tensions persisted between Modocs and Euroamerican settlers following the return of Jack's band to the plateau, they were not violent. Rather, they were petty disputes between employers and employees and between property owners disputing title to the land.

As Canby reasoned, disputes over wages, land title, and rent were hardly grounds for an Indian war. Yet nine months later, Canby allowed himself to be persuaded by settlers and by Indian agents such as Applegate to attempt the removal of the Modocs to Oregon. The effort to make an example of the Modocs in order to permit the process of enclosure to proceed

ultimately led Canby to authorize the November 1872 attack on Jack's winter camp.

Once a general in the Civil War, by 1872 Canby commanded merely 1,200
troops dispersed across the state of Oregon and the territories of Washington
and Idaho. Following the failure of the Army's attack on Jack's winter camp,
Canby was forced to commit four hundred of his troops to the siege of the
Modocs in the lava beds. Given the limitations of his force, Canby adhered to
the standard tactics of fighting Indians in the 1870s. Rather than pressing
battles, he opted for starving his enemy into submission—pursuing by military
means what enclosure had accomplished by treaty. Indeed, a few days before
the Good Friday parley, during a truce one of Canby's officers had driven
off the Modocs' horses. Canby had refused to return them, on the grounds that
the loss of the horses would "shorten their subsistence"—under the conditions
of the siege, the Modocs used the horses not as mounts but as rations.[91]

Like Canby, Jack, once an advocate of compromise and negotiation, was
persuaded by his aides against his better judgment to violence. The two other
tyees in the lava beds stronghold, Hooker Jim and Shacknasty Jim, had been
among the most ardent advocates of the plan to murder the commissioners.
Jack had continued to urge negotiation until the very end, but his already tenuous authority had eroded under the conditions of the siege. Conscious that
the majority of the tyees favored the murder plan and were determined to go
forward with or without him, Jack only acceded at the last moment. In a desperate attempt to maintain his titular status as the Modocs' leader, he had insisted on the privilege of personally killing Canby.[92]

Writing in 1877, the amateur California ethnologist Stephen Powers theo-
rized that the Modocs had killed the peace commissioners because "they believed that the death of our leaders would strike terror into the hearts of their
followers, and cause them to disperse in wild dismay."[93] Instead, the killing of
Canby and Thomas prompted calls in the California and national press for the
extermination of the Modocs. The *Alta California* reported a few days after
the killings that in San Francisco, "thousands of volunteers could be obtained
to go to the front to wipe out the entire band." The newspaper added fuel to
this fire, advocating on April 16 the "annihilation of the band that committed
these dastardly murders." On April 19 the newspaper called again for "A
War of Extermination."[94] Colonel Alvan Gillem, who succeeded to Canby's
command, was prepared to oblige such sentiments. He instructed his subor-

dinates on April 16 to attack the Modoc positions, urging, "Let us extermi-
nate the tribe."[95]

The Modocs were a formidable enemy, however. William Murray, a
soldier in Gillem's force, described the Modocs as excellent marksmen–and
markswomen, as many of the women in the stronghold also defended the
Modoc positions–who kept up accurate sniper fire on the Army's line. Murray complained that the soldiers were, by contrast, overloaded with unnecessary supplies and undermotivated to fight. At night, some Modoc women
infiltrated the Army's lines and exchanged sex for food and ammunition. The
Modocs mocked the soldiers across the no-man's-land between the opposing
forces, shouting confusing orders and taunting the soldiers in "tolerable English" to pick up their dead and go home.[96] Determined to avenge the peace
commissioners but well aware that his regular troops were no match for the
Modocs, Gillem augmented his force with a detachment of Warm Springs Indian scouts.[97]

Assisted by the Indian auxiliaries and supported by mortar fire, the troops
began an assault on the Modoc barricades on April 15. After four days of heavy
fighting, the Modocs withdrew, escaping during the night through a gap in
the Army's line. In the abandoned fortress, the soldiers discovered the effectiveness of Canby's siege. Murray reported that the caves of the fortress were
"reeking with human filth and swarming with disgusting vermin; the putrid
carcasses of beeves and horses, old decaying and decayed bones of every animal known in the surrounding country." The desperate conditions within the
fortress had doubtless contributed to the Modocs' decision to kill the peace
commissioners. Most of the victorious Euroamericans were in no mood to reflect on the causes of the Indians' treachery, however. Two of the Modocs'
rear guard had been killed covering the retreat from the stronghold. Just as
the Modocs had stripped and mutilated the bodies of the peace commissioners, the Euroamericans desecrated the Modocs' bodies. According to Murray, during the Euroamericans' celebration of their victory, the heads of the
two Indians "were kicked about like footballs by soldiers, citizens, [and]
newspaper reporters."[98]

The Modocs' retreat from the lava beds did not mark the end of the war,
however. The Modocs dispersed throughout the Tule Lake region; against
such small, moving groups Gillem could concentrate neither his forces nor
his mortar fire.[99] The pursuit of the elusive Modocs across an unfamiliar ter-

rain increased Army casualties: on April 26, the Modocs trapped a squad of soldiers in a cul-de-sac, killing twenty-two and wounding twelve.[100] As the costs of defeating the Modocs rose, so too did criticism of the war. In mid-May, the *Sacramento Daily Union* called the Modoc War "a series of blunders from the beginning." Among the errors the *Daily Union* enumerated were the 1864 treaty that had relegated the Modocs to Oregon against their will; the failure to allow the Modocs a small reservation in northeastern California in 1869 and 1870; the bungled effort to arrest the Modoc leaders to force a return to Oregon in 1872; and the failed peace commission. The "greatest blunder," according to the newspaper, was Gillem's order "for the extermination of the entire tribe. This was alike cruel and impolitic and if possible in excess of the savagery of the Modoc chiefs."[101]

Ignoring such criticisms, Gillem and Colonel Jefferson C. Davis, who was appointed as Canby's permanent replacement as commander of the Department of the Columbia, pursued the war against the Modocs to its conclusion. In early May, the Warm Springs auxiliaries engaged some Modocs in a skirmish in which Ellen's Man George was killed. In late May, Hooker Jim and Shacknasty Jim, weary of the conflict, surrendered with their bands. Mindful that he needed Indian auxiliaries to augment his forces, Davis offered the captive tyees the choice of either facing execution for the murders of Canby and Thomas or assisting the Army in tracking down Jack. Ironically, in the days before Good Friday, Hooker Jim and Shacknasty Jim had persuaded Jack to murder Canby, but as the erstwhile leader of the Modocs and as Canby's murderer, Jack was the Army's primary quarry. With the help of Hooker Jim and the Hot Creek Modocs, Jack was apprehended quietly on June 1. Some sporadic violence continued—settlers lynched one group of four Modocs after they had surrendered—but the Modoc War was effectively over. On October 3, 1873, after a brief trial, Jack, John Schonchin, and two other Modocs who had held out with Jack to the last were hanged.

Following the execution, plateau ranchers hoped to restore the status quo ante, with Modocs available for hire as ranch hands and domestic servants. Several ranchers wrote to the secretary of the interior in 1873 that the remaining Modocs "are useful farm hands capable of and fully competent intellectually to trade for and take care of themselves." They asked the secretary to assign the defeated Modocs to the care of the former sheriff of Siskiyou County, "who is a large farmer near Yreka."[102] They sought to create a system much like the one in place in southern California, where Indian agents such as B. D. Wilson and Cave Couts bound Indians to service on the ranchos. Instead, to preclude further violence, the Modocs who had helped to apprehend Jack were granted a new reservation. The reservation was not in California, nor across the border in Oregon, but far to the east in the Indian Territory (later the state of Oklahoma).[103]

The exile of the Modocs permitted the enclosure of the plateau to continue. In 1860, only two farms in Siskiyou County had been greater than one thousand acres in size. By 1870 nine farms were so large. In 1880, by which time Modoc County had been carved out of Siskiyou County, the two counties together had 29 farms larger than one thousand acres. By 1890 there were 82 such farms in the two counties. Farms smaller than one hundred acres fell from 192 in 1870, to 119 in 1880, to only 88 in 1890. The average farm size in Modoc County was just under three hundred acres in 1880; it had risen to over four hundred acres by 1890.[104]

The social discipline imposed by the Euroamerican victory came at a great price. The Modoc War cost the United States roughly $500,000. Eighteen Modocs—only 7 of whom were men—died in the conflict. For the United States, the brief war claimed the lives of 47 soldiers, 16 volunteers, 2 Indian scouts, and 18 civilian settlers.[105] The two thousand acres that Jack had requested for a reservation in northern California were worth approximately $20,000.[106]

TABLE 3.

FARM SIZE IN SISKIYOU AND MODOC COUNTIES, 1860–90

		No. of farms 3–99 acres	No. of farms 100–199 acres	No. of farms 500–999 acres	No. of farms 1000 acres or more	Avg. farm size
1860	Siskiyou	95	178	22	2	—
1870	Siskiyou	192	153	18	9	—
1880	Modoc	28	399	38	7	299
	Siskiyou	91	179	49	22	369
	Total	119	578	87	29	—
1890	Modoc	36	478	51	48	411
	Siskiyou	52	365	66	34	443
	Total	88	843	117	82	—

The United States endured the costs of the war to make an example of the Modocs. As one Indian agent in Oregon put it, "Let Captain Jack dictate his own terms, and it may not be long before the Klamaths, the Snakes, some of the Umatillas, and others feign to be aggrieved and follow Jack's precedent."[107] That sentiment was widespread. L. B. Applegate, a longtime resident of the region and brother of the Indian agent at the Yainax Indian Agency, urged the governor of California, Newton Booth:

> If they are not crushed at once, the Pitt Rivers, and Indians on the Klam-ath Reservation, may be encouraged to join them in force, in which case the whole country embracing the Klamath, Rhett, Clear, and Goose lakes and the Pitt River Country will be involved in a terrible Indian war. If Capt Jack's band can be destroyed, or captured (and the winter is the time to do it) it will end the war, and be a wholesome les-son to the other Indians.[108]

Yet a widespread Indian war in the Northwest was unlikely: to the contrary, the Modocs' neighbors joined the U.S. Army in defeating their old enemies. By Easter 1873, the aim of making an example of the Modocs focused on bringing the murderers of Canby and Thomas to justice. Yet some of the most unreconciled enemies of the Euroamericans, including Hooker Jim, who led the attack on settlers in November, escaped punishment.

In the minds of contemporaries, the Modoc War ended with Jack's execu-tion and the exile of the remaining Modocs to the Indian Territory. Long be-fore those events, however, the fundamental prize of the war—control over the plateau environment—had been won by the Euroamericans. The Modocs cer-tainly understood what was at issue in the war—so, too, did the Klamaths, when they denied the use of their resources to the Modocs. While the Modocs staked a claim to only a small and remote parcel of land and while they otherwise integrated themselves into the Euroamerican economy, their defiance of the economic and ecological conquest put them on the path toward violence.

The roots of the conflict can be understood neither as a Euroamerican frontier conquest nor simply as a defense by the Modocs of their cultural tra-ditions. Such interpretations, emphasizing the cultural distance between In-dians and Euroamericans, offer little understanding of Modoc cultural and economic adaptations to the presence of settlers. The Modoc War did not arise between two groups that lived in separate worlds. Instead, and far more poignantly, it involved two groups characterized as much by cultural interaction as by cultural conflict. Euroamericans and Modocs were employers and employees, the landed and the newly landless. It was the process of enclosure that created both the shared world of the plateau ranching economy and the conditions for conflict.

Epilogue: Economic Development and the California Environment

In June 1874 a group of farmers in Tulare County formed a corporation, the Settlers' Ditch Company, with a modest capital stock of $10,000. They began work on an irrigation ditch to draw water from Cross Creek, completing their ditch in December 1875. By the early 1880s the ditch provided water to nearly eight thousand acres producing wheat, barley, and alfalfa. The cost to farmers who drew water from the ditch was a mere $1.50 per acre; the irrigated fields yielded bumper crops of twenty to forty bushels of wheat per acre. Irrigated farming was so profitable that by 1883 the Settlers' Ditch was only one of seven irrigation canals operating in Tulare County. By that time, Tulare County farmers were irrigating almost fifty thousand acres.[1]

Over 60 percent of that acreage in Tulare County was planted in wheat. In 1879, according to the federal census, California's wheat production was seventh in the nation. In 1889 it was second only to Minnesota. The apex was in 1884, when California led the nation in wheat production with over 57 million bushels.[2] California emerged as an agricultural empire just in time for the frontier historian Frederick Jackson Turner to incorporate it into his agrarian paradigm for western American history. Turner's 1893 essay, "The Significance of the Frontier in American History," envisioned a linear progression from wilderness to farming to cities and industry that conflated Daniel Boone's path to Kentucky with overland emigrants' route to California: "Stand at Cumberland Gap and watch the procession of civilization," Turner wrote. "Stand at South Pass in the Rockies a century later and see the same procession."[3]

Yet the economic development of nineteenth-century California was hardly linear. An industrial frontier in the 1850s, Anglo California did not have extensive lands under cultivation until the 1870s—in the 1850s, the most profitable and extensive ranches were those of Mexican southern California. The incorporation of those ranchos into the Anglo economy was complicated and contested. Moreover, California before the gold rush had never been a real wilderness in any meaningful sense of the term: its native population had been dense and complex, followed by nearly a century as a Spanish colony and Mexican province. Yet at the end of the nineteenth century, Californians, recoiling from the ugliness as well as from the social costs of the resource-intensive industrialization that had brought economic prosperity to the state, preserved landscapes from exploitation and imagined them as wilderness. Anglo California's economic development thus began with industry, later included agriculture, and still later invented wilderness.

By the time the Tulare County wheat farmers had started to tap rivers to irrigate their fields, California had already become a "hydraulic society." Gold production, the state's largest industry, depended on the control of water. Hydraulic mining, in turn, created demands for further industrial pro-

Mechanized wheat production in the Central Valley

duction: hydraulic miners were not only the largest customers for mercury, the second-largest industry in California, but helped to sustain other industries including lumbering and ironworking. California's nineteenth-century industrial "hydraulic society" was not, however, of the kind that the historian Donald Worster wrote of in a 1982 essay, "Hydraulic Society in California." Worster was writing of large-scale, commercial, irrigated agriculture in California's Central Valley, which started with organizations such as the Settlers' Ditch Company.[4]

The large-scale control of water in California emerged not for the purpose of agriculture but for the industrial exploitation of gold deposits. The 1887 Wright Act in California, which formally inaugurated the state's ultimately extensive irrigation system by allowing localities to establish irrigation districts and levy taxes for their operation, was enacted long after hydraulic mining had developed its own extensive system of reservoirs and distributing ditches. California's twentieth-century hydraulic system was in many ways the legacy of hydraulic mining: many of the engineers who had created the network of reservoirs and distributing ditches for the mines went to work in the 1880s creating California's irrigation and municipal water supply system.[5]

Some Californians both understood and resented the water companies' early and rapid consolidation of economic power in the Sierra Nevada. In 1857, the Tuolumne County Water Company offered $1,000 for the apprehension of those responsible for breaching one of their reservoirs. The company made a similar offer in response to another breach in October 1860. Their call for civic vigilance apparently had little effect; in December 1860 a person or persons blew up one of the company's flumes, causing several thousand dollars worth of damage and, more significantly, depriving the local mining district of water for two months.[6] The destruction of dams tapped into English and American custom—embedded in the common law—that regarded industrial impediments of rivers as public nuisances and as violations of an agrarian people's traditional right to unfettered watercourses.[7]

Anonymous Californians' destruction of corporate reservoirs as early as the 1850s demonstrated their recognition of the concentration of economic power in the hands of those who controlled water. Their destruction of flumes and reservoirs presaged the legal challenge to the hydraulic miners in the 1870s and 1880s by a Sacramento Valley farmers' organization, the Anti-Debris Association.

Although the historian Robert Kelley has described the Anti-Debris Association as "representing populist democracy in the traditional sense," the image of protopopulists opposing corporate mining is as much a romantic myth as the image of the lone prospector.[8] Many of the members of the Anti-Debris Association were not hardscrabble homesteaders but large-scale commercial farmers. The group was organized at the behest of one of the largest and most influential engines of economic development in California, the Southern Pacific Railroad. The owners of the Southern Pacific conglomerate, the so-called Big Four of Charles Crocker, Mark Hopkins, Collis Huntington, and Leland Stanford, had determined by the late 1860s that California's economic future was in agriculture rather than mining. They employed the newspaper they controlled, the *Sacramento Record-Union*, to editorialize against hydraulic mining. In the summer of 1878, the editor of the *Record-Union*, William Mills, was instrumental in organizing the Anti-Debris Association, whose purpose was to pursue a lawsuit against hydraulic miners.[9]

Two years before the founding of the Anti-Debris Association, hydraulic mining companies had organized to resist legal challenges. In the summer of 1876, J. P. Pierce of the Excelsior Water Company, Egbert Judson of Spring Valley Water Company and Milton Mining and Water Company, Lester L. Robinson of the Union Gravel Mining Company (also the president of the North Bloomfield mine), Thomas Smith of the El Dorado and Blue Tent mines, and Hamilton Smith, Jr., of the North Bloomfield mine met in San Francisco to form an association of "owners either in gravel mines, or of canals for the supply of water to such mines," for "the general purpose of mutual benefit and protection." Anticipating legal challenges, the association agreed to cooperate in "the defense or protection of any one of its members who may be legally attacked, and where the point at issue involves some general principle."[10]

The eventual Hydraulic Miners' Association, like the Anti-Debris Association, attempted to sway public opinion. Tapping into the developmentalist notions that Turner later codified, the hydraulic mining companies proclaimed in 1881 that "the only way by which the pristine purity of the waters of the State can be brought back, is by driving out the present population, and restoring the land to the nomadic Indian, for when civilized man touches the soil the rivers inevitably become muddy."[11] The miners' proclamation was consistent with the policy that had guided federal land policy since the discovery of gold in California: to exploit natural resources for industrial growth. Pollution, industrialists argued, was inevitable if the American economy was to expand. Pollution was not to be wished for, perhaps, but it was a condition willingly tolerated for the sake of wealth.

In the conflict between the hydraulic miners and the Anti-Debris Association, the law provided no easy solution to the conflict over water rights. Statutes favored the miners. The California water code of 1872 embraced the doctrine of "prior appropriation." The judiciary, however, tempered this doctrine by recognizing the older common law doctrine of riparian rights. The latter protected farmers' vested rights to the undisturbed "natural" flow of the river.[12] The guiding purpose of the common law was to restrain uses of the land to agricultural purposes. Instrumental uses of the land such as dams and mills, for instance, ran counter to one of the common law's cardinal principles: Use your land without harming another's (*Sic utere tuo ut alienum non laedas*).

The confusion of the legal system was evident in an 1857 California Supreme Court case involving a dispute between two hydraulic mining companies over the diversion of water from the Bear River. Associate Justice Peter Burnett, the former governor of California and before that a real estate developer in Sacramento, complained:

> The mining interest of the State has grown up under the force of new
> and extraordinary circumstances, and in the absence of any specific
> and certain legislation to guide us. Left without any direct precedent,
> as well as without specific legislation, we have been compelled to ap-
> ply to this anomalous state of things the analogies of the common law,
> and the more expanded principles of equitable justice.

He concluded, "In these mining cases, we are virtually projecting a new system." Nonetheless, he wrote, "we are compelled to decide these cases, because they must be settled in some way, whether we can say after it is done, that we have given a just decision or not." Unable to untangle the claims and counterclaims of the mining companies, the justices opted to affirm the simple expedient of prior appropriation. While the doctrine offered clarity, the justices were clearly unnerved by its potential for concentrating power in the hands of a single corporation.[13]

Ironically, the plaintiff in the suit, the Bear River and Auburn Mining Company, whose prior right to divert the waters of the Bear River the court ultimately affirmed, unintentionally provided the court with the opportunity to express its misgivings over the "new system" that hydraulic mining had created. Overreaching in its arguments before the court, the company maintained that by its prior appropriation, it had acquired "a positive vested right" to an undiminished and unaltered flow of water in the Bear River, just as a farmer or rancher had a right to an uncorrupted flow of water to irrigate crops or water stock. The court rejected this contention in unequivocal terms. "The use of water for domestic purposes, and for the watering of stock, are *preferred uses*, because essential to sustain life. Other uses must be subordinate to these," Burnett wrote. "In our mineral region we have a novel use of water, that cannot be classed with the preferred uses."[14] In 1857 agriculturalists' rights to water in the gold country were largely hypothetical; rather, the court asserted those rights as a check on the otherwise absolute rights to divert water that the hydraulic mining companies held under the doctrine of prior appropriation.

Economically and politically, California was likewise divided. Representatives to the California Assembly from the agricultural districts of the Central Valley were the leading opponents of hydraulic mining. The miners were well represented both by their own Assembly members from the Sierra and those from the urban districts of San Francisco and Sacramento, where the investors, industrialists, and merchants who profited from mining were concentrated.

By 1878 farmers' representatives had succeeded in creating a special Committee on Mining Debris. The committee convened in February 1878 to hear testimony. The engineers and mining company executives who testified at the hearings, including Lester L. Robinson, the president of the largest mine in the state, the North Bloomfield mine, dissembled impressively. Sediment was but a consequence of a natural process of erosion, claimed one. Slickens contributed to the fertility of the soil, maintained another. Finally, they blamed their accusers for the pollution of the rivers. Robinson claimed that all but an insignificant fraction of the mining debris was deposited just below the mines themselves. Pollution farther downstream, he suggested, was the consequence of erosion caused by farmers.[15]

The majority of the committee explicitly rejected this suggestion, noting in its final report that the Sacramento River, above its confluence with the Feather River, flowed southward through over one hundred miles of Central

Valley farmland. Through this entire length, the river was clear. Not until the Sacramento joined the Feather, which drained some of the mines of the Sierra, did it become polluted.[16] Indeed, for the Anti-Debris Association, the only significant accomplishment of the legislative hearings was publicly to discredit the hydraulic mining companies' contention that they were not responsible for the debris in California's rivers.

Even the Minority Report of the Committee on Mining Debris, composed of Assembly members friendly to the business interests of the miners, conceded that "a very considerable portion" of the debris originated at the mines. Too politically astute to endorse the mine owners' transparently disingenuous denials of responsibility for the debris, the minority adopted a more persuasive defense of the mines. While the damage to farmers from debris amounted to about $2 million annually, the minority argued, the hydraulic mines contributed between $12 million and $15 million to the state's economy each year. "The industry from which a large part of the damage proceeds," wrote the minority, "gives employment and sustenance to a considerable portion of the State."[17]

This argument prevailed when in March the Assembly considered a bill prohibiting the dumping of mining debris in rivers. The Assembly rejected the bill by a ratio of five to one. Every member of the Assembly from the urban districts of Sacramento and San Francisco voted against it.[18] San Francisco's reliably pro-mining *Alta California* celebrated this result, editorializing that the bill was "properly killed." The editors argued, "The miners have a legal right to use the natural channels for the outlet of their sluices, and even if they had not, it would be policy to give them that right, for the State could not afford to do without the $10,000,000 or $12,000,000 obtained from the hydraulic mines annually."[19]

As a compromise measure, the legislature passed a Drainage Act in 1880, which provided for the building of dams to impound the debris from the mines. The act won backing from the supporters of hydraulic mining because it promised not only to protect farmers and city dwellers downstream of the mines from slickens, but to protect the hydraulic miners from the conditions that would provoke an expensive lawsuit. Indeed, for precisely that reason, a year before the passage of the Drainage Act, the North Bloomfield mine had begun construction on a levee, which ultimately cost $85,000, designed to contain their debris.

Debris dam

Unfortunately, the dams built under the auspices of the Drainage Act failed utterly to contain mining debris. A fourteen-foot-high, two-mile-long dam across the Yuba River, eight miles above Marysville, constructed at a cost of $120,000, broke in three places during the rains of 1881. The water poured through with such force that it crushed the ten-ton boulders used to construct the dam. During the dry summer that followed, much of the remainder of the dam caught fire and burned down. A dam on the Bear River also collapsed. Altogether, the state expended $500,000 on the failed effort to impound mining debris.[20]

The Anti-Debris Association was more successful in the state courts, where it could appeal to common law riparian rights. In 1876, James Keyes, the president of the Anti-Debris Association, had initiated a suit in the Tenth District Court against the Little York mine, charging it for the damages to his farm resulting from the debris the mine deposited in the Bear River. On March 10, 1879, Judge Phil Keyser delivered a ruling resoundingly in Keyes's favor. Keyser's findings of fact concluded that in January 1875 debris consisting of "fine and coarse sand, small stones and a sticky compound composed of clay and sand, called slickens," from the Little York had inundated 400 of Keyes's more than 1,000 acres. As a matter of law, Keyser, drawing directly on riparian doctrine, ruled that the owners of the Little York mine "have not acquired any right to use the bed of the Bear River, nor the beds of its branches and tributaries, as a place of deposit of their mining tailings." Their actions, therefore, "constitute a nuisance." Keyser enjoined the miners from depositing further debris in the river.[21] In November, however, the California Supreme Court reversed Keyser's decision on a legal technicality; the defendants, they ruled, had been "misjoined," as it was impossible to determine the exact source of the debris.[22]

When the state supreme court overruled Keyser, hydraulic mining was still the leading industry in the state. In the 1880s, however, steam-powered tractors, reapers, and threshers manufactured in Stockton spurred the exponential expansion of wheat cultivation in the Central Valley. Farmers grew much of this wheat in the Sacramento Valley, in precisely the region subject to slickens.[23] The expansion of agriculture undercut the hydraulic miners' claim to be indispensable to the California economy.

By 1882, when Edwards Woodruff, who owned 1,700 acres of wheatland near Marysville on both banks of the Yuba River, sued the largest hydraulic mine in the state, the North Bloomfield mine, for inundating his lands with slickens, the economic landscape had changed markedly: the wheat farmers who opposed hydraulic mining debris had become one of the leading economic sectors in the state.

Yet in many ways Woodruff, a native of New York who had come to California in 1849, was an unlikely opponent of hydraulic mining; his fortune was heavily implicated in California's urban and industrial economy. In the early 1850s Woodruff made considerable profits as a landlord and real estate speculator in Marysville, resulting especially from his control of a prime commercial structure, the "Empire Block," on the city's Old Plaza. By the 1860s his investment portfolio included holdings in the Spring Valley Water Company, which provided water to hydraulic mines as well as to municipalities; a copper mine in Calaveras County; and a silver mine in Mexico. In the mid-1870s he invested in the Ophir mining district in Utah Territory.[24]

The lawyers argued their positions before Judge Lorenzo Sawyer of the Ninth U.S. Circuit Court. Sawyer had written rhapsodically of the beauty of the Sierra when he first migrated to California in 1850. "Insensible indeed must that man be who can stand upon this place and gaze upon the sublimities of nature around him without forgetting self in admiration of this display of Almighty power," Sawyer wrote in December 1850. He juxtaposed the beauty of nonhuman nature with the ugliness of "the work of man." "By his persever-

Lorenzo Sawyer

ing and indefatigable labors the forests are uprooted and prostrated, the lowest depths of earth yields up her treasures, mountains themselves are removed." In 1850, Sawyer had been cognizant of the social as well as the environmental costs of mining. Almost immediately after his arrival in California, he wrote to friends warning them not to emigrate. The lone prospector was already a thing of the past, he said. "Mining without capital is becoming unprofitable."[25]

While Sawyer decried the degradation of the gold country, still more Californians romanticized its forests. As early as 1857, the owner of a stand of sequoias in the Sierra Nevada advertised his property as a tourist destination: "The Proprietor of Mammoth Tree Grove begs leave to inform the traveling public that he is now prepared to furnish the best of accommodations to visitors and others at reasonable prices." The owner made his pitch directly to urbanites: "During the summer months, thousands from the Cities and Plains of California can meet for relaxation from the dust and turmoil of the crowded thoroughfares." Among the sequoias, the "air of quiet serenity in which the whole landscape reposes . . . [invests] it with a charm eminently desirable to those who, for so many months of the year, are circumscribed by high walls of brick and stone."[26] Long before the founding of Yellowstone and Yosemite national parks, Californians imagined the wilderness as an antidote to urban, industrial society.

Californians exhibited an equal fascination with the redwoods. An observer who surveyed the redwood industry in 1884 commended the industry for its productivity, but nonetheless lamented,

> Almost the first thought passing in one's mind, as he enters a virgin forest of redwoods, is one of pity, that such a wonderful creation of nature should be subject to the greed of man for gold. The same feelings of awe pervade one's being upon his first introduction to this apparently inexhaustible army of giants, that impress the beholder of Niagara, Yosemite, and the near relative of the redwoods—the Big Trees of Calaveras and Merced.[27]

Redwood lumber companies eventually apprehended the tourist value of their holdings. For years, the Pacific Lumber Company had hauled redwood logs to its mill on its railroad along the Eel River. By 1887, when the amount of available timber along the Eel River had declined, the Pacific Lumber Company transformed its holdings into a scenic tourist attraction. The company preserved a few redwoods on a scenic spot, and carted tourists to the site on its Eel River Railroad.[28]

By the middle of the 1880s, the California State Board of Forestry had undertaken both to urge the timber industry to conserve forest resources, and to preserve scenic groves. One of the board's first acts following its creation in 1885 was to call on the California naturalist John Muir to petition Congress to create a national park in the Sierra to protect the sequoias; Congress created two preserves—Sequoia National Park and General Grant National Park—in 1890. The agency also addressed itself to forest conservation. In 1886 it implored timber companies to avoid logging in the Sierra, where the forests reduced runoff into rivers, prevented floods, and mitigated "violent winds and extremes of temperature and humidity." Board members rued that "wasteful and destructive methods of cutting timber now prevail and no regard is paid to the reproductive power of the forests" and urged the creation of a "forest reservation" in the mountains where "the cutting of timber and fuel should be regulated in such a reasonable way as will preserve the reproductive capacity of the forests." A year later, concerned in particular that timber companies were logging public lands, the board created a "Forestry Police" to patrol the public domain. In 1886, the board proposed the system later adopted by the United States Forest Service in the national forests: "all of the Timber land in the State should be withdrawn from sale or entry and the lumber interest provided for by the European system of the sale of the timber alone, leaving the title to the land in the Gov. with the responsibility of establishing a new growth as fast as the timber is cut."[29]

Judge Sawyer reflected this emerging concern for forests, valleys, and rivers. As a member of the California Supreme Court in the 1860s, Sawyer had voted with a majority of the court in decisions that eroded the legal privileges of hydraulic mining companies. In 1864 the court determined that the Tuolumne County Water Company had been negligent when, during an exceptionally heavy flood season in 1862, it had intentionally opened a breach in an embankment to remove excess water in one of its ditches. Water flowed through the breach and flooded nearby farms.[30]

In the same year, the court extended to farmers legal protection against slickens, in a ruling in *John Wixon* v. *The Bear River and Auburn Water and Mining Company*. Wixon's orchard, which he had established in 1854, was situated in a ravine that the mining company, which was established in 1860, used to deposit sediment and runoff from its reservoir. The company had argued that "in granting to the people of the State the right to mine, the Legislature and laws of the State grant the right to the enjoyment of *such privileges as are necessary to the enjoyment of the right*." According to the mining company, those privileges included the right to dispose of waste in the ravine—indeed, they contended that the ravine was meant for such a purpose: "A ravine is one of the natural drains of the earth's land surface, and should no more be obstructed from the purpose of its natural creation than the bed of a river." Just as the Bear River company's lawyers had overreached in 1857, prompting the court to declare that farmers had a preferred right to the diversion of water, the court in 1864 resoundingly rejected the company's arguments, and instead declared that mining companies must use rivers so as "not to injure or destroy orchards or gardens bordering on the stream, which have been inclosed and planted before the water was appropriated."[31] Having thus loosened the strictures for negligence and injury, in 1866 the court returned to county courts jurisdiction over actions to prevent or abate nuisances.[32] By the time that Sawyer heard Woodruff's case against the North Bloomfield mine, several other cases supported by the Anti-Debris Association were also proceeding through the courts.

Ironically, one of the strongest legal precedents for a ruling against the hydraulic mining companies emerged from an 1875 lawsuit in which Lester L. Robinson, the president of the North Bloomfield mine, sued the Black Diamond Coal Company for inundating his ranch in Contra Costa County with sand, clay, and other debris. Robinson charged that the coal mine discharged "a large quantity of the refuse of the product of the mining ground—a large quantity of water, as well as smaller and finer portions of the coal, together with sand and clay and other refuse mixed with water—the whole forming a flowing mass," which rendered Robinson's land "incapable of profitable vegetation." The California Supreme Court ruled unequivocally against the mine.[33]

As the legal and economic environment turned against the hydraulic mining companies, the collapse of a dam turned public opinion against the companies as well. In the summer of 1883, the English Dam on the Yuba River, belonging to the North Bloomfield mine, collapsed, bringing a flood of water that reached a point eighty-five miles downstream of the dam in a mere ten hours. In narrow canyons, the water swelled to a height of ninety feet. At Marysville, the river was two feet above its normal level. Fortunately, the breach occurred during the summer, when the river was at its low point; had it occurred during the winter, it might well have been disastrous. Cognizant that such accidents raised public ire, the Anti-Debris Association persuaded the U.S. secretary of war not to expend $250,000 on levees. Rather than putting their hopes in dams or levees, the lobby hoped for a favorable ruling from Sawyer.[34]

In January 1884, Sawyer ruled in Woodruff's favor. He declared mining debris a nuisance and perpetually enjoined miners from discharging debris in rivers.[35] Sawyer's decision, although it drew on riparian doctrine, hardly marked a return to California's preindustrial landscape. He had ruled against one part of California's industrial economy, the hydraulic miners, because their debris harmed the economic interests of another, and increasingly important, part of the industrial economy, the heavily mechanized farmers of the Central Valley. Moreover, he left open the possibility that in the future, a more "safe and effective" technology might emerge, in which case he would lift the injunction. Acting on Sawyer's ruling, mining companies transformed the artificial craters of hydraulic mines into ponds and installed floating, steam-powered dredges, which scooped and sorted auriferous gravel by the bucketful. By 1914, 120 dredges in California produced over $12.5 million worth of gold. Dredging created as much debris as hydraulic mining, but impounded the materials at the mining site.[36] Moreover, the specter of a return to hydraulic mining persisted. Miners continued to lobby for the restoration of hydraulic mining into the 1890s.[37]

According to the census of 1890, the rise of irrigated wheat production in California owed itself to Sawyer's decision. "Water is obtained to a large extent from the flumes and ditches constructed for working the placers and other deposits in which the hill country abounds," wrote F. H. Newell in his *Report on Agriculture by Irrigation*. According to Newell, who had been one of John Wesley Powell's assistants in the U.S. Geological Survey and later became chief of that bureau, following Sawyer's decision, "many of these ditches fell into disuse and would have become entirely abandoned had not the discovery been made that the climate and soil of adjacent localities were singularly favorable" for agriculture.[38] Yet long before Sawyer's decision, hydraulic mining companies had anticipated profits from selling water to farms and municipalities. In 1878, for instance, the authors of the Excelsior Water and Mining Company prospectus presented the company's control of water as its most valuable long-term asset; when the gold in its claim had been exhausted, it could lease water to other mining operations, farmers, and cities.[39]

California in the second half of the nineteenth century initiated the industrial transformation of the nineteenth-century western environment. Banned in California, hydraulic mining technology nonetheless spread to placer deposits throughout the West, particularly in Idaho, Montana, and South Dakota. More enduringly, the hydraulic engineering pioneered in California to deliver water to the mines, and to protect cities from inundation, likewise diffused throughout the West; it was a onetime Californian, Francis Newlands, who legislated the extension of California's hydraulic society to the rest of the West with the passage of the Newlands Reclamation Act in 1902.[40] Likewise, the donkey engine, the steam-powered apparatus for moving large felled trees that James Dolbeer invented to transport redwoods in the early 1880s, spread to the Pacific Northwest and the forests of the interior West, accelerating deforestation. The technologically grounded, resource-intensive industrialization of nineteenth-century California remade the western environments and the western economy in the nineteenth and early twentieth century.

Resource-intensive industry also set the terms for the preservation of the natural environment. The preservation and conservation movements beginning in the late nineteenth century were in many ways a reaction to the industrial transformation of the West, particularly in California. Farmers' opposition to hydraulic mining in the 1870s was one of the earliest legal challenges to industrial pollution in the United States. California was among the first states to regulate logging, fishing, and hunting, in large part because of the scale and rapidity of the transformation of the state's environment. California's State Board of Forestry proposed forest conservation measures long before Gifford Pinchot took charge of the national forest system. John Muir, an early opponent of hydraulic mining, led the Sierra Club, which he had helped to found, in opposition to logging, sheep-grazing, and dam-building in the Sierra. In short, much of the agenda of the wilderness movement in the United States can be understood as a reaction to or a negation of the most prominent forms of industrial resource exploitation in the nineteenth-century West: mining, dam-building, commercial ranching, and logging.

Early wilderness advocates such as Muir defined wilderness as places free of mines, dams, livestock, and loggers. Wilderness was not to be a place without human beings, but rather a place set apart from industrial production. The oppositional, even reactionary character of the ideology of wilderness has persisted. Always a fuzzy concept, wilderness is still most clearly defined not by what qualities it possesses, but by what it rejects: wilderness is by definition a place unchanged by dams, mining, logging, ranching, and other forms of resource exploitation.

The environmental history of California between 1850 and 1900 was indicative of the industrial transformation of the American West in the nineteenth century. The impetus of the California gold rush compressed mining, ranching, lumbering, urban growth, and, ultimately, Indian war into a single state and a relatively brief span of time. Californians repeatedly discovered that their alterations of nature were not without consequence: hydraulic mining led to extensive pollution; deforestation and overgrazing caused erosion; centers of commerce harbored deadly disease and were liable to flooding. Nonetheless, throughout the nineteenth-century West, in the mining centers of Nevada, Colorado, Montana, South Dakota, and Alaska; in the instant cities of the Pacific Coast and the interior West; in the forests of the Pacific Northwest; in the ranchlands of the Great Plains; and ultimately in the creation of national parks as landscapes nominally protected from industrial exploitation, Euroamericans reinscribed the political ecology of California upon the landscape of the West.

Notes

◄▬

Introduction: The Political Economy of California Industrialization

1. John H. Eagle to Margaret H. Eagle, June 13, 1852, John H. Eagle Correspondence, HUN; John Thompson Kincade to James and Hannah Kincade, May 20, 1853, John Thompson Kincade Correspondence, HUN. Admiration for the beauty of the natural environment was typical of settlers in the Willamette Valley of Oregon in the mid-nineteenth century. See Peter Boag, *Environment and Experience: Settlement Culture in Nineteenth-Century Oregon* (Berkeley: University of California Press, 1992).

2. Lorenzo Sawyer, *Way Sketches* (New York: Edward Beerstadt, 1926), 122.

3. For California environmental history, see Raymond F. Dasmann, *California's Changing Environment* (San Francisco: Boyd and Fraser, 1981); Dasmann, "Environmental Changes Before and After the Gold Rush," in James J. Rawls and Richard J. Orsi, eds., *A Golden State: Mining and Economic Development in Gold Rush California* (Berkeley: University of California Press, 1998), 105–22; William Preston, *Vanishing Landscapes: Land and Life in the Tulare Lake Basin* (Berkeley: University of California Press, 1981); Preston, "Serpent in the Garden: Environmental Change in Colonial California," in Ramón A. Gutiérrez and Richard J. Orsi, eds., *Contested Eden: California Before the Gold Rush* (Berkeley: University of California Press, 1998), 260–98; Arthur F. McEvoy, *The Fisherman's Problem: Ecology and Law in the California Fisheries, 1850–1980* (New York: Cambridge University Press, 1986); Carolyn Merchant, ed., *Green Versus Gold: Sources in California's Environmental History* (Washington, D.C.: Island Press, 1998); Donald Worster, "Hydraulic Society in California: An Ecological Interpretation," *Agricultural History,* 56 (July 1982), 503–15.

4. See Elna Bakker, *An Island Called California: An Ecological Introduction to Its Natural Communities,* 2d ed. (Berkeley: University of California Press, 1984); David Rockwell, *The Nature of North America* (New York: Berkley Books, 1998), 188, 275, 308–9; Peter Steinhart, *California's Wild Heritage: Threatened and Endangered Species in the Golden State* (San Francisco: Sierra Club Books, 1990).

5. M. Kat Anderson, Michael G. Barbour, and Valerie Whitworth, "A World of Balance and Plenty: Land, Plants, Animals, and Humans in a Pre-European California," in Gutiérrez and Orsi, *Contested Eden,* 12–47.

6. See Crane S. Miller and Richard S. Hyslop, *California: The Geography of Diversity* (Mountain View, Calif.: Mayfield, 1983), 17.

7. Scott Stine, "Extreme and Persistent Drought in California and Patagonia During Mediaeval Time," *Nature,* 369 (June 16, 1994), 546–49.

8. Miller and Hyslop, *California: The Geography of Diversity,* 17, 66; Mike Davis, *Ecology of Fear: Los Angeles and the Imagination of Disaster* (New York: Vintage, 1998), 10–14, 98; Orman Granger, "Increasing Variability in California Precipitation," *Annals of the Association of American Geographers,* 69 (December 1979), 533–43.

9. McEvoy, *Fisherman's Problem,* 19–23; Dasmann, "Environmental Changes Before and After the Gold Rush," 105–22.

10. Martin A. Baumhoff, "Environmental Background," in Robert F. Heizer, ed., *Handbook of North American Indians*, vol. 8, *California* (Washington, D.C.: Smithsonian Institution Press, 1978), 22–24.

11. McEvoy, *Fisherman's Problem,* 19–21.

12. *Stockton City Directory and Emigrants' Guide to the Southern Mines* (Stockton: San Joaquin Republican, 1852), 23–25. For an excellent analysis of the boosters' role in the promotion of western settlement, see William Cronon, *Nature's Metropolis: Chicago and the Great West* (New York: Norton, 1991), 31–46.

13. Kenneth Thompson, "Insalubrious California: Perception and Reality," *Annals of the Association of American Geographers* (March 1969), 50–64.

14. John Thompson Kincade to James Kincade, September 7, 1853, Kincade Correspondence, HUN; Carol A. O'Connor, "A Region of Cities," in Clyde A. Milner II, Carol A. O'Connor, and Martha A. Sandweiss, eds., *The Oxford History of the American West* (New York: Oxford University Press, 1994).

15. "California in '49 and '74," *Placer Herald,* January 16, 1875. The classic study of the idea of the West as a "garden" is Henry Nash Smith, *Virgin Land: The American West as Symbol and Myth* (Cambridge, Mass.: Harvard University Press, 1950).

16. J. D. Borthwick, *Three Years in California* (Oakland, Calif.: Biobooks, 1948), 193; John H. Eagle to Margaret H. Eagle, November 14, 1852, Eagle Correspondence, HUN.

17. Sawyer, *Way Sketches,* 122–23.

18. "Salmon Fishery," *Sacramento Daily Union,* July 10, 1858; "Salmon Fishery," ibid., July 15, 1858; "Salmon Fishery," ibid., September 9, 1858.

19. P. A. Heartstrand et al., "Petition of the Citizens of Siskiyou County, in Relation to the Game Laws of California," *Appendix to the Journals of the Senate and Assembly of the Twenty-second Session of the Legislature of the State of California,* vol. 4 (Sacramento: F. P. Thompson, 1878).

20. John Frederick Morse, *History of Sacramento* (1853; Sacramento: Sacramento Book Collectors Club, 1945), 37; "Transactions of the California State Agricultural Society, 1870 and 1871," in *Appendix to the Journals of the Senate and Assembly of the Nineteenth Session of the Legislature of the State of California,* vol. 3 (Sacramento: T. A. Springer, 1872), 20–21.

21. E. E. Tucker, George A. Atherton, and Marsden Manson, *Report on a Plan of Sewerage for the City of Stockton, California* (*Stockton Daily Independent,* 1888), 7.

22. Frederick Jackson Turner, "The Significance of the Frontier in American History," *American Historical Association Annual Report* (1893), 199–227.

23. See Charles A. Beard, "The Frontier in American History," *New Republic*, 25 (February 16, 1921), 349–50; Fred Shannon, "The Homestead Act and the Labor Surplus," *American Historical Review*, 41 (July 1936), 637–51.

24. Efforts to modernize Turner include William Cronon, "Revisiting the Vanishing Frontier: The Legacy of Frederick Jackson Turner," *Western Historical Quarterly*, 18 (April 1987), 157–76; Stephen Aron, "Lessons in Conquest: Towards a Greater Western History," *Pacific Historical Review*, 63 (May 1994), 125–47.

25. Walter Prescott Webb, "The American West: Perpetual Mirage," *Harper's Magazine*, 214 (May 1957), 25–31.

26. For instance, the 1997 *Atlas of the New West*, a publication inspired by the work of New Western Historians, drew the western boundary of "the West" at California's eastern border with Nevada and Arizona. William Riebsame, *Atlas of the New West: Portrait of a Changing Region* (New York: Norton, 1997).

27. Worster, "Hydraulic Society in California," 503–15.

28. Rodman Paul, *California Gold: The Beginning of Mining in the Far West* (Cambridge, Mass.: Harvard University Press, 1947), vii. For other early studies of industry in the West, see Samuel Hays, *Conservation and the Gospel of Efficiency: The Progressive Conservation Movement, 1890–1920* (Cambridge, Mass.: Harvard University Press, 1959); Earl Pomeroy, *The Pacific Slope: A History of California, Oregon, Washington, Idaho, Utah, and Nevada* (New York: Knopf, 1965); J. Willard Hurst, *Law and the Conditions of Freedom in the Nineteenth-Century United States* (Madison: University of Wisconsin Press, 1956). For more recent work, see Mark Wyman, *Hard Rock Epic: Western Miners and the Industrial Revolution* (Berkeley: University of California Press, 1979); William F. Deverell, *Railroad Crossing: Californians and the Railroad, 1850–1910* (Berkeley: University of California Press, 1994); David Igler, *Industrial Cowboys: Miller & Lux and the Transformation of the Far West, 1850–1920* (Berkeley: University of California Press, 2001); Kathryn Morse, *The Nature of Gold: An Environmental History of the Klondike Gold Rush* (Seattle: University of Washington Press, 2003). Igler has recently revived the industrial paradigm of the West. See David Igler, "The Industrial Far West: Region and Nation in the Late Nineteenth Century," *Pacific Historical Review*, 69 (May 2000), 159–92.

29. See Walter Nugent, "Comparing Wests and Frontiers," in Milner, O'Connor, and Sandweiss, *Oxford History of the American West*, 813.

30. See Keith L. Bryant, "Entering the Global Economy," in Milner, O'Connor, and Sandweiss, *Oxford History of the American West*, 195–235.

31. Carroll Pursell, *The Machine in America: A Social History of Technology* (Baltimore: Johns Hopkins University Press, 1995), 115–16.

32. See Carl Abbott, "Frontiers and Sections: Cities and Regions in American Growth," *American Quarterly*, 37 (1985), 395–96. For census data, see Inter-University Consortium for Political and Social Research, *Study 00003: Historical Demographic, Economic, and Social Data*, U.S., 1790–1970 (Ann Arbor, Mich.: ICPSR).

33. See Paul Kennedy, *The Rise and Fall of the Great Powers: Economic Change and Military Conflict from 1500 to 2000* (New York: Vintage, 1987), 149.

34. See Graham Bannock, R. E. Baxter, and R. Rees, *The Penguin Dictionary of Economics*, 3d ed. (New York: Penguin, 1984), 166–67. Some economists subdivide these three

categories, for instance distinguishing "land" from "raw materials." Others add cultural categories such as "technology" or "entrepreneurship."

35. Herbert O. Brayer, "The Influence of British Capital on the Western Cattle-Range Industry," *Journal of Economic History,* 9 (1949), 85–98.

36. Inter-University Consortium for Political and Social Research, *Study 00003.*

37. Campbell J. Gibson and Emily Lennon, "Historical Census Statistics on the Foreign-born Population of the United States: 1850–1990," Population Division Working Paper No. 29, U.S. Bureau of the Census, 1999. Of course, industrial society in California was, despite its rapid growth, smaller and less dense than industrial society in the Northeast and Upper Midwest. While California's industries and laboring population were scattered relatively thinly across the landscape compared to such places as western Pennsylvania or the English Midlands, most industrial societies in the second half of the nineteenth century departed from the British and eastern North American models in one or more respects. France had few natural resources and slow population growth; German industrialization was hampered by a relatively small middle class and the late abolition of serfdom and guilds; Russia and Japan abolished serfdom later still; Japan had the added disadvantage of few natural resources. Within each of these nations, as in the United States, considerable regional variation prevailed. See Peter N. Stearns, *The Industrial Revolution in World History* (Boulder, Colo.: Westview Press, 1993), 45–47, 74, 116–24.

38. Stanley L. Engerman and Robert E. Gallman, *The Cambridge Economic History of the United States*, vol. 2, *The Long Nineteenth Century* (New York: Cambridge University Press, 2000), 16.

39. Gavin Wright, "The Origins of American Industrial Success, 1879–1940," *American Economic Review,* 80 (September 1990), 651–68.

40. W. H. Hutchinson, *California: Two Centuries of Man, Land, and Growth in the Golden State* (Palo Alto, Calif.: American West, 1969), 15–17.

41. See Andrew C. Isenberg, "Environment and the Nineteenth-Century West; or, Process Encounters Place," in William Deverell, ed., *A Companion to the History of the American West* (Oxford: Blackwell, 2004), 77–92; Donald J. Pisani, *Water, Land, and Law in the West: The Limits of Public Policy, 1850–1920* (Lawrence: University Press of Kansas, 1996); Charles F. Wilkinson, *Crossing the Next Meridian: Land, Water, and the Future of the West* (Washington, D.C.: Island Press, 1992).

42. See Alan Trachtenberg, *The Incorporation of America: Culture and Society in the Gilded Age* (New York: Hill and Wang, 1982); Lawrence Goodwyn, *The Populist Moment: A Short History of the Agrarian Revolt in America* (New York: Oxford University Press, 1978).

43. For examples, see David Lopez, "Cowboy Strikes and Unions," *Labor History,* 18 (1977), 325–40; Carlos A. Schwantes, "Protest in a Promised Land: Unemployment, Disinheritance, and the Origin of Labor Militancy in the Pacific Northwest, 1885–1886," *Western Historical Quarterly,* 13 (October 1982), 373–90; Melvin Dubofsky, *We Shall Be All: A History of the Industrial Workers of the World* (New York: Quadrangle, 1969), 5–56, 291–346.

44. Exceptions include McEvoy, *Fisherman's Problem,* 123–32; Duane Smith, *Mining America: The Industry and the Environment* (Lawrence: University Press of Kansas, 1987);

Andrew C. Isenberg, *The Destruction of the Bison: An Environmental History, 1750–1920* (New York: Cambridge University Press, 2000); and Igler, *Industrial Cowboys*.

45. Robert L. Kelley, *Gold vs. Grain: The Hydraulic Mining Controversy in California's Sacramento Valley* (Glendale, Calif.: Arthur H. Clark, 1959).

46. Cronon, *Nature's Metropolis*.

47. John Muir, *My First Summer in the Sierra* (Boston: Houghton Mifflin, 1944), 157.

48. The literature on these subjects is vast. It includes Smith, *Mining America*; Thomas Cox, *Mills and Markets: A History of the Pacific Coast Lumber Industry to 1900* (Seattle: University of Washington Press, 1974); Terry Jordan, *North American Cattle-Ranching Frontiers: Origins, Diffusion, Differentiation* (Albuquerque: University of New Mexico Press, 1993); Randall E. Rohe, "Hydraulicking in the American West: The Development and Diffusion of a Mining Technique," *Montana: The Magazine of Western History* (Spring 1985), 18–35.

49. See Patricia Nelson Limerick, *Legacy of Conquest: The Unbroken Past of the American West* (New York: Norton, 1987).

Part I: The Nature of Industry

1. Carl O. Sauer, "Theme of Plant and Animal Destruction in Economic History," in Sauer, *Land and Life* (Berkeley: University of California Press, 1963), 154.

2. For the influence of geography on environmental history, see Andrew C. Isenberg, "Historicizing Natural Environments: The Deep Roots of Environmental History," in Lloyd Cutler and Sarah Maza, eds., *A Companion to Western Historical Thought* (Oxford: Blackwell, 2002), 372–89.

3. William Cronon, *Changes in the Land: Indians, Colonists, and the Ecology of New England* (New York: Hill and Wang, 1983).

4. See Alan Taylor, "'Wasty Ways': Stories of American Settlement," *Environmental History*, 3 (July 1998), 291–310; Jon T. Coleman, *Vicious: Wolves and Men in America* (New Haven: Yale University Press, 2004).

5. James Beith Letterbook, December 18, 1857, BAN.

6. Arthur F. McEvoy, *The Fisherman's Problem: Ecology and Law in the California Fisheries, 1850–1980* (New York: Cambridge University Press, 1986), 9.

1. The Alchemy of Hydraulic Mining: Technology, Law, and Resource-Intensive Industrialization

1. Rodman Paul, *California Gold: The Beginning of Mining in the Far West* (Cambridge, Mass.: Harvard University Press, 1947), 120, 345.

2. Sullivan Osborne Diary, July 24, 1857, August 3, 1857, HUN.

3. In placer deposits, the rock encasing the gold has partly eroded, exposing the precious mineral. In the case of so-called lode deposits, miners resort to tunneling and then processing gold-bearing quartz with stamp mills that crush the rock. This chapter focuses on hydraulic mining in placer deposits.

4. John Thompson Kincade to James Kincade, June 28, 1871, John Thompson Kincade Correspondence, HUN.

5. For a discussion of the place of technology in labor history, see Donald MacKenzie, "Marx and the Machine," *Technology and Culture*, 25 (July 1984), 473–502. See also Bruce Laurie, *Artisans into Workers: Labor in Nineteenth-Century America* (New York: Noonday, 1989).

6. Thomas P. Hughes, "The Evolution of Large Technological Systems," in Wiebe E. Bijker, Thomas P. Hughes, and Trevor J. Pinch, eds., *The Social Construction of Technological Systems: New Directions in the Sociology and History of Technology* (Cambridge, Mass.: MIT Press, 1987), 53.

7. Richard White, *The Organic Machine: The Remaking of the Columbia River* (New York: Hill and Wang, 1995); John F. Kasson, *Civilizing the Machine: Technology and Republican Values in America* (New York: Grossman, 1976).

8. For the intersection of technology and imperialism, see Daniel R. Headrick, *The Tools of Empire: Technology and European Imperialism in the Nineteenth Century* (New York: Oxford University Press, 1981); Michael Ades, *Machines as the Measure of Men: Science, Technology, and Ideologies of Western Dominance* (Ithaca, N.Y.: Cornell University Press, 1989).

9. For the geological formation of the Sierra Nevada, see John McPhee, *Assembling California* (New York: Farrar, Straus and Giroux, 1993), 12–36; Elna Bakker, *An Island Called California: An Ecological Introduction to Its Natural Communities*, 2d ed. (Berkeley: University of California Press, 1984), 183–84; Allan A. Schoenherr, *A Natural History of California* (Berkeley: University of California Press, 1992), 73–75; Crane S. Miller and Richard S. Hyslop, *California: The Geography of Diversity* (Mountain View, Calif.: Mayfield, 1983), 51–56.

10. Edward J. Tarbuck and Frederick K. Lutgens, *Earth Science*, 4th ed. (Columbus, Ohio: Merrill, 1985), 189–92.

11. McPhee, *Assembling California*, 42–43; Bakker, *Island Called California*, 183–84; Schoenherr, *Natural History of California*, 79; Mary Hill, *Geology of the Sierra Nevada* (Berkeley: University of California Press, 1975), 80–81.

12. Bakker, *Island Called California*, 146–48.

13. Jeffrey F. Mount, *California Rivers and Streams: The Conflict Between Fluvial Process and Land Use* (Berkeley: University of California Press, 1995), 8; Schoenherr, *Natural History of California*, 69–70, 517–18; Bakker, *Island Called California*, 144–45.

14. Joseph Pownall to Dr. O. C. Pownall, May 1850, Joseph Pownall Collection, HUN.

15. For too much water, see John Eagle to Margaret H. Eagle, May 11, 1853, John Eagle Correspondence, HUN; Seymour D. Beach to Amos Parmalee Catlin, April 3, 1855, Amos Parmalee Catlin Papers, Box 2, HUN. For too little, see Beach to Catlin, April 5, 1855, July 18, 1855, and August 27, 1855, Catlin Papers, Box 2, HUN; John Thompson Kincade to James Kincade, April 8, 1855, and May 24, 1855, Kincade Correspondence, HUN.

16. Maureen A. Jung, "Capitalism Comes to the Diggings: From Gold-Rush Adventure to Corporate Enterprise," in James J. Rawls and Richard J. Orsi, eds., *A Golden State: Mining and Economic Development in Gold Rush California* (Berkeley: University of California Press, 1998), 52–77.

17. Ira B. Cross, *Financing an Empire: History of Banking in California*, vol. 1 (Chicago: S. J. Clarke, 1927), 121–23, 172–83.

18. Gerald D. Nash, *State Government and Economic Development: A History of Administrative Policies in California, 1849–1933* (Berkeley: Institute of Governmental Studies, 1964), 30.

19. Lance E. Davis and Robert J. Cull, "International Capital Movements, Domestic Capital Markets, and American Economic Growth, 1820–1914," in Stanley L. Engerman and Robert E. Gallman, eds., *The Cambridge Economic History of the United States*, vol. 2, *The Long Nineteenth Century* (New York: Cambridge University Press, 2000), 733–812.

20. Albin Joachim Dahl counted eight such companies in London between 1848 and 1853. See Dahl, "British Investment in California Mining, 1870–1890" (Ph.D. dissertation, University of California, Berkeley, 1961), 62–63. Clark Spence found thirty-two firms between 1851 and 1853 registered to invest in mining throughout the United States. See Spence, *British Investments and the American Mining Frontier, 1860–1901* (Ithaca, N.Y.: Cornell University Press, 1958), 3. The discrepancy points not only to the different geographical scope of the two studies (Dahl investigated only California, Spence's figure encompasses the entire United States) but to the ephemeral quality of such investment companies. Dahl and Spence agree that most British investment in American mining came after the Civil War.

21. A. H. Gilmore to James Gilmore, December 12, 1851, Pioneer Manuscript Collection, CSL.

22. Joseph Pownall, "History of Tuolumne County Water Company," c. 1880, Joseph Pownall Collection, HUN.

23. "Map of the American River and Natoma Water and Mining Company Canals" (c. 1857–68), and Sacramento County Records, Book A, Pre-emption Claims, Natoma Company Collection, and Amos P. Catlin Papers, CSL; "Natoma Ditch," Miscellaneous Working Papers, William Hammond Hall Papers, CSA.

24. For Chinese labor, see Hamilton Smith, Jr., to V. G. Bell, July 4, 1876, Milton Mining and Water Company Records, CSL: "We have employed upon the Bonham dam a very fair quality of Chinese labor, to whom we pay $1.15 per day."

25. "Natoma Ditch," Hall Papers, CSA.

26. Hamilton Smith., Jr., to V. G. Bell, March 31, 1876, Milton Mining and Water Company Records, CSL.

27. James D. Hague, *The Water and Gravel Mining Properties Belonging to the Eureka Lake & Yuba Canal Company* (San Francisco, December 22, 1876), 20.

28. Taliesin Evans, "Hydraulic Mining in California," *Century Magazine*, 25 (January 1883), 331.

29. The control of water is a major theme in the history of the American West. See Donald Worster, *Rivers of Empire: Water, Aridity, and the Growth of the American West* (New York: Pantheon, 1985); White, *The Organic Machine*; Wallace Stegner, *Beyond the Hundredth Meridian: John Wesley Powell and the Second Opening of the West* (Boston: Houghton Mifflin, 1954); Marc Reisner, *Cadillac Desert: The American West and Its Disappearing Water* (New York: Viking, 1986).

30. Malcolm Rohrbough, *Days of Gold: The California Gold Rush and the American Nation* (Berkeley: University of California Press, 1997), 125–27. For claim clubs, see Lawrence M. Friedman, *A History of American Law*, 2d ed. (New York: Simon and Schuster, 1985), 366.

31. *James W. Tartar* v. *The Spring Creek Water and Mining Company*, 5 California 399 (1855).

32. Ibid. See also *Irwin* v. *Phillips*, 5 California 140 (1855).

33. *William Parsons* v. *The Tuolumne County Water Company*, 5 California 43 (1855).

34. *E. Hoffman et al.* v. *The Tuolumne County Water Company*, 10 California 413 (1858).

35. *Wolf et al.* v. *St. Louis Independent Water Company*, 10 California 541 (1858).

36. *Lexington & Ohio Railroad* v. *Applegate*, 8 Kentucky 289 (1839), in Morton Horwitz, *The Transformation of American Law, 1785–1850* (Cambridge, Mass.: Harvard University Press, 1976), 74–75.

37. J. Willard Hurst, *Law and the Conditions of Freedom in the Nineteenth-Century United States* (Madison: University of Wisconsin Press, 1956), 3–32.

38. John S. Hittell, *Mining in the Pacific States of North America* (San Francisco: H. H. Bancroft, 1861), 145.

39. G. H. Mendell, "Report Upon a Project to Protect the Navigable Waters of California from the Effects of Hydraulic Mining," H.ex.doc. 98, 47th Cong., 1st Sess. (1882), 13.

40. See *Edwards Woodruff* v. *North Bloomfield Gravel Mining Company*, 18 F. 9 753 (1884).

41. "Annual Review of the Mining Interests of California," *Mining Magazine and Journal of Geology*, 2 (April 1861), 138. For hydraulic mining technology, see Hunter Rouse, *Hydraulics in the United States, 1776–1976* (Iowa City: Institute of Hydraulic Research, 1976), 50–52.

42. Albert H. Hayes, *Report on the Red Hill Hydraulic Gold Mines* (Boston: Alfred Mudge, 1882), 9.

43. Thomas Price and William Ashburner, "Prospectus of the Excelsior Water and Mining Company," 1878.

44. Dahl, "British Investment in California Mining," 64, 130–31.

45. The ten wealthiest counties in 1860 were San Francisco, Nevada, Tuolumne, Sacramento, Calaveras, Mariposa, Amador, Placer, Siskiyou, and Sierra.

46. David J. St. Clair, "The Gold Rush and the Beginnings of California Industry," in Rawls and Orsi, *A Golden State*, 185–208.

47. Rossiter Raymond, *Statistics of Mines and Mining in the States and Territories West of the Rocky Mountains* (Washington, D.C.: Government Printing Office, 1874), 39–47.

48. Thomas H. Thompson and Albert Augustus West, *History of Sacramento County, California* (Oakland: Thompson and West, 1880), 150–51, 157.

49. Rossiter Raymond, *Silver and Gold: An Account of the Mining and Metallurgical Industry of the United States* (New York: J. B. Ford, 1873), 32.

50. Inter-University Consortium for Political and Social Research, *Study 00003: Historical Demographic, Economic, and Social Data*, U.S., 1790–1970 (Ann Arbor, Mich.: ICPSR).

51. The environmental implications of the iron and steel industry are discussed authoritatively in Andrew Hurley, *Environmental Inequalities: Race, Class, and Industrial Pollution in Gary, Indiana, 1945–1980* (Chapel Hill: University of North Carolina Press, 1995), 19–27.

52. "Second Biennial Report of the State Board of Health of California, for the Years 1871, 1872, and 1873," *Appendix to the Journals of the Senate and Assembly of the Twentieth Session of the Legislature of the State of California*, vol. 5 (Sacramento: G. H. Springer, 1874), 30–31; "Fourth Biennial Report of the State Board of Health of California, for the

Years 1876 and 1877," *Appendix to the Journals of the Senate and Assembly of the Twenty-second Session of the Legislature of the State of California*, vol. 3 (Sacramento: F. P. Thompson, 1878), 14–15.

53. "Second Biennial Report of the State Board of Health," 37.

54. "Mines and Mining," *Marysville Herald*, January 27, 1854.

55. "Hydraulic Mining," *Sacramento Daily Union*, July 11, 1854.

56. B. Silliman and George D. MacLean, *Reports on the Blue Tent Consolidated Hydraulic Gold Mines of California, Limited* (London: D. P. Croke, 1873), 13; George Black, *Report on the Middle Yuba Canal and Eureka Lake Canal, Nevada County, California* (San Francisco: Towne and Bacon, 1864), 8; John S. Hittell, *The Resources of California*, 6th ed. (San Francisco: A. Roman, 1874; New York: W. J. Widdleton, 1874), 17; Titus Fey Cronise, *The Natural Wealth of California* (San Francisco: H. H. Bancroft, 1868), 547; John Kincade to James Kincade, December 28, 1856, Kincade Correspondence, HUN.

57. T. Evans, "Hydraulic Mining," 326.

58. John Kincade to James Kincade, December 28, 1856, Kincade Correspondence, HUN.

59. Hamilton Smith, Jr., "North Bloomfield Gravel Mining Company Report" (October 1871), 6, BAN.

60. *California Daily Express*, October 23, 1858; "Immense Mining Enterprise," ibid., November 2, 1858.

61. Charles Waldeyer, "Report," in R. H. Stretch, *Report on the Cherokee Flat Blue Gravel and Spring Valley Mining and Irrigating Company's Property* (New York: Mining Record Press, 1879), 21–24.

62. F. A. Bishop to S. A. Garnett, November 10, 1875, Francis Augustus Bishop Papers, HUN.

63. *California Daily Express*, October 5, 1858.

64. Raymond, *Silver and Gold*, 131.

65. Ibid., 21.

66. Hamilton Smith, Jr., "Testimony Taken by the Committee on Mining Debris, as Reported to the Assembly," *Appendix to the Journals of the Senate and Assembly of the Twenty-second Session of the Legislature of the State of California*, vol. 4, 47.

67. "Industrial Condition of the Slope," *Alta California*, April 1, 1878; "Minority Report of the Committee on Mining Debris," *Appendix to the Journals of the Senate and Assembly of the Twenty-second Session of the Legislature of the State of California*, vol. 4, 5.

68. A. L. Williams, *Description of the Property of the Yuba Hydraulic Gold Mining Company* (Cincinnati: Moore, Wilstack, and Baldwin, 1867); Hamilton Smith, Jr., *An Account of the Operations of the North Bloomfield Gravel Mining Company* (San Francisco, 1875); Silliman and MacLean, *Blue Tent Gold Mines*, 11–13; W.M.R. Wood, "California: Its Mining and Industrial Resources" (1864), 10–18, BAN; "Annual Review of the Mining Interests of California," 140.

69. John Muir, quoted in *Prospectus of the Cataract and Wide West Hydraulic Gravel Mining Company* (San Francisco: Fluto, 1876), 4–6.

70. Cronise, *Natural Wealth of California*, 547. See also Hittell, *Resources of California*, 81; Black, *Middle Yuba Canal*, 4.

71. G. L. Gilley and S. D. Merchant to Natoma Water Company, May 14, 1852, Catlin Papers, HUN; James L. Cheeseman, Sacramento, to Amos Parmalee Catlin, May 22, 1852, Catlin Papers, HUN.

72. T. Evans, "Hydraulic Mining," 328, 333–34.

73. "Transactions of the California State Agricultural Society, 1870 and 1871," *Appendix to the Journals of the Senate and Assembly of the Nineteenth Session of the Legislature of the State of California*, vol. 3 (Sacramento: T. A. Springer, 1872), 20–21.

74. Hittell, *Mining in the Pacific States*, 145.

75. Raymond, *Silver and Gold*, 17.

76. R. H. Stretch, Charles Waldeyer, and Hamilton Smith, Jr., *Reports on the Spring Valley Hydraulic Gold Mining Company, Comprising the Cherokee Flat Blue Gravel and Spring Valley Mining and Irrigating Company's Property* (New York: John J. Caulon, 1879). For gold in the debris, see also Louis Janin, *Report on the Excelsior Water and Mining Company, Smartsville, California* (San Francisco, May 16, 1879), 8.

77. Otto von Geldern, *An Analysis of the Problem of the Proposed Rehabilitation of Hydraulic Mining in California* (Sutter County, January 3, 1928), 4.

78. "Accumulation of Tailings," *Placer Herald*, April 6, 1872.

79. W. H. Drum, "Testimony Taken by the Committee on Mining Debris," 77.

80. Charles W. Hendel, *Report on the Alturas Gold Mine in Slate Creek Basin, Sierra and Plumas Counties, California* (San Francisco: A. L. Bancroft, 1872), 6.

81. von Geldern, *Hydraulic Mining*, 4.

82. A. T. Arrowsmith, James H. Keyes, J. H. Jewett, and Joseph Johnson, "Testimony Taken by the Committee on Mining Debris," 4–5, 80–82, 100, 105, 141.

83. *James H. Keyes v. Little York Gold Washing and Water Company* (Sacramento: H. S. Crocker, 1879), 15–16; N. S. Hanlin and W. H. Drum, "Testimony Taken by the Committee on Mining Debris," 77, 137–38. See also *Address of George Cadwalader, Delivered at Sacramento, February 28 and March 1st, 1882, in the Case of the State of California vs. Gold Run Hydraulic Mining Company* (Sacramento: H. S. Crocker, 1882), 43.

84. W. H. Drum, "Testimony Taken by the Committee on Mining Debris," 76–77; *Keyes v. Little York*, 16.

85. George Ohlyer, James H. Keyes, H. M. Larue, "Testimony Taken by the Committee on Mining Debris," 95, 143, 155–56.

86. "Mining Debris in California," H.ex.doc. 267, 51st Cong., 2d Sess. (1891), 14.

87. von Geldern, *Hydraulic Mining*, 9.

88. Joseph Johnson, W. H. Parks, and George Ohlyer, "Testimony Taken by the Committee on Mining Debris," 86–88, 96–98.

89. See Arthur F. McEvoy, *The Fisherman's Problem: Ecology and Law in the California Fisheries, 1850–1980* (New York: Cambridge University Press, 1986), 22, 47.

90. "Fisheries," *Alta California*, November 18, 1850; "Salmon," *California Daily Express*, September 18, 1858.

91. Charles Nordhoff, *California for Health, Pleasure, and Residence: A Book for Travellers and Settlers* (New York: Harper, 1872), 102.

92. "Report of the Commissioners of Fisheries of the State of California, 1870 and 1871," *Appendix to the Journals of the Senate and Assembly of the Nineteenth Session of the Legislature of the State of California*, vol. 2 (Sacramento: T. A. Springer, 1872), 8; "Report of the Commissioners of Fisheries of the State of California for the Years 1876 and 1877," *Appendix to the Journals of the Senate and Assembly of the Twenty-second Session of the Legislature of the State of California*, vols. 3, 5; see also Hittell, *Resources of California*, 193.

93. Ibid. 64.

94. Francis Augustus Bishop to John P. Clough, May 3, 1873, Bishop Letterbook, 49–50, Francis Augustus Bishop Papers, HUN.

95. "Auburn Reservoir," *Placer Herald*, January 13, 1872; "Lake Tahoe," ibid., January 20, 1872.

96. "Second Biennial Report of the State Board of Health, 138–39.

97. Thompson, R. W., "Sand Bars and Deposits Near Mare Island," Letter from the Secretary of the Navy, H.ex.doc. 31, 46th Cong., 2d Sess., 1880.

98. B. S. Alexander and W. M. Pierce, "Testimony Taken by the Committee on Mining Debris," 28, 148.

99. See Schoenherr, *Natural History of California*, 264–69; Tarbuck and Lutgens, *Earth Science*, 192–204.

100. "California in '49 and '74," *Placer Herald*, January 16, 1875; Hittell, *Resources of California*, 328.

101. *Facts Concerning the Quicksilver Mines in Santa Clara County, California* (New York: R. C. Root, Anthony, 1859), 7; *The Quicksilver Mining Company* (New York: Sun Job Printing House, 1868), 18; *The Quicksilver Mining Company* (New York: Sun Job Printing House, 1869), 5; *The Quicksilver Mining Company* (New York: E. S. Dodge, 1871), 13; *The Quicksilver Mining Company* (New York: William F. Jones, 1873), 5; *The Quicksilver Mining Company* (New York: D. Murphy, 1874), 7; *The Quicksilver Mining Company* (New York: D. Murphy, 1875), 5; *The Quicksilver Mining Company Annual Report* (New York: D. Murphy, 1876), 6; *The Quicksilver Mining Company Annual Report* (New York: D. Murphy, 1877), 6; Hennen Jennings, *The Quicksilver Mines of Almaden and New Almaden: A Comparative View of their Extent, Production, Costs of Work, Etc.* (1886), 9. For New Almaden's production, see also David J. St. Clair, "New Almaden and California Quicksilver in the Pacific Rim Economy," *California History*, 73 (Winter 1994), 278–94; J. Ross Brown, "Down the Cinnabar Mines," *Harper's New Monthly Magazine*, 31 (October 1865), 545–60.

102. F. E. Spencer, *A Mining Accident at New Almaden, California* (San Francisco, 1888), 1.

103. *California Quicksilver* (San Francisco, 1890), 10.

104. William V. Wells, "The Quicksilver Mines of New Almaden, California," *Harper's New Monthly Magazine*, 27 (June 1863), 27–39.

105. United States Environmental Protection Agency, *Mercury Study Report to Congress*, vol. 5, *Health Effects of Mercury and Mercury Compounds*, EPA-452/R-97-007 (December 1997), ES 1–9.

106. Augustus Jesse Bowie, Jr., *A Practical Treatise on Hydraulic Mining in California* (New York: Van Nostrand, 1885), 244–45; J. Ross Brown, *Resources of the Pacific Slope* (San Francisco: H. H. Bancroft, 1869), 151; Silliman and MacLean, *Blue Tent Gold Mines*, 11.

107. Rossiter Raymond, "Mineral Resources of the States and Territories West of the Rocky Mountains, H.ex.doc. 54," 40th Cong., 1st Sess. (1869), 10; Hittell, *Resources of California*, 329.

108. "Accumulation of Tailings," *Placer Herald*, April 6, 1872.

109. *The Bear River Tunnel Company* (Boston: Alfred Mudge, 1881), 10, 16–17.

110. United States Environmental Protection Agency, *Mercury Study Report*, ES 1–9.

111. Donald E. Trimble, *The Geologic Story of the Great Plains* (Bismarck, N.D.: Theodore Roosevelt Nature and History Association, 1980), 39–40.

2. Banking on Sacramento: Urban Development, Flood Control, and Political Legitimization

1. Elisha Oscar Crosby Memoirs, HUN.
2. For the founding of Sacramento, see J. S. Holliday, *Rush for Riches: Gold Fever and the Making of California* (Berkeley: University of California Press, 1999), 77.
3. Charles Brown, "Statement of recollections of early events in California, 1878," BAN. For Russian exploitation of aquatic mammals, see Adele Ogden, *The California Sea Otter Trade, 1784–1848* (Berkeley: University of California Press, 1941).
4. See James A. Sandos, "Between Crucifix and Lance: Indian-White Relations in California, 1769–1848," in Ramón A. Gutiérrez and Richard J. Orsi, eds., *Contested Eden: California Before the Gold Rush* (Berkeley: University of California Press, 1998), 213; Allan A. Schoenherr, *A Natural History of California* (Berkeley: University of California Press, 1992), 660–62. For the ecological consequences of the near extinction of the sea otter, see Arthur F. McEvoy, *The Fisherman's Problem: Ecology and Law in the California Fisheries, 1850–1980* (New York: Cambridge University Press, 1986), 74–76, 81–82.
5. *Stockton City Directory and Emigrants' Guide to the Southern Mines* (Stockton, Calif.: San Joaquin Republican, 1852), 25.
6. Schoenherr, *Natural History of California*, 538–39.
7. *Sacramento Illustrated* (Sacramento: Barker and Barker, 1855), 15. For Indian labor at Sutter's fort, see Albert L. Hurtado, *Indian Survival on the California Frontier* (New Haven: Yale University Press, 1988), 55–71.
8. Isaac Owen Diary, November 10, 1850, HUN.
9. Elisha Oscar Crosby Memoirs, HUN.
10. Isaac Perkins to Daniel Perkins, January 13, 1852, Isaac Perkins Correspondence, CSL.
11. Geographers call such places "breaks in transport": such places have become the sites of major North American cities. See Richard C. Wade, *The Urban Frontier: The Rise of Western Cities, 1780–1830* (Cambridge, Mass.: Harvard University Press, 1959); William Cronon, *Nature's Metropolis: Chicago and the Great West* (New York: Norton, 1991); Ari Kelman, *A River and Its City: The Nature of Landscape in New Orleans* (Berkeley: University of California Press, 2003).
12. J. D. Borthwick, *Three Years in California* (Oakland: Biobooks, 1948), 80.
13. See Carl Abbott, "Frontiers and Sections: Cities and Regions in American Growth," *American Quarterly*, 37 (1985), 395–96. For nodal regions in the American West, see Donald W. Meinig, *Imperial Texas: An Interpretive Essay in Cultural Geography* (Austin: University of Texas Press, 1969); Cronon, *Nature's Metropolis*.
14. For examples of the idea of cities as organisms, see Spenser W. Havelick, *The Urban Organism* (New York: Macmillan, 1974); Peter G. Goheen, "Industrialization and the Growth of Cities in Nineteenth-Century America," *American Studies*, 14 (Spring 1973), 49–65. For an analysis of the history of this idea, see Graeme Davison, "The City as a Natural System: Theories of Urban Society in Nineteenth-Century Britain," in Derek Fraser and Anthony Sutcliffe, eds., *The Pursuit of Urban History* (London: Arnold, 1983).
15. *Marysville Herald*, March 24, 1854.
16. Such enterprises were common in the American West. See J. Christopher Schnell and Katherine Clinton, "The New West: Themes in Nineteenth-Century Urban Promotion,

1815–1880," *Missouri Historical Society Bulletin*, 30 (July 1974), 75–88; Gilbert Stelter, "The City and Westward Expansion: A Western Case Study," *Western Historical Quarterly*, 4 (April 1973), 187–202.

17. *Hale & Emory's Marysville City Directory* (Marysville, Calif.: *Marysville Herald*, 1853), 13.

18. The railroad was to cost $800,000; the plank road $350,000. Benicia later voted to subscribe $250,000 to the cost of the railroad. *Marysville Herald*, February 28, 1854; ibid., March 6, 1854; ibid., March 10, 1854.

19. City Council Minutes, January 29, 1853, SAC.

20. The Sacramento Valley Railroad Company's line was superseded by the Central Pacific Railroad, which reached Sacramento by an alternate route. By 1870, the Central Pacific had driven the Sacramento Valley Railroad Company into a steep decline in business. See Francis A. Bishop to Placerville and Sacramento Valley Railroad Company, February 19, 1870, Bishop Letterbook, Francis Augustus Bishop Papers, HUN.

21. For urban public health and epidemics, particularly with respect to cholera, see Charles Rosenberg, *The Cholera Years: The United States in 1832, 1849, and 1866* (Chicago: University of Chicago Press, 1987). See also Richard Evans, *Death in Hamburg: Society and Politics in the Cholera Years, 1830–1910* (New York: Oxford University Press, 1987).

22. *Sacramento Illustrated*, 24–26; Mark A. Eifler, *Gold Rush Capitalists: Greed and Growth in Sacramento* (Albuquerque: University of New Mexico Press, 2002), 52.

23. *Sacramento Illustrated*, 38–39; Eifler, *Gold Rush Capitalists*, 64.

24. Thomas H. Thompson and Albert Augustus West, *History of Sacramento County, California* (Oakland: Thompson and West, 1880), 146.

25. John Frederick Morse, *History of Sacramento* (Sacramento: Book Collectors Club, 1945), 31–32.

26. Isaac Perkins to Daniel Perkins, April 28, 1850, Isaac Perkins Correspondence, CSL.

27. *Sacramento Illustrated*, 38–39; Eifler, *Gold Rush Capitalists*, 64.

28. "Lumbermen Cutting Saw-Logs on the American," *Sacramento Daily Union*, November 17, 1854.

29. Isaac Perkins to Daniel Perkins, September 26, 1852, Isaac Perkins Correspondence, CSL; W. L. Messinger to Catlin, November 15, 1852; Luther C. Cutler to Catlin, April 23, 1853; Messinger to Catlin, June 1, 1853, Amos P. Catlin Papers, CSL.

30. Samuel Nichols to Sarah Ann Nichols, May 8, 1850, Samuel Nichols Collection, HUN.

31. Kenneth Thompson, "Riparian Forests of the Sacramento Valley, California," *Annals of the Association of American Geographers*, 51 (September 1961), 294–315.

32. For deforestation by steamboats, see Kelman, *A River and Its City*, 67.

33. "Lumbermen Cutting Saw-Logs on the American."

34. Jeffrey F. Mount, *California Rivers and Streams: The Conflict Between Fluvial Process and Land Use* (Berkeley: University of California Press, 1995), 56–57, 236.

35. Mount, *California Rivers and Streams*, 83–100, 145–60; Thompson, "Riparian Forests of the Sacramento Valley," 300.

36. Mount, *California Rivers and Streams*, 52–82.

37. "Flood at Sacramento City," *Alta California*, January 14, 1850; "Sacramento and Placer Intelligence," ibid., February 6, 1850.

38. John Plumbe, *The Settlers and Land Speculators of Sacramento* (1851), 13. See also *Sacramento Illustrated*, 42.

39. Israel Lord quoted in Peter Blodgett, *Land of Golden Dreams: California in the Gold Rush Decade, 1848–1858* (San Marino, Calif.: Huntington Library, 1999), 90.

40. "To the People of Sacramento City" (August 8, 1850), *Sacramento Illustrated*, 43–46.

41. See "Terrible Riot at Sacramento," *Alta California*, August 15, 1850; "Latest from Sacramento! Cessation of Hostilities," ibid., August 16, 1850; Benjamin Stillman, "Seeking the Golden Fleece," *Overland Monthly*, 11 (November 1873), 417–21; Donald Pisani, "Squatter Law in California, 1850–1858," *Western Historical Quarterly*, 25 (Autumn 1994), 277–310.

42. *Sacramento Illustrated*, 33.

43. John H. Eagle to Margaret H. Eagle, April 10, 1852, John H. Eagle Correspondence, HUN.

44. Morse, *History of Sacramento*, 43–46.

45. Samuel Nichols to Sarah Ann Nichols, October 7, 1850, Samuel Nichols Collection, HUN.

46. Morse, *History of Sacramento*, 43–46. For the city's efforts to confront public health, see City Council Minutes, November 5, November 14, November 16, November 20, and December 15, 1849, SAC.

47. J. Roy Jones, *Memories, Men, and Medicine: A History of Medicine in Sacramento, California* (Sacramento: Society for Medical Improvement, 1950), 34–35.

48. Morse, *History of Sacramento*, 46.

49. Robert A. Devlin, ed., *Statutes of the State of California Relating to the City of Sacramento* (Sacramento: Valley Press, 1881), 61.

50. See Martin Melosi, "'Out of Sight, Out of Mind': The Environment and Disposal of Municipal Refuse, 1860–1920," *The Historian*, 35 (August 1973), 622.

51. Israel Lord Journal, October 20, 1850, HUN.

52. Morse, *History of Sacramento*, 48–61.

53. John D. Unruh, *The Plains Across: The Overland Emigrants and the Trans-Mississippi West, 1840–1860* (Urbana: University of Illinois Press, 1979), 403.

54. Rosenberg, *Cholera Years*, 2–3.

55. Isaac Perkins to Daniel Perkins, October 27, 1850, Isaac Perkins Correspondence, CSL.

56. Israel Lord Journal, October 23, 1850, HUN.

57. Morse, *History of Sacramento*, 91.

58. Jones, *Memories, Men, and Medicine*, 34–35.

59. Israel Lord Journal, October 23, 1850; October 31, 1850; November 6, 1850; November 11, 1850; December 22, 1850, HUN; "Sacramento," *Alta California*, November 3, 1850.

60. Stanley K. Schultz and Clay McShane, "To Engineer the Metropolis: Sewers, Sanitation, and City Planning in Late Nineteenth-Century America," *Journal of American History*, 65 (September 1978), 389–411.

61. "Sewerage," *Sacramento Daily Union*, December 1, 1854; "Sewerage," ibid., October 10, 1856.

62. John Kincade to James Kincade, August 15, 1857, Kincade Correspondence, HUN.

63. Eifler, *Gold Rush Capitalists*, 97–100.

64. *Sacramento Illustrated*, 54–56.

65. City Council Minutes, July 23, 1850, SAC.

66. *G. and O. Amy's Marysville Directory* (San Francisco: Monson and Valentine, 1856), 4–7.

67. "Disastrous Visitation! Great Freshet! Breaks in the Levee!" *Alta California*, March 8, 1852; "The Flood! Sacramento Completely Inundated!" ibid., March 9, 1852; "The Overflow," ibid., March 10, 1852; "The Inundation," ibid., March 11, 1852; "State of the Inundation," ibid., March 12, 1852.

68. "Rain," *Sacramento Daily Union*, November 13, 1861; "The American," ibid., November 18, 1861; "Severe on Rats," ibid., November 20, 1861; "Rain in Grass Valley," ibid., November 30, 1861.

69. "Great Rise in the Rivers," *Sacramento Daily Union*, March 28, 1861; "A Great Calamity–Sacramento Deluged," ibid., December 10, 1861.

70. "Mines and Mining," *Marysville Herald*, January 27, 1854; G. H. Mendell, "Report Upon a Project to Protect the Navigable Waters of California from the Effects of Hydraulic Mining," H.ex.doc. 98, 47th Cong., 1st Sess. (1882), 13; Rossiter Raymond, *Silver and Gold: An Account of the Mining and Metallurgical Industry of the United States* (New York: J. B. Ford, 1873), 17.

71. "The Flood: Destruction in the Interior," *Sacramento Daily Union*, December 11, 1861; ibid., December 13, 1861.

72. "A Great Calamity–Sacramento Deluged."

73. Ibid.

74. "The Flood in Sacramento," *Sacramento Daily Union*, December 11, 1861; "Dead Animals," ibid., December 13, 1861.

75. "The Flooded Portion," *Sacramento Daily Union*, December 13, 1861; "The Rivers," ibid., January 1, 1862; "The Levee Near R Street," ibid., January 3, 1862; "The Condition of the City" and "Levee Repairs," ibid., January 4, 1862; "The Levee Work" and "Railroad Lumber," ibid., January 7, 1862; "Communication with the Interior," ibid., January 10, 1862.

76. "Another Destructive Flood," *Sacramento Daily Union*, January 11, 1862; "Deaths from Drowning" and "The Rise and Fall of the Flood," ibid., January 13, 1862; "Dead Bodies Found," ibid., January 14, 1862; "The Levee at the Tannery," ibid., January 21, 1862; "The Levee at Rabel's Gone," ibid., January 23, 1862; "The Flood," ibid., January 24, 1862.

77. Thompson and West, *History of Sacramento County*, 74–75.

78. William L. Willis, *History of Sacramento County, California* (Los Angeles: Historic Record Company, 1913), 116.

3. Capitalizing on Nature: Innovation and Production in the Redwood Forests

1. Isaac Branham Reminiscences, BAN; Charles Brown, Statement of recollections of early events in California, 1878, BAN. For family migration to the Far West in the mid-nineteenth century, see John Unruh, *The Plains Across: The Overland Emigrants and the Trans-Mississippi West, 1840–60* (Urbana: University of Illinois Press, 1979); John Mack Faragher, *Women and Men on the Overland Trail* (New Haven: Yale University Press, 1979).

2. G. C. Taplin Diary, July 11, July 23, July 24, July 25, July 26, July 27, July 30, July 31, 1855, BAN.

3. Sullivan Osborne Diary, July 24, August 3, 1857, HUN; Nathan Blanchard Journal, December 24, 1854, HUN.

4. Richard Goss Stanwood Journals and Letters, April 3, 1853, January 4, 1857, January 3, 1858, BAN.

5. John S. Hittell, *The Resources of California*, 6th ed. (San Francisco: A. Roman, 1874; New York: W. J. Widdleton, 1874), 189.

6. "Transactions of the California State Agricultural Society, 1870 and 1871," *Appendix to the Journals of the Senate and Assembly of the Nineteenth Session of the Legislature of the State of California*, vol. 3 (Sacramento: T. A. Springer, 1872), 20–21.

7. "Lumber Business," *Humboldt Times*, October 2, 1858.

8. A. Kellogg, *Forest Trees of California* (Sacramento: J. D. Young, 1882), 47–49; Everett Russell Stanford, "A Short History of California Lumbering" (M.S. thesis, University of California, 1924), 23.

9. "Lumber for the Navy Yard," *Sacramento Daily Union*, November 20, 1856; Stanford, "History of California Lumbering," 59, 63.

10. "Lumbering on the Eastern Slope of the Sierra Nevada—Forest Destruction and Reproduction," *Pacific Coast Wood and Iron*, 12 (December 1889), 168; "Timber Getting Scarcer," ibid., 21 (January 1894), 8.

11. Kellogg, *Forest Trees of California*, 24–26.

12. W. G. Bonner, *The Redwoods of California: A Glimpse at the Wonder-Land of the Golden West* (San Francisco: California Redwood Company, 1884), 21–22.

13. Reed F. Noss, ed., *The Redwood Forest: History, Ecology, and Conservation of the Coast Redwoods* (Washington, D.C.: Island Press, 2000), xxi, 39; Raymond F. Dasmann, *California's Changing Environment* (San Francisco: Boyd and Fraser, 1981), 29–38. For logging in the Upper Midwest, see William Cronon, *Nature's Metropolis: Chicago and the Great West* (New York: Norton, 1991), 148–206.

14. See Michael Williams, *Americans and Their Forests: A Historical Geography* (New York: Cambridge University Press, 1989), 299–300; Richard White, *Land Use, Environment, and Social Change: The Shaping of Island County, Washington* (Seattle: University of Washington Press, 1980), 77–112; Robert Bunting, *The Pacific Raincoast: Environment and Culture in an American Eden, 1778–1900* (Lawrence: University Press of Kansas, 1997), 135–63.

15. See Thomas R. Cox, *Mills and Markets: A History of the Pacific Coast Lumber Industry to 1900* (Seattle: University of Washington Press, 1974).

16. Noss, *Redwood Forest*, 86, 114; Allan A. Schoenherr, *A Natural History of California* (Berkeley: University of California Press, 1992), 287.

17. Noss, *Redwood Forest*, 82–84; Crane S. Miller and Richard S. Hyslop, *California: The Geography of Diversity* (Mountain View, Calif.: Mayfield, 1983), 121.

18. Elna Bakker, *An Island Called California: An Ecological Introduction to Its Natural Communities*, 2d ed. (Berkeley: University of California Press, 1984), 106; Howard Brett Melendy, "One Hundred Years of the Redwood Lumber Industry, 1850–1950" (Ph.D. dissertation, Stanford University, 1952), 12.

19. Noss, *Redwood Forest*, 45, 101–5; Schoenherr, *Natural History of California*, 231, 284–85; Bakker, *Island Called California*, 107.

20. Bonner, *Redwoods of California*, 8.

21. "The Redwood Trees of California," *Pacific Coast Wood and Iron*, 11 (April 1889), 89.

22. *Redwood and Lumbering in California Forests* (San Francisco: Edgar Cherry, 1884), 4–6.

23. Bonner noted that a market for redwood lumber had developed in Chile and Peru, where "there are ants and other insects which destroy the native woods, as well as pine and other kinds of wood from this country; but redwood is never molested–a fact which is thoroughly appreciated in those countries." Bonner, *Redwoods of California*, 11.

24. "Land Sales," *Humboldt Times*, August 14, 1858.

25. "Monopoly of Timber Lands," *Humboldt Times*, February 1, 1868.

26. Ralph Thomas Wattenburger, "The Redwood Lumbering Industry on the Northern California Coast, 1850–1900" (M.A. thesis, University of California, Berkeley, 1931), 6–12; Leigh H. Irvine, *History of Humboldt County, California* (Los Angeles: Historic Record Company, 1915), 112.

27. James Beith Letterbook, September 1, 1854, BAN.

28. "To the Capitalists of California," *Humboldt Times*, January 25, 1868.

29. William McDaniels Interview, in Benjamin Allen, "Notes on the Pacific Lumber Company and Lumbering in Humboldt County," BAN.

30. "Lumbering in Humboldt," *Pacific Coast Wood and Iron*, 12 (December 1889), 170; McDaniels Interview, BAN.

31. Melendy, "Redwood Lumber Industry," 44.

32. Titus Fey Cronise, *The Natural Wealth of California* (San Francisco: H. H. Bancroft, 1868), 191; Wattenburger, "Redwood Lumbering Industry," 14–18.

33. Beith to Helen McDougal, November 1, 1861; Beith to Richard Deighton, January 10, 1862; Beith to Hugh Hansen, January 14, 1862, James Beith Letterbook, BAN.

34. Wattenburger, "Redwood Lumbering Industry," 20.

35. "Logging on Mad River," *Humboldt Times*, May 1, 1858.

36. W. H. Wilde, "Chronology of the Pacific Lumber Company, 1869–1945," 9, BAN.

37. Melendy, "Redwood Lumber Industry," 57.

38. Cronise, *Natural Wealth of California*, 190–92.

39. Irving Slade to C. V. Slade, June 29, 1873; Irving Slade to C. V. Slade, May 10, 1874, Irving T. Slade Letters, BAN.

40. Cronise, *Natural Wealth of California*, 190–99; Wilde, "Chronology of the Pacific Lumber Company," 10, BAN.

41. Hittell, *Resources of California*, 189.

42. Bonner, *Redwoods of California*, 18.

43. "Accident," *Humboldt Times*, August 6, 1859; "Sad Accident," ibid. September 10, 1859; "Leg Broken," ibid. January 1, 1870; Jerome Ford Diary, February 26, 1867, BAN.

44. "Lumbermen's Protective Union," *Humboldt Times*, February 22, 1868. For the occupational hazards of the timber industry, see Andrew Mason Prouty, *More Dangerous Than War: Pacific Coast Logging, 1827–1981* (New York: Garland, 1985).

45. *Redwood and Lumbering*, 44.

46. Oscar F. Redfield to Lucretia M. Carpenter Redfield, August 7, 1887, Carpenter Family Papers, BAN. For the donkey engine, see also Hugh Bower, "Notes on Lumbering Methods, c. 1950," and George Douglas, "History of the Pacific Lumber Company," as told to Derby Bendorf, both in Allen, "Notes on the Pacific Lumbering Company," BAN. For the use of donkey engines in the Pacific Northwest, see White, *Land Use, Environment, and Social Change*, 96, 106.

47. *Redwood and Lumbering*, 48.

48. Irvine, *History of Humboldt County*, 112.

49. Bonner, *Redwoods of California*, 14.

50. *Pacific Coast Wood and Iron*, 17 (March 1892), 120–21.

51. Wilde, "Chronology of the Pacific Lumber Company," 10, BAN; *Redwood and Lumbering*, 17.

52. Dolbeer estimated 75 percent efficiency, as did the mill owner Alexander Duncan; another mill owner, C. A. Hooper, estimated 70 percent. See H. W. Plummer, *Redwood Lands of California* (San Francisco, 1887), 5–6. Wattenburger claimed, without solid evidence, that loggers had reduced waste to 30–40 percent. Wattenburger, "Redwood Lumbering Industry," 22, 34–35.

53. "Waste in Cutting Timber," *Pacific Coast Wood and Iron*, 11 (January 1889), 10.

54. Oscar F. Redfield to Lucretia M. Carpenter Redfield, August 7, 1887, Carpenter Family Papers, BAN.

55. Bonner, *Redwoods of California*, 18.

56. "Saw Mill Refuse," *Pacific Coast Wood and Iron*, 10 (November 1888), 80; "The Timber Waste," ibid., 26 (November 1896), 177.

57. Wilde, "Chronology of the Pacific Lumber Company," 15, BAN.

58. J. M. Eddy, *In the Redwood's Realm* (San Francisco: D. S. Stanley, 1893), 21–22.

59. For chain migration, see Charles Tilly, "Transplanted Networks," in Virginia Yans-McLaughlin, ed., *Immigration Reconsidered: History, Sociology, and Politics* (New York: Oxford University Press, 1990), 79–95.

60. Interview with A. P. Alexanderson, August 23, 1944, in Allen, "Notes on the Pacific Lumber Company," BAN.

61. Bonner, *Redwoods of California*, 15.

62. *Redwood and Lumbering*, 35, 50.

63. Wattenburger, "Redwood Lumbering Industry," 16.

64. Irving Slade to C. V. Slade, November 14, 1873; Irving Slade to C. V. Slade, January 3, 1875, Slade Letters, BAN.

65. Kathleen Neils Conzen, "A Saga of Families," in Clyde A. Milner II, Carol A. O'Connor, and Martha A. Sandweiss, eds., *The Oxford History of the American West* (New York: Oxford University Press, 1994), 315–57.

66. "Free Lumber," *Pacific Coast Wood and Iron*, 10 (September 1888), 42.

67. By comparison, over 60 percent of Italian immigrants to the United States returned to Italy, and perhaps 30 percent of English immigrants returned to England. Sucheng Chan, "European and Asian Immigration into the United States in Comparative Perspective, 1820s to 1920s," in Yans-McLaughlin, *Immigration Reconsidered*, 37–75.

68. Ping Chiu, *Chinese Labor in California, 1850–1880: An Economic Study* (Madison: Historical Society of Wisconsin, 1967); Liping Zhu, *A Chinaman's Chance: The Chinese on the Rocky Mountain Mining Frontier* (Niwot: University Press of Colorado, 1997); Ronald Takaki, *Strangers from a Different Shore: A History of Asian Americans* (Boston: Little, Brown, 1998); Yong Chen, "The Internal Origins of Chinese Emigration to the United States Reconsidered," *Western Historical Quarterly*, 28 (Winter 1997), 521–46.

69. Daniel Cornford, *Workers and Dissent in the Redwood Empire* (Philadelphia: Temple University Press, 1987), 42.

70. "Anti-Coolie Association," *Humboldt Times*, January 25, 1862.

71. Carlos A. Schwantes, "Protest in a Promised Land: Unemployment, Disinheritance, and the Origin of Labor Militancy in the Pacific Northwest, 1885–1886," *Western Historical Quarterly*, 13 (October 1982), 373–90.

72. Alexander Saxton, *The Indispensable Enemy: Labor and the Anti-Chinese Movement in California* (Berkeley: University of California Press, 1971), 201–5.

73. See Eric Foner, *Free Soil, Free Labor, Free Men: The Ideology of the Republican Party Before the Civil War* (New York: Oxford University Press, 1970); Lawrence Goodwyn, *The Populist Moment: A Short History of the Agrarian Revolt in America* (New York: Oxford University Press, 1978).

74. Humboldt County, which had voted reliably Republican in the 1860s, sent a slate of Workingmen's candidates to the state constitutional convention in 1878 and endorsed every Workingmen's candidate for state office in 1879. In 1880, although the Greenback-Labor presidential candidate, James Weaver, received only 2 percent of the California vote, he received 25 percent of the vote in Humboldt County. Cornford, *Workers and Dissent*, 43–59.

75. "Is It Right?," *Western Watchman* (Eureka), April 23, 1887.

76. Cornford, *Workers and Dissent*, 72–98. For the Knights, see Craig Phelan, *Grand Master Workman: Terence Powderly and the Knights of Labor* (Westport, Conn.: Greenwood Press, 2000); Robert Weir, *Knights Unhorsed: Internal Conflict in a Gilded Age Social Movement* (Detroit: Wayne State University Press, 2000).

77. See Terry L. Anderson and Donald R. Leal, *Enviro-Capitalists: Doing Good While Doing Well* (Lanham, Md.: Rowman and Littlefield, 1997); Anderson and Leal, *Free Market Environmentalism*, rev. ed. (New York: Palgrave, 2001); Richard L. Stroup, *Eco-Nomics: What Everyone Should Know About Economics and the Environment* (Washington, D.C.: Cato Institute, 2003).

78. Redfield to Lucretia Redfield Carpenter, August 7, 1887, Carpenter Family Papers, BAN.

79. Wattenburger, "Redwood Lumbering Industry," 25. See also Wilde, "Chronology of the Pacific Lumber Company," 14, BAN.

80. *Certificate of Incorporation and By-Laws of the Redwood Lumber Association* (San Francisco: Women's Union Print, 1871), 3–4.

81. "Consumption of Redwood Lumber by San Francisco Market," *Pacific Coast Wood and Iron*, 15 (May 1891), 211.

82. D. J. Flanigan, "California Lumber," c. 1890, BAN.

83. Wilde, "Chronology of the Pacific Lumber Company," 16, BAN.

84. "Logs Hauled into Elk River for D. R. Jones & Co. and Dolbeer & Carson," Dolbeer and Carson Lumber Company Records, vol. 55, BAN.

85. "Consumption of Redwood," 211.

86. California Lumber Exchange Agreement, March 24, 1882, Hans Henry Buhne Miscellaneous Papers, 1865–1897, BAN. See also *By-Laws of the California Lumber Exchange* (San Francisco, 1884), 3, which states, "The object of this Exchange is to maintain uniform prices and terms at which Pine and Redwood Lumber and building material shall be sold at retail."

87. Wattenburger, "Redwood Lumbering Industry," 33–34.

88. Dorothy Weidberg, "The History of John Kentfield and Company, 1854–1925, a Lumber Manufacturing Firm of San Francisco" (M.A. thesis, University of California, Berkeley, 1940), 25.

89. Plummer, *Redwood Lands*, 1.

90. Interview with Weyerhaeuser, *San Francisco Examiner*, April 12, 1887, reprinted in Plummer, *Redwood Lands*, 6.

91. "The Inevitable," *Pacific Coast Wood and Iron*, 20 (September 1893), 114; "The Lumber Trade," ibid., 20 (October 1893), 154; "The Lumber Trade," ibid., 20 (November 1893), 193.

92. Plummer, *Redwood Lands*, 2; "The Fate of the Redwoods," *Pacific Coast Wood and Iron*, 11 (June 1889), 150.

93. G. Namkuong and J. H. Roberts, "Extinction Probabilities and the Changing Age Structure of Redwood Forests," *The American Naturalist*, 108 (May–June 1974), 355–68.

94. Noss, *Redwood Forest*, 119–63, 236.

95. Ibid., 166–74; Schoenherr, *Natural History of California*, 614.

Part II: The Industrial Frontier

1. See Jonathan Prude, *The Coming of Industrial Order: Town and Factory Life in Rural Massachusetts, 1810–1860* (New York: Cambridge University Press, 1983); Christopher Clark, *The Roots of Rural Capitalism: Western Massachusetts, 1780–1860* (Ithaca, N.Y.: Cornell University Press, 1990).

2. For a comparative study of the effect of industrialization and ranching on the non-Anglo societies of the western North American periphery, see Andrew Graybill, "Instruments of Incorporation: Rangers, Mounties, and the North American Frontier, 1875–1910" (Ph.D. dissertation, Princeton University, 2003).

3. See David Igler, *Industrial Cowboys: Miller & Lux and the Transformation of the Far West, 1850–1920* (Berkeley: University of California Press, 2001).

4. Gambling on the Grassland: Kinship, Capital, and Ecology in Southern California

1. Cave J. Couts to William Bandini Couts, October 30, 1873, Cave J. Couts Collection, Box 6, HUN.

2. "Transactions of the Agricultural Society of the State of California, 1859," *Appendix to the Journals of the Senate and Assembly of the Eleventh Session of the Legislature of the State of California* (Sacramento: C. T. Botts, 1860), 344–45.

3. For a recent interpretation of the Californios, see Albert L. Hurtado, *Intimate Frontiers: Sex, Gender, and Culture in Old California* (Albuquerque: University of New Mexico Press, 1999).

4. Leonard Pitt, *The Decline of the Californios: A Social History of the Spanish-Speaking Californians, 1846–1890* (Berkeley: University of California Press, 1966).

5. Raymond V. Padilla, "A Critique of Pittian History," *El Grito: A Journal of Contemporary Mexican-American Thought*, 6 (Fall 1972), 3–41; Albert Camarillo, *Chicanos in a Changing Society: From Mexican Pueblos to American Barrios in Santa Barbara and Southern California, 1848–1930* (Cambridge, Mass.: Harvard University Press, 1979); Richard Griswold del Castillo, *The Los Angeles Barrio, 1850–1890: A Social History* (Berkeley: University of California Press, 1979); Tomás Almaguer, *Racial Fault Lines:*

The Historical Origins of White Supremacy in California (Berkeley: University of California Press, 1994); Lisbeth Haas, *Conquests and Historical Identities in California, 1769–1936* (Berkeley: University of California Press, 1995).

6. Griswold del Castillo, *Los Angeles Barrio*, 23. The older interpretation also sees the Anglo-American ranchers as transitional figures. Note, for instance, the title of Philip Fedewa's 1970 dissertation, a biography of Couts's brother-in-law Abel Stearns: "Abel Stearns in Transitional California, 1848–1871" (Ph.D. dissertation, University of Missouri, 1970).

7. See Richard White, *The Middle Ground: Indians, Empires, and Republics in the Great Lakes Region, 1650–1815* (New York: Cambridge University Press, 1991); Gary C. Anderson, *Kinsmen of Another Kind: Dakota-White Relations in the Upper Mississippi Valley, 1650–1862* (Lincoln: University of Nebraska Press, 1984).

8. Fedewa, "Abel Stearns in Transitional California," 125; Pitt, *Decline of the Californios*, 105, 109–10; R. H. Allen, "The Spanish Land Grant System as an Influence in the Agricultural Development of California," *Agricultural History*, 9 (July 1935), 127–42; Paul W. Gates, "Public Land Disposal in California," *Agricultural History*, 49 (January 1975), 158–78; Gates, *California Ranchos and Farms, 1846–1862* (Madison: State Historical Society of Wisconsin, 1967), 15; Ellen Liebman, *California Farm Land: A History of Large Agricultural Landholdings* (Totowa, N.J.: Rowman and Allanheld, 1983), 12.

9. Camarillo, *Chicanos in a Changing Society*, 114; Pitt, *Decline of the Californios*, 106; Paul W. Gates, *Land and Law in California: Essays on Land Policies* (Ames: Iowa State University Press, 1991), 158.

10. For a discussion of different ranching techniques in the history of the North American West, see Terry Jordan, *North American Cattle-Ranching Frontiers: Origins, Diffusion, Differentiation* (Albuquerque: University of New Mexico Press, 1993); Richard White, "Animals and Enterprise," in Clyde A. Milner II, Carol A. O'Connor, and Martha A. Sandweiss, eds., *The Oxford History of the American West* (New York: Oxford University Press, 1994), 252–69.

11. United States Census Office, *Agriculture of the United States in 1860* (Washington, D.C.: Government Printing Office, 1864), 10–13.

12. For grasslands, see Paul Sears, *Lands Beyond the Forest* (Englewood Cliffs, N.J.: Prentice-Hall, 1969); Lauren Brown, *Grasslands* (New York: Knopf, 1985); for rainfall in Los Angeles, see Mike Davis, *Ecology of Fear: Los Angeles and the Imagination of Disaster* (New York: Vintage, 1998), 10–14.

13. For the California grasslands, see Elna Bakker, *An Island Called California: An Ecological Introduction to Its Natural Communities*, 2d ed. (Berkeley: University of California Press, 1984), 350–51; Allan A. Schoenherr, *A Natural History of California* (Berkeley: University of California Press, 1992), 39, 315–17, 341–432.

14. For drought in southern California, see Crane S. Miller and Richard S. Hyslop, *California: The Geography of Diversity* (Mountain View, Calif.: Mayfield, 1983), 75–77.

15. Hubert Howe Bancroft, *California Pastoral, 1769–1848* (San Francisco: A. L. Bancroft, 1888), 337–38.

16. For ecological invasions, see Charles Elton, *The Ecology of Invasions by Plants and Animals* (London: Methuen, 1958); Alfred W. Crosby, *Ecological Imperialism: The Biological Expansion of Europe, 900–1900* (New York: Cambridge University Press, 1986).

17. Steven W. Hackel, "Land, Labor, and Production: The Colonial Economy of Spanish and Mexican California," in Ramón A. Gutiérrez and Richard J. Orsi, eds., *Contested Eden: California Before the Gold Rush* (Berkeley: University of California Press, 1998), 116; Jordan, *North American Cattle-Ranching Frontiers*, 163.

18. For the Great Plains, see Andrew C. Isenberg, *The Destruction of the Bison: An Environmental History, 1750–1920* (New York: Cambridge University Press, 2000). For New Mexico, see James F. Brooks, *Captives and Cousins: Slavery, Kinship, and Community in the Southwest Borderlands* (Chapel Hill: University of North Carolina Press, 2002).

19. See Elinor G. K. Melville, *A Plague of Sheep: Environmental Consequences of the Conquest of Mexico* (New York: Cambridge University Press, 1994).

20. See Hazel Adele Pulling, "A History of California's Range-Cattle Industry, 1770–1912" (Ph.D. dissertation, University of Southern California, 1944), 201.

21. M. Kat Anderson, Michael G. Barbour, and Valerie Whitworth, "A World of Balance and Plenty: Land, Plants, Animals, and Humans in a Pre-European California," in Gutiérrez and Orsi, *Contested Eden*, 23.

22. C. E. Grunsky Monthly Rainfall Records, William Hammond Hall Papers, CSA.

23. John T. Kincade to James Kincade, October 29, 1873, Kincade Correspondence, HUN.

24. Bancroft, *California Pastoral*. For Mexican California's integration into the global market, see David Igler, "Diseased Goods: Global Exchanges in the Eastern Pacific Basin, 1770–1850," *American Historical Review*, 109 (June 2004), 693–719.

25. For haciendas, see Magnus Morner, "The Spanish American Hacienda: A Survey of Recent Research and Debate," *Hispanic American Historical Review*, 53 (May 1973), 183–216. For Mexican ranchos, see Frans J. Schryer, "A Ranchero Economy in Northeastern Hidalgo, 1880–1920," *Hispanic American Historical Review*, 59 (August 1979), 418–43.

26. David Hornbeck, "Land Tenure and Rancho Expansion in Alta California, 1784–1846," *Journal of Historical Geography*, 4 (October 1978), 371–90.

27. Pulling, "California's Range-Cattle Industry," 75.

28. *An Historical Sketch of Los Angeles County, California* (Los Angeles: Louis Lewin, 1876), 32; Robert Cowan, *Ranchos of California: A List of Spanish Concessions, 1775–1822, and Mexican Grants, 1822–1846* (Fresno: Academy Library Guild, 1956); Martin Cole and Henry Welcome, eds., *Don Pio Pico's Historical Narrative* (Glendale, Calif.: Arthur H. Clarke, 1973), 39–52.

29. For Mexico's northern provinces, see David J. Weber, *The Spanish Frontier in North America* (New Haven: Yale University Press, 1992).

30. "To California Over Southern Trails: Doctor Joseph Pownall's Overland Diary, Being an 1849 Narrative and His Life at the Gold Diggins," Joseph Pownall Collection, HUN. See also John J. Werth, *A Dissertation on the Resources and Policy of California: Mineral, Agricultural, and Commercial* (Benicia, Calif.: St. Clair and Pinkerton, 1851), 1.

31. Charles Nordhoff, *California for Health, Pleasure, and Residence* (New York: Harper, 1872; New York: Berkley, 1974), 238–41; Richard Henry Dana, *Two Years Before the Mast*, ed. Thomas Philbrick (New York: Penguin, 1981); Charles Loring Brace, *The New West: California in 1867–1868* (New York: Putnam, 1869), 287; "Transactions of the California State Agricultural Society, 1863," *Appendix to the Journals of the Senate and Assembly of the Fifteenth Session of the Legislature of the State of California*, vol. 2 (Sacramento: O. M. Clayes, 1864), 146; Hackel, "Land, Labor, and Production," 132–33;

Jordan, *North American Cattle-Ranching Frontiers*, 166–68. A similar ranching economy emerged in nineteenth-century Venezuela to produce beef for markets in Cuba. See J. S. Otto and N. E. Anderson, "Cattle Ranching in the Venezuelan Llanos and the Florida Flatwoods," *Comparative Studies in Society and History*, 28 (October 1986), 672–83.

32. Nordhoff, *California for Health*, 242.

33. See Robert Glass Cleland, *The Cattle on a Thousand Hills: Southern California, 1850–1880*, 2d ed. (San Marino, Calif.: Huntington Library, 1951), 30–31.

34. David A. Brading, *Miners and Merchants in Bourbon Mexico, 1763–1810* (Cambridge: Cambridge University Press, 1971), 219. For the variety of Mexican haciendas, see Brading, *Haciendas and Ranchos in the Mexican Bajío: León, 1700–1860* (Cambridge: Cambridge University Press, 1978), 1–12.

35. Some cotton planters of the American South shared this speculative mentality. See Edward Phifer, "Slavery in Microcosm: Burke County, North Carolina," *Journal of Southern History*, 28 (May 1962), 137–65.

36. Doris Marion Wright, *A Yankee in Mexican California: Abel Stearns, 1798–1848* (Santa Barbara, Calif.: Wallace Hebberd, 1977).

37. Cleland, *Cattle on a Thousand Hills*, 184–87.

38. Fedewa, "Abel Stearns in Transitional California," 104, 132; Cleland, *Cattle on a Thousand Hills*, 196–97, 332.

39. Gates, *California Ranchos and Farms*, 5–6.

40. United States Census Office, *Census of the City and County of Los Angeles, California, for the Year 1850* (Los Angeles: Times-Mirror Press, 1929), 44, 117.

41. José Anaz, quoted in Wright, *Yankee in Mexican California*, 93.

42. Hurtado, *Intimate Frontiers*, 21–44.

43. The house, which featured a one-hundred-foot-long ballroom, was maintained by a staff of nineteen servants. Fedewa, "Abel Stearns in Transitional California," 61; Albert L. Hurtado, *Indian Survival on the California Frontier* (New Haven: Yale University Press, 1988), 199.

44. David Montejano, *Anglos and Mexicans in the Making of Texas, 1836–1986* (Austin: University of Texas Press, 1994), 36–37. For Robinson, see Alfred Robinson, *Life in California* (New York, 1846; London: H. G. Collins, 1851); Maynard Geiger, ed., *The Letters of Alfred Robinson to the De la Guerra Family of Santa Barbara, 1834–1873* (Los Angeles: Zamorano Club, 1972).

45. Pitt, relying on snide observations such as those of José Anaz, emphasized discord. Pitt described "constant friction" between the Bandinis on one side and Don Juan's Anglo-American sons-in-law on the other. According to Pitt, Stearns, Couts, and Johnson deplored the "false pride, laziness, [and] ingratitude" of the Bandinis. Pitt, *Decline of the Californios*, 110–16.

46. Camarillo derided the cross-cultural marriages, dismissing the historical significance of the unions. According to Camarillo in his study of Santa Barbara, by 1853 only a few Anglos had married into ranchero families, while most landowners remained California-born. Camarillo, *Chicanos in a Changing Society*, 26–29.

47. Pitt, *Decline of the Californios*, 124.

48. Charles Johnson to Stearns, May 26, 1851, Abel Stearns Collection, Box 36, HUN; Cleland, *Cattle on a Thousand Hills*, 196–97.

49. "Last Will and Testament of Juan Bandini," 1859, BAN.

50. For the exchanges of land and cattle between Stearns and Couts, see Stearns to Couts, February 5, 1853; Stearns to Couts, March 23, 1853; Stearns to Couts, April 9, 1853; Stearns to Couts, May 2, 1853; "Articles of Agreement made and entered into . . . between Abel Stearns . . . & Cave J. Couts," July 11, 1853; Stearns to Couts, January 11, 1854; Stearns to Couts, October 19, 1855; Stearns to Couts, July 8, 1856, Couts Collection, Box 36, HUN.

51. Fedewa, "Abel Stearns in Transitional California," 161–63.

52. Johnson to Stearns, June 7, 1853, Stearns Collection, Box 36, HUN.

53. For the American South, see Harry L. Watson, "Conflict and Collaboration: Yeomen, Slaveholders, and Politics in the Antebellum South," *Social History*, 10 (October 1985), 273–98. For the Yucatán, see Allen Wells, "Family Elites in a Boom-and-Bust Economy: The Molinas and Peons of Porfirian Yucatán," *Hispanic American Historical Review*, 62 (May 1982), 224–53; Fred Carstensen and Diane Roazen, "Foreign Markets, Domestic Initiatives, and the Emergence of a Monocrop Economy: The Yucatecan Experience, 1825–1903," *Hispanic American Historical Review*, 72 (November 1992), 555–92; Juan Carlos Garavaglia and Juan Carlos Grosso, "Mexican Elites of a Provincial Town: The Landowners of Tepeaca (1700–1870)," *Hispanic American Historical Review*, 70 (May 1990), 255–93.

54. Stearns to Couts, May 2, 1853, Couts Collection, Box 36, HUN.

55. For labor on Mexican haciendas, see Morner, "The Spanish American Hacienda," 199. For Paraguay, see John Hoyt Williams, "Black Labor and State Ranches: The Tabapi Experience in Paraguay," *Journal of Negro History*, 62 (October 1977), 378–89. For a comparison between California and Argentina, see Ricardo D. Salvatore, "Modes of Labor Control in Cattle-Ranching Economies: California, Southern Brazil, and Argentina, 1820–1860," *Journal of Economic History*, 51 (June 1991), 441–51.

56. See *Narrative of B. D. Wilson* (Lake Vineyard, Calif., December 6, 1877), Benjamin Davis Wilson Collection, HUN. For Wilson's landholdings, see United States Census Office, *Census of Los Angeles*, 117.

57. Wilson to Couts, June 13, 1853, Wilson Collection, HUN; B. D. Wilson, *The Indians of Southern California in 1852* (Lincoln: University of Nebraska Press, 1995), 57; Couts to the Editor, *San Diego Herald*, June 13, 1855, Couts Collection, Box 6, HUN. For violence to compel labor, see Abel Stearns to Cave J. Couts, April 4, 1854, Couts Collection, HUN.

58. Couts petitioned for the assignment of seven Indians to his custody in 1861. See Couts to D. B. Hollister, January 10, 1861, Couts Collection, Box 6, HUN. For labor regimes in other ranching economies, see Silvio R. Duncan and John Markoff, "Civilization and Barbarism: Cattle Frontiers in Latin America," *Comparative Studies in Society and History*, 20 (October 1978), 602.

59. Wilson, *Indians of Southern California in 1852*, 26. For Indian labor at the missions and ranchos, see Hackel, "Land, Labor, and Production," 121–34; William S. Simmons, "Indian Peoples of California," in Gutiérrez and Orsi, *Contested Eden*, 48–77; Hurtado, *Indian Survival on the California Frontier*.

60. Stearns to Couts, July 6, 1855; Stearns to Couts, May 9, 1856; Stearns to Couts, July 8, 1856; Stearns to Couts, February 15, 1857; Stearns to Couts, April 7, 1857; Stearns to Couts, June 23, 1857, Couts Collection, Box 36, HUN.

61. Johnson to Stearns, July 1, 1856, Stearns Collection, Box 36, HUN; Couts to Stearns, December 6, 1852, Stearns Collection, Box 18, HUN.

62. Couts to Stearns, February 9, 1852, Stearns Collection, Box 18, HUN; Pulling, "California's Range-Cattle Industry," 82.

63. Couts to Stearns, February 14, 1852; Couts to Stearns, May 12, 1852; Couts to Stearns, June 15, 1852; Couts to Stearns, July 12, 1852; Couts to Stearns, July 22, 1852; Couts to Stearns, August 14, 1852; Couts to Stearns, December 6, 1852, Stearns Collection, Box 18, HUN.

64. Couts to Stearns, April 20, 1856, Stearns Collection, Box 18, HUN.

65. Johnson to Stearns, July 21, 1856, Stearns Collection, Box 36, HUN.

66. Stearns to Couts, May 7, 1857; Stearns to Couts, February 4, 1858; Stearns to Couts, February 21, 1858, Couts Collection, Box 36, HUN.

67. Couts to Francisco Rodriguez, March 14, 1856, Stearns Collection, Box 18, HUN; Couts to Stearns, March 15, 1856, Stearns Collection, Box 18, HUN.

68. Stearns to David Spence, December 2, 1852, Stearns Collection, Box 62, HUN; see also Stearns to Andrew Randall, October 14, 1853, Stearns Collection, Box 62, HUN.

69. Stearns to Randall, October 14, 1853, Stearns Collection, Box 62, HUN; Stearns to Couts, April 7, 1857; Stearns to Couts, April 23, 1857, Couts Collection, Box 36, HUN.

70. Fedewa, "Abel Stearns in Transitional California," 165.

71. Gates, *California Ranchos and Farms*, 23.

72. Johnson to Stearns, February 13, 1862; Johnson to Stearns, February 23, 1862, Stearns Collection, Box 36, HUN. For the decline of the beef market in the 1860s, see also John S. Hittell, *The Resources of California*, 6th ed. (San Francisco: A. Roman, 1874; New York: W. J. Widdleton, 1874), 276.

73. L. T. Burcham, "Cattle and Range Forage in California: 1770-1880," *Agricultural History*, 35 (July 1961), 140-49.

74. "Stock Dying from Poverty," *Sacramento Daily Union*, December 10, 1861.

75. Stearns to Couts, April 4, 1860; Stearns to Couts, February 3, 1861, Couts Collection, Box 36, HUN; Stearns to Couts, March 4, 1862; Stearns to Couts, February 16, 1863, Couts Collection, Box 37, HUN.

76. Grunsky Rainfall Records, Hall Papers, CSA.

77. "Rain" and "Grass," *Los Angeles Star*, November 16, 1861; "Rain," and "Mud," ibid., November 23, 1861; "The Rain," and "The River," ibid., January 4, 1862; "Rain," ibid., January 11, 1862.

78. "The Rains–The Flood," *Los Angeles Star*, January 25, 1862; "From San Diego" and "Santa Barbara," ibid., February 1, 1862.

79. Johnson to Stearns, September 9, 1862, Stearns Collection, Box 36, HUN; Johnson to Couts, April 21, 1862, Couts Collection, Box 20, HUN.

80. Fedewa, "Abel Stearns in Transitional California," 186-89.

81. Johnson to Stearns, January 11, 1863; Johnson to Stearns, February 6, 1863; Johnson to Stearns, March 4, 1863; Johnson to Stearns, March 14, 1863, Stearns Collection, Box 36, HUN.

82. Johnson to Couts, March 10, 1863; Johnson to Couts, March 25, 1863, Couts Collection, Box 20, HUN.

83. Johnson to Stearns, June 13, 1863, Stearns Collection, Box 36, HUN.

84. Johnson to Stearns, June 2, 1863; Johnson to Stearns, June 13, 1863, Stearns Collection, Box 36, HUN.

85. Stearns to Couts, April 8, 1863, Couts Collection, Box 37, HUN; Johnson to Stearns, June 13, 1863, Stearns Collection, Box 36, HUN.

86. See David Rockwell, *The Nature of North America: A Handbook of the Continent; Rocks, Plants, and Animals* (New York: Berkley, 1998), 236–37.

87. *California Daily Express*, August 6, 1858. See also "Grasshoppers," *Daily California Express*, August 3, 1860; *Placer Herald*, May 11, 1870.

88. "Grasshoppers," *Los Angeles Star*, June 6, 1863.

89. Johnson to Stearns, June 13, 1863, Stearns Collection, Box 36, HUN.

90. Grunsky Rainfall Records, Hall Papers, CSA.

91. "The Weather," *Los Angeles Star*, January 23, 1864.

92. Stearns to Couts, February 9, 1864, Couts Collection, Box 37, HUN.

93. Johnson to Couts, April 21, 1864, Couts Collection, Box 20, HUN.

94. Hittell, *Resources of California*, 218, 276.

95. United States Census Office, *Agriculture of the United States in 1860* (Washington, D.C.: Government Printing Office, 1864), 10–11; United States Census Office, *The Statistics of Wealth and Industry of the United States, Ninth Census*, vol. 3 (Washington, D.C.: Government Printing Office, 1872), 104–5.

96. Stearns to Couts, January 25, 1866, Couts Collection, Box 37, HUN. See also John Kincade to James Kincade, March 13, 1864; John Kincade to James Kincade, July 6, 1864, Kincade Correspondence, HUN.

97. Katherine Bixby Hotchkis, *Rancho Los Alamitos* (Balboa, Calif., 1964).

98. Johnson to Couts, July 6, 1864, Couts Collection, Box 20, HUN.

99. Stearns to Couts, November 16, 1864, Couts Collection, Box 37, HUN; Couts to Juan Bautista Bandini, July 6, 1865, Stearns Collection, Box 19, HUN; "Agreement between Abel Stearns, of Los Angeles and Henry D. Bacon, of St. Louis," December 22, 1864, Huntington Manuscript, HUN. For Parrott, see David Igler, *Industrial Cowboys: Miller & Lux and the Transformation of the Far West, 1850–1920* (Berkeley: University of California Press, 2001), 41–45.

100. Stearns to Couts, January 25, 1866; Stearns to Couts, March 8, 1866; Stearns to Couts, April 5, 1866, Couts Collection, Box 37, HUN. See also Johnson to Couts, March 15, 1865, Couts Collection, Box 21, HUN.

101. Stearns to Don Pablo de la Guerra, April 28, 1866, Huntington Manuscript, HUN.

102. Fedewa, "Abel Stearns in Transitional California," 224–40.

103. Couts to Stearns, July 24, 1856, Stearns Collection, Box 18, HUN.

104. United States Census Office, *Agriculture of the United States in 1860*, 10–11.

105. Johnson to Couts, January 13, 1863; Johnson to Couts, February 17, 1863; Johnson to Couts, February 24, 1863, Couts Collection, Box 20, HUN.

106. Joseph Weed, *A View of California As It Is* (San Francisco: Bynon and Wright, 1874), 110.

107. See Augustus Simon Bixby Diary, HUN.

108. Fedewa, "Abel Stearns in Transitional California," 199.

109. "Sheep," *Los Angeles Star*, April 27, 1861; John J. Powell, *The Golden State and Its Resources* (San Francisco: Bacon, 1874), 56; Brace, *New West*, 237; Hittell, *Resources of California*, 275.

110. David N. Cole and Peter B. Landres, "Threats to Wilderness Ecosystems: Impacts and Research Needs," *Ecological Applications*, 6 (February 1996), 168–84.

111. John Muir, "The Bee Pastures of California," *The Century*, 24 (June 1882), 228.

112. George G. Mackenzie, "The Pressing Need of Forest Reservation in the Sierra," *The Century*, 44 (June 1892), 318–19.

113. Donald Pisani, *From Family Farm to Agribusiness: The Irrigation Crusade in California and the West, 1850–1931* (Berkeley: University of California Press, 1984), 4.

114. Powell, *Golden State and Its Resources*, 54.

115. See Igler, *Industrial Cowboys*, 35–91, 147–78.

5. The Enclosure of the Plateau: Land and Labor in the High Lake Country

1. William Simpson, "The Modoc Region, California," *National Geographic*, 19 (1874–75), 292.

2. Newton Booth to U.S. War Department, January 1, 1873, Military Department, Adjutant General, Indian War Papers, CSA.

3. For a summary of the history of the Modoc War, particularly the events of April 11, 1873, see Keith A. Murray, *The Modocs and Their War* (Norman: University of Oklahoma Press, 1959).

4. Alfred Benjamin Meacham, *The Tragedy of the Lava-Beds* (Hartford, Conn.: privately printed, 1877), 8.

5. K. Murray, *Modocs and Their War*, 82–97.

6. Meacham, "The Tragedy of the Lava-Beds," lecture delivered at the Park Street Church, Boston, Mass., May 24, 1874, BAN.

7. Alfred Benjamin Meacham, *Wi-ne-ma* (Hartford, Conn.: American Publishing Company, 1876), 137–38.

8. Ibid., 138.

9. James McLaughlin, *My Friend the Indian* (Boston: Houghton Mifflin, 1910), 325.

10. Meacham, *Tragedy of the Lava-Beds*, 14; Meacham, *Wi-ne-ma*, 57–59.

11. The best source for the events of April 11, 1873, is the transcript of Jack's trial. See "Proceedings of a Military Commission Convened at Fort Klamath, Oregon, for the Trial of Modoc Prisoners" (July 1878), H.ex.doc. 122, 43d Cong., 1st Sess. (1874), 136–77. See also Meacham, *Wi-ne-ma*, 59–62; K. Murray, *Modocs and Their War*, 188–91.

12. For the Sioux, see Robert G. Utley, *Lance and Shield: The Life and Times of Sitting Bull* (New York: Henry Holt, 1993); Gary Clayton Anderson, *Sitting Bull and the Paradox of Lakota Nationhood* (New York: HarperCollins, 1996); for the Nez Perce, see Alvin M. Josephy, *The Nez Perce Indians and the Opening of the Northwest* (New Haven: Yale University Press, 1965).

13. During the 1950s and 1960s, when popular, narrative-driven western history prevailed, historians produced a few studies devoted to the Modoc War. Strongly influenced by the prevailing frontier paradigm of western history, these accounts tended to depict the murders of the peace commissioners as prima facie evidence of Indian barbarity. By far the best of these studies is K. Murray, *Modocs and Their War*; others include William Samuel Brown, *California Northeast, the Bloody Ground* (Oakland, Calif.: Biobooks, 1951); Hugh R. Wilson, *The Causes and Significance of the Modoc War* (Klamath Falls,

Ore.: Guide Print Co., 1953); Richard Dillon, *Burnt-Out Fires: California's Modoc Indian War* (Englewood Cliffs, N.J.: Prentice-Hall, 1973).

By the 1970s, ethnohistory, the study of Indian cultures and cultural persistence, had come to replace the older western history. Yet most ethnohistorical studies of American Indian civil and military resistance to Euroamerican conquest pointedly excluded Captain Jack and the Modocs. See Alvin M. Josephy, *The Patriot Chiefs* (New York: Viking, 1958); R. David Edmunds, ed., *American Indian Leaders: Studies in Diversity* (Lincoln: University of Nebraska Press, 1980); and James A. Clifton, ed., *Being and Becoming Indian: Biographical Studies of the North American Frontier* (Chicago: Dorsey Press, 1989).

The few studies that have included the Modocs have struggled unsuccessfully to explain their assimilation to the Euroamerican economy and to justify Jack's perfidy. See, for instance, Dee Brown, *Bury My Heart at Wounded Knee: An Indian History of the American West* (New York: Washington Square Press, 1970), 213–34. Most ethnohistorians have abandoned the subject, leaving the Modocs in a kind of historical limbo.

14. For an analogous case, see Martha C. Knack, "A Short Resource History of Pyramid Lake, Nevada," *Ethnohistory*, 24 (Winter 1977), 47–63. For a new approach to Indians and the environment, see Richard White, "Indian Peoples and the Natural World: Asking the Right Questions," in Donald L. Fixico, ed., *Rethinking American Indian History* (Albuquerque: University of New Mexico Press, 1997), 87–100.

15. G. M. Trevelyan, *English Social History* (New York: Pelican, 1967), 391. For enclosure, see also Keith Wrightson, *Earthly Necessities: Economic Lives in Early Modern Britain* (New Haven: Yale University Press, 2000), 209–12.

16. Beginning in the early twentieth century, British historians produced two sorts of studies of enclosure. One type, including Edward C. K. Gonner's *Common Land and Inclosure* (London: Macmillan, 1912), focused on the spatial and macroeconomic consequences of enclosure. Gonner viewed small farmers as inefficient and thus doomed to be replaced in an increasingly commercialized countryside. While Gonner conceded that in the short run some small farmers were impoverished, in the long run, "the beneficial effect on farming taken as a whole is undoubted." The other type of study, best exemplified by John L. Hammond and Barbara Hammond's *The Village Labourer, 1760–1832: A Study in the Government of England Before the Reform Bill* (London: Longman, 1912), centered on the injustice of the process. They described "disinherited" peasants, "exiled" laborers, and villages reduced to "poverty and crime." The impoverishment of rural laborers eventuated in a series of rural revolts, one of the last of which occurred in 1830. My understanding of the early twentieth-century historiography of enclosure comes in part from Michael Turner, *Enclosures in Britain, 1750–1830* (London: Macmillan, 1984), 11–15. See also Gilbert Slater, *The English Peasantry and the Enclosure of Common Fields* (London: Constable, 1907); and Arthur H. Johnson, *The Disappearance of the Small Landowner* (London: Merlin Press, 1963).

In succeeding years most historians have interpreted enclosure either, like the Hammonds, as an injustice that produced a range of social problems, or, like Gonner, as an economic inevitability that ultimately worked to the benefit of the vast majority. Most enclosures, and the most opposition to the process, occurred between 1760 and 1815, the period of rapid English industrialization, as Harold Perkin noted. See Perkin, *Origins of Modern English Society* (London: Ark, 1969), 124–33. While the Hammonds focused on this period, when the social costs of enclosure were most acute, scholars who have followed Gonner have argued, that enclosures extended over a much longer period, beginning as early as the fifteenth century and extending in rare cases into the early twentieth. Enclosure, they argued, was as often a consequence as a cause of the rise of commercialism and manufacturing. They pointed to the variety of types of enclosure: by agreement, Chancery proceeding, or Parliamentary act. By taking the focus off the most coercive period of enclosure in the late eighteenth and early nineteenth century, these scholars have diluted some of the force of the arguments of the Hammonds and their followers. See J. A. Yelling, *Common Field and Enclosure in England, 1450–1850* (London: Macmillan, 1977); G. E. Mingay, *Parliamentary Enclosure in England: An Introduction to Its Causes, Incidence, and Impact, 1750–1850* (London: Longman, 1997). Studies that generally support the more critical view of enclosure include J. M. Neeson, *Commoners: Common Right, Enclosure, and Social Change in England, 1700–1820* (Cambridge: Cambridge University Press, 1993); Robert C. Allen, *Enclosure and the Yeoman* (London: Clarendon, 1992).

17. E. P. Thompson, *The Making of the English Working Class* (New York: Vintage, 1963), 219.

18. Allan Kulikoff, *From British Peasants to Colonial American Farmers* (Chapel Hill: University of North Carolina Press, 2000), 131. See also Kulikoff, "The Transition to Capitalism in Rural America," *William and Mary Quarterly*, 3d ser., 46 (January 1989), 120–44.

19. See, for instance, Timothy J. Shannon, "The Ohio Company and the Meaning of Opportunity in the American West, 1786–1795," *New England Quarterly*, 64 (September 1991), 393–413.

20. Nathaniel Sheidley, "Unruly Men: Indians, Settlers, and the Ethos of Frontier Patriarchy in the Upper Tennessee Watershed, 1763–1815" (Ph.D. dissertation, Princeton University, 1999).

21. John Mack Faragher, *Sugar Creek: Life on the Illinois Prairie* (New Haven: Yale University Press, 1986); Paul W. Gates, *Landlords and Tenants on the Prairie Frontier: Studies in American Land Policy* (Ithaca, N.Y.: Cornell University Press, 1973), 3.

22. See Ellen Liebman, *California Farmland: A History of Large Agricultural Landholdings* (Totowa, N.J.: Rowman and Allanheld, 1983), 30.

23. Paul W. Gates, "Public Land Disposal in California," *Agricultural History*, 49 (January 1975), 158–78.

24. For Indians' hunting and gathering areas as "commons," see Louis Warren, *The Hunter's Game: Poachers and Conservationists in Twentieth-Century America* (New Haven: Yale University Press, 1997); Stephen Aron, "Pigs and Hunters: 'Rights in the Woods' on the Trans-Appalachian Frontier," in Andrew R. L. Cayton and Frederike Teute, eds., *Contact Points: American Frontiers from the Mohawk Valley to the Mississippi, 1750–1830* (Chapel Hill: University of North Carolina Press, 1998), 175–204.

25. Gregory A. Reed, in *An Historical Geography Analysis of the Modoc Indian War* (Chico, Calif.: ANCRR, 1991), treated the war as largely a result of changes to the land, but he did not consider the Modocs' adaptations to the Euroamerican economy.

26. William M. Turner, "Scraps of Modoc History," *Overland Monthly*, 11 (July 1873), 21.

27. Stan Turner, *The Years of Harvest: A History of the Tule Lake Basin*, 3d ed. (Eugene, Ore.: Spencer Creek Press, 2002), 17–21.

28. Crane S. Miller and Richard S. Hyslop, *California: The Geography of Diversity* (Mountain View, Calif.: Mayfield, 1983), 41–44; Allan A. Schoenherr, *A Natural History of California* (Berkeley: University of California Press, 1992), 11.

29. S. Turner, *Years of Harvest*, 35.

30. Carrol B. Howe, *Ancient Modocs of California and Oregon* (Portland, Ore.: Binford and Mort, 1979), 6.

31. Robert W. Pease, *Modoc County: A Geographic Time Continuum on the California Volcanic Tableland* (Berkeley: University of California Press, 1965), 38–42; Reed, *Historical Geography Analysis*, 20.

32. Schoenherr, *Natural History of California*, 11.

33. Howe, *Ancient Modocs*, 102.

34. For native uses of nettles, see Richard White, *Land Use, Environment, and Social Change: The Shaping of Island County, Washington* (Seattle: University of Washington Press, 1980), 20.

35. For native fishing in California, see Arthur F. McEvoy, *The Fisherman's Problem: Ecology and Law in the California Fisheries, 1850–1980* (New York: Cambridge University Press, 1986), 19–62. For Modoc subsistence, see A. L. Kroeber, *Handbook of the Indians of California* (New York: Dover, 1976), 318–35.

36. W. Turner, "Scraps of Modoc History," 21–25; Verne F. Ray, *Primitive Pragmatists: The Modoc Indians of Northern California* (Seattle: University of Washington Press, 1963), 180–82; Stephen Powers, *Tribes of California* (1877; Berkeley: University of California Press, 1976), 255–56; K. Murray, *Modocs and Their War*, 9–11.

37. For the diffusion of horses northward from New Mexico and its ecological, economic, and social consequences, see Andrew C. Isenberg, *The Destruction of the Bison: An Environmental History, 1750–1920* (New York: Cambridge University Press, 2000), 39–46.

38. See W. Raymond Wood, "Plains Trade in Prehistoric and Protohistoric Intertribal Relations," in W. Raymond Wood and Margot Liberty, eds., *Anthropology on the Great Plains* (Lincoln: University of Nebraska Press, 1980), 99–102; Joseph E. Taylor III, *Making Salmon: An Environmental History of the Northwest Fisheries Crisis* (Seattle: University of Washington Press, 1999), 24–26.

39. Schoenherr, *Natural History of California*, 50–51.

40. Reed, *Historical Geography Analysis*, 31–32.

41. K. Murray, *Modocs and Their War*, 12–13.

42. For a recent study of Indian slavery in the Southwest, see James F. Brooks, *Captives and Cousins: Slavery, Kinship, and Community in the Southwest Borderlands* (Chapel Hill: University of North Carolina Press, 2002).

43. Meacham, *Tragedy of the Lava-Beds*, 8.

44. See Peter Boag, *Environment and Experience: Settlement Culture in Nineteenth-Century Oregon* (Berkeley: University of California Press, 1992); Dean May, *Three Frontiers: Family, Land, and Society in the American West, 1850–1900* (New York: Cambridge University Press, 1994).

45. K. Murray, *Modocs and Their War*, 17–18. For the effect of epidemics on Indians, see Alfred W. Crosby, Jr., "Virgin Soil Epidemics as a Factor in the Aboriginal Depopulation of America," *William and Mary Quarterly*, 33 (April 1976), 289–99.

46. Powers, *Tribes of California*, 254.

47. See *Kit Carson's Autobiography*, ed. Milo Quaife (Lincoln: University of Nebraska Press, 1966), 77–78, 94–105.

48. W. N. Davis, Jr., "Sagebrush Corner: The Opening of California's Northeast," in *California Indians*, vol. 5 (New York: Garland, 1974), 68.

49. For a comparative example, consider the effects of emigrants along the Platte and Santa Fe trails on the bison's habitat. See Elliott West, *The Way to the West: Essays on the Central Plains* (Albuquerque: University of New Mexico Press, 1995), 72–78.

50. J. H. Holeman to L. Lea, June 28, 1852, quoted in Knack, "A Short Resource History," 49.

51. James Beith Letterbook, July 10, 1858, BAN.

52. Joel Palmer, quoted in "Statements of Inhabitants of Southern Oregon and Northern California in Regard to the Character and Conduct of the Modoc Indians, also a Statement of Gen'l Joel Palmer to the Same Subject While He Was Superintendent of Indian Affairs of Oregon" (1857), 2, BAN.

53. *Report of Governor Grover to General Schofield on the Modoc War* (Salem, Ore.: Mart V. Brown, 1874), 4.

54. John D. Unruh, *The Plains Across: The Overland Emigrants and the Trans-Mississippi West, 1840–60* (Urbana: University of Illinois Press, 1979), 144.

55. Elisha Steele, quoted in "Statements of Inhabitants of Southern Oregon and Northern California," 20.

56. W. S. Kirshaw, quoted in "Statements of Inhabitants of Southern Oregon and Northern California," 47–51; K. Murray, *Modocs and Their War*, 26–27.

57. Theodora Kroeber, *Ishi in Two Worlds: A Biography of the Last Wild Indian in North America* (Berkeley: University of California Press, 1961), 46; Sherburne Cook, *The Conflict Between the California Indian and White Civilization* (Berkeley: University of California Press, 1976).

58. John Thompson Kincade to James Kincade, March 13, 1864, Kincade Correspondence, HUN.

59. Giles French, *Cattle Country of Peter French* (Portland, Ore.: Binford and Mort, 1972), 41.

60. W. Davis, "Sagebrush Corner," 200.

61. Pease, *Modoc County*, 80.

62. "Surprise Valley," *Sacramento Daily Union*, July 14, 1864.

63. Titus Fey Cronise, *The Natural Wealth of California* (San Francisco: H. H. Bancroft, 1868), 211.

64. Inter-University Consortium for Political and Social Research, *Study 00003: Historical Demographic, Economic, and Social Data*, U.S., 1790–1970 (Ann Arbor, Mich.: ICPSR).

65. Simpson, "Modoc Region," 295–96.

66. Stephen Powers, "A Pony Ride on Pit River," *Overland Monthly*, 13 (October 1874), 344–46; W. Davis, "Sagebrush Corner," 313–16.

67. Hazel Adele Pulling, "A History of California's Range-Cattle Industry, 1770–1912" (Ph.D. dissertation, University of Southern California, 1944), 125.

68. W. Davis, "Sagebrush Corner," 303–4.

69. Powers, "Pony Ride," 347.

70. Thomas P. Vale, "Forest Changes in the Warner Mountains, California," *Annals of the Association of American Geographers*, 67 (March 1977), 28–45.

71. P. A. Heartstrand et al., "Petition of the Citizens of Siskiyou County, in Relation to the Game Laws of California," *Appendix to the Journals of the Senate and Assembly of the Twenty-second Session of the Legislature of the State of California*, vol. 4 (Sacramento: F. P. Thompson, 1878).

72. Albert L. Hurtado, *Intimate Frontiers: Sex, Gender, and Culture in Old California* (Albuquerque: University of New Mexico Press, 1999), 75–81.

73. *Alturas Modoc Independent*, December 25, 1875, cited in W. Davis, "Sagebrush Corner," 414.

74. Simpson, "Modoc Region," 295–96.

75. Albert L. Hurtado, *Indian Survival on the California Frontier* (New Haven: Yale University Press, 1988), 169–92.

76. K. Murray, *Modocs and Their War*, 36–37.

77. Meacham, *Tragedy of the Lava-Beds*. For the text of the treaty, see Charles Kappler, ed., *Indian Affairs: Laws and Treaties*, vol. 2 (Washington, D.C.: Government Printing Office, 1904), 865–68.

78. E. Steele and A. M. Rosborough to Commanding Officer at Fort Klamath, August 28, 1865, in Olaf Theodore Hagen, *Modoc War: Official Correspondence and Documents, 1865–1878* (San Francisco, 1942), 1–2, BAN.

79. A. M. Rosborough, April 4, 1868, in Hagen, *Modoc War*, 5.

80. See Isenberg, *Destruction of the Bison*, 123–30.

81. Kappler, *Indian Affairs*, vol. 2, 866–67.

82. Jeff C. Riddle, *The Indian History of the Modoc War, and the Causes That Led to It* (San Francisco: Marnell and Company, 1914), 34–38. See also E. W. Pollack to O. C. Applegate, May 24, 1870; John Meacham to Alfred B. Meacham, August 21, 1871; R. S. Canby to Assistant Adjutant General, Military Division of the Pacific, February 2, 1872, in Hagen, *Modoc War*, 20–21, 46–47.

83. Simpson, "Modoc Region," 292.

84. Maj. C. G. Huntt, July 29, 1871, in Hagen, *Modoc War*, 43–44.

85. J.E.P. to the *Oregonian* Editor, February 22, 1872, in Hagen, *Modoc War*, 100.

86. K. Murray, *Modocs and Their War*, 58.

87. Ivan D. Applegate to Thomas B. Odeneal, May 8, 1872, in Hagen, *Modoc War*, 141.

88. Thomas Odeneal, *The Modoc War: Statement of Its Origins and Causes* (Portland, Ore.: Bulletin Printing Office, 1873), 9.

89. Henry Miller, April 3, 1872, in Hagen, *Modoc War*, 115, 125. One of Miller's neighbors contradicted this account, claiming that Miller abandoned his ranch between July 1870 and February 1871 because of fear of the Indians. Miller would seem to have little reason to misrepresent himself before the Indian agents, however. By all accounts, including that of Hooker Jim, the Modocs liked and trusted Miller. Jim accidentally shot and killed Miller in November 1872, during the opening violence of the Modoc War. Jim claimed that he did not recognize Miller until too late.

90. Mr. Ball, Joseph Seeds, in Hagen, *Modoc War*, 117–19.

91. Meacham, *Tragedy of the Lava-Beds*, 24; Meacham, *Wi-ne-ma*, 44. See also William Murray, "The Modoc Campaign" (1873), 6, HUN. For Canby, see K. Murray, *Modocs and Their War*, 60.

92. Meacham, *Wi-ne-ma*, 55–56.

93. Powers, *Tribes of California*, 263.

94. "Indian Treachery," *Alta California*, April 14, 1873; "Retribution. Latest from the Lava Beds. Gen Gillem in Pursuit of the Assassins. His Purpose Extermination," ibid., April 14, 1873; "Resources of the Modocs," ibid., April 16, 1873; "The Modoc War," ibid., April 19, 1873.

95. Gillem to Mason, April 16, 1873; "Dispatches sent by signal between Gen. Gillem's camp and Col. Mason's camp during the Modoc Indian War, Apr. 6–May 8, 1873, near Tule Lake, Calif.," Fort Dalles Papers, HUN.

96. W. Murray, "Modoc Campaign." See also Meacham, *Wi-ne-ma*, 84–85.

97. Canby had made the original decision to recruit the Warm Springs auxiliaries from their reservation in Oregon in March, but they did not arrive in California until Gillem had assumed temporary command. See K. Murray, *Modocs and Their War*, 198–200; Meacham, *Wi-ne-ma*, 52.

98. W. Murray, "Modoc Campaign."

99. "The Modocs," *Alta California*, April 22, 1873.

100. Adams to Mason, April 26, 1873; Mason to Adams, April 27, 1873; "Dispatches sent," Fort Dalles Papers, HUN.

101. "The Modocs–A Blundering War," *Sacramento Daily Union*, May 12, 1873.

102. Elisha Steele, William H. Morgan, John A. Fairchild, and H. Wallace Atwell to Columbus Delano, July 30, 1873, in Francis S. Landrum, ed., *Guardhouse, Gallows, and Graves: The Trial and Execution of Indian Prisoners of the Modoc Indian War by the U.S. Army* (Klamath Falls, Ore.: Klamath County Museum, 1988), 56–57.

103. K. Murray, *Modocs and Their War*, 259–63.

104. For agricultural census data, see Inter-University Consortium for Political and Social Research, *Study 00003: Historical Demographic, Economic, and Social Data*, U.S., 1790–1970 (Ann Arbor, Mich.: ICPSR).

105. Dillon, *Burnt-Out Fires*, 339–40.

106. Albert Britt, *Great Indian Chiefs: A Study of Indian Leaders in the Two Hundred Year Struggle to Stop the White Advance* (New York: McGraw-Hill, 1938), 247–48.

107. Odeneal, *Modoc War*, 9–10.

108. L. B. Applegate to Newton Booth, January 2, 1873, Military Department, Adjutant General, Indian War Papers, CSA.

Epilogue: Economic Development and the California Environment

1. Settlers' Ditch Company Records, CSL; *History of Tulare County, California* (San Francisco: Wallace W. Elliott, 1883), 108–10; Eugene L. Menefee and Fred A. Dodge, *History of Tulare and Kings Counties* (Los Angeles: Historic Record Company, 1913), 192. After the California legislature passed the Wright Act in 1887, which allowed localities to establish irrigation districts and levy taxes for their operation, the Settlers' Ditch Company sold its Cross Creek water rights to the Tulare Irrigation District and purchased a share of the larger People's Ditch Company, which drew water from the Kings River. The People's Ditch Company had been established in 1873 with a capital stock of $10,000. That amount was gradually increased to $100,000 to cover rising construction costs.

2. Donald J. Pisani, *From Family Farm to Agribusiness: The Irrigation Crusade in California and the West, 1850–1931* (Berkeley: University of California Press, 1984), 9; Rodman Paul, *The Far West and Great Plains in Transition, 1859–1900* (New York: Harper and Row, 1988), 227.

3. Frederick Jackson Turner, "The Significance of the Frontier in American History," *American Historical Association Annual Report* (1893), 199–227.

4. Donald Worster, "Hydraulic Society in California: An Ecological Interpretation," *Agricultural History*, 56 (July 1982), 503–15.

5. See Gray Brechin, *Imperial San Francisco: Urban Power, Earthly Ruin* (Berkeley: University of California Press, 1999), 71–84.

6. J. McChesney, President, Tuolumne County Water Company, "$1,000 Reward!," July 13, 1857, Huntington Manuscript, HUN; "Tuolumne County Water Company," *Daily California Express*, October 24, 1860; "Flume Blown Up," ibid., December 6, 1860.

7. See Gary Kulik, "Dams, Fish, and Farmers: Defense of Public Rights in Eighteenth-Century Rhode Island," in Steven Hahn and Jonathan Prude, eds., *The Countryside in the Age of Capitalist Transformation: Essays in the Social History of Rural America* (Chapel Hill: University of North Carolina Press, 1985), 25–50.

8. Robert L. Kelley, *Gold vs. Grain: The Hydraulic Mining Controversy in California's Sacramento Valley* (Glendale, Calif.: Arthur H. Clark, 1959), 116.

9. Richard J. Orsi, "*The Octopus* Reconsidered: The Southern Pacific and Agricultural Modernization in California, 1865–1915," *California Historical Quarterly*, 54 (Fall 1975), 200–2.

10. Hamilton Smith, Jr., Chairman, Temporary Organization, July 1876, Milton Mining and Water Company Records, CSL.

11. Thomas Bell et al., *The Mining Debris Question: A Statement by the Miners' Association* (San Francisco, August 1, 1881), 6.

12. George A. Blanchard and Edward P. Weeks, *The Law of Mines, Minerals, and Mining Water Rights* (San Francisco: Sumner Whitney, 1877), 627–31; M. Catherine Miller, *Flooding the Courtrooms: Law and Water in the Far West* (Lincoln: University of Nebraska Press, 1993), 6.

13. *The Bear River and Auburn Water and Mining Company* v. *The New York Mining Company*, 8 California 327 (1857).

14. Ibid.

15. Lester L. Robinson and James O'Brien, "Testimony Taken by the Committee on Mining Debris, as Reported to the Assembly," *Appendix to the Journals of the Senate and Assembly of the Twenty-second Session of the Legislature of the State of California*, vol. 4 (Sacramento: F. P. Thompson, 1878), 16–20.

16. "Majority Report of the Committee on Mining Debris," *Appendix to the Journals of the Senate and Assembly of the Twenty-second Session*, vol. 4, 4.

17. Ibid., 3–5.

18. Kelley, *Gold vs. Grain*, 106.

19. "Industrial Condition of the Slope," *Alta California*, April 1, 1878.

20. *Edwards Woodruff* v. *North Bloomfield Gravel Mining Company*, 18 F9 753 (1884).

21. *James H. Keyes* v. *Little York Gold Washing and Water Company* (Sacramento: H. S. Crocker, 1879).

22. Kelley, *Gold vs. Grain*, 121.

23. Taliesin Evans, "Hydraulic Mining in California," *Century Magazine*, 25 (January 1883), 336.

24. Woodruff's investments from 1851 to 1878 are detailed in the Decker-Jewett Bank Papers, CSL.

25. Lorenzo Sawyer, *Way Sketches* (New York: Edward Beerstadt, 1926), 114, 122–23.

26. A. Smith Hayes, "The 'Mammoth Trees' of Calaveras" (San Andreas, 1857), Huntington Manuscript, HUN.

27. *Redwood and Lumbering in California Forests* (San Francisco: Edgar Cherry, 1884), 34.

28. George Douglas, "History of the Pacific Lumber Company," as told to Derby Bendorf, BAN.

29. Minute Records, California State Board of Forestry, December 1, 1885; May 22, 1886; July 1, 1887; July 18, 1887; July 19, 1887; July 20, 1887; July 21, 1887, CSA.

30. *S. S. Turner and H.G. Platt* v. *The Tuolumne County Water Company*, 25 California 397 (1864).

31. *John Wixon* v. *The Bear River and Auburn Water and Mining Company*, 24 California 367 (1864).

32. *George Courtwright* v. *The Bear River and Auburn Water and Mining Company*, 30 California 573 (1866).

33. *Lester L. Robinson and William T. Coleman* v. *The Black Diamond Coal Company*, 50 California 460 (1875).

34. *Woodruff* v. *North Bloomfield*.

35. Kelley, *Gold vs. Grain*, 229–40.

36. Clark C. Spence, "The Golden Age of Dredging: The Development of an Industry and Its Environmental Impact," *Western Historical Quarterly* (October 1980), 401–14.

37. "Memorial of Miners and Farmers at San Francisco, California, January 21, 1892, Praying such Legislation as Will Promote the Construction of Dams to Protect the Navigable Waters of Said State from Mining Debris," Huntington Manuscript, HUN.

38. F. H. Newell, *Report on Agriculture by Irrigation* (Washington, D.C.: Government Printing Office, 1894), 35.

39. Thomas Price and William Ashburner, "Prospectus of the Excelsior Water and Mining Company" (1878); and Louis Janin, *Report on the Excelsior Water and Mining Company, Smartsville, California* (San Francisco, 1879), 9, HUN.

40. See Brechin, *Imperial San Francisco,* 92–98.

Bibliography

MANUSCRIPT COLLECTIONS

Bancroft Library, Berkeley, California (BAN)
Allen, Benjamin, "Notes on the Pacific Lumber Company and Lumbering in Humboldt County"
Anthony, E. M., Reminiscences
Bandini, Juan, "Last Will and Testament of Juan Bandini"
Beith, James, Letterbook
Branham, Isaac, Reminiscences
Brown, Charles, Recollections
Buhne, Hans Henry, Papers
Carpenter Family Papers
Dolbeer and Carson Lumber Company Records
Flanigan, D. J., "California Lumber" (c. 1890)
Ford, Jerome, Diary
Joy, T. B., and Company Records
Morrill, J. C., and Company Business Records
Pacific Lumber Company Records
Slade, Irving T., Letters
Stanwood, Richard Goss, Journals and Letters
Taplin, G. C., Diary
Wilde, W. H., "Chronology of the Pacific Lumber Company, 1869–1945"

California State Archives, Sacramento (CSA)
Hall, William Hammond, Papers
Military Department, Adjutant General, Indian War Papers
Minute Records, California State Board of Forestry, 1885–92

California State Library, Sacramento (CSL)
Bidwell, John, Collection
Catlin, Amos P., Papers

Chaffee, Joseph B., Collection
Decker-Jewett Bank Papers
Gallup, Josiah, Collection
Gibson, John C., Collection
Lanchlin McLaine Bank Collection
Milton Mining and Water Company Records
National Bank of D.O. Mills and Company Records
Natoma Company Collection
New Almaden Mines Collection
New Idria Mining Company Records
Parker, Henry A., Letters
Perkins, Isaac, Correspondence
Pioneer Manuscript Collection
Settlers' Ditch Company Records
Sutter, John A., Collection

Huntington Library, San Marino, California (HUN)
Bishop, Francis Augustus, Papers
Bixby, Augustus Simon, Diary
Blanchard, Nathan, Journal
Catlin, Amos Parmalee, Papers
Couts, Cave Johnson, Collection
Crosby, Elisha Oscar, Memoirs
Eagle, John H., Correspondence
Fort Dalles Papers
Hague Collection
Kincade, John Thompson, Correspondence
Lord, Israel, Journal
Murray, William, Manuscript
New Almaden Mine Collection
Nichols, Samuel, Collection
Osborne, Sullivan, Diary
Owen, Isaac, Diary
Pownall, Joseph, Collection
Stearns, Abel, Collection
Stone, Andrew J., Correspondence
Wilson, Benjamin Davis, Collection

Sacramento City Archives (SAC)
City Council Minutes, 1849–67

GOVERNMENT DOCUMENTS

"Biennial Message of Governor William Irwin." *Appendix to the Journals of the Senate and Assembly of the Twenty-third Session of the Legislature of the State of California*, vol. 5. Sacramento: F. P. Thompson, 1880.

"California Detritus Question." House Report No. 760, 46th Cong., 2d Sess., 1880.

Devlin, Robert A., ed. *Statutes of the State of California Relating to the City of Sacramento.* Sacramento: Valley Press, 1881.

"Fourth Biennial Report of the State Board of Health of California, for the Years 1876 and 1877." *Appendix to the Journals of the Senate and Assembly of the Twenty-second Session of the Legislature of the State of California*, vol. 3. Sacramento: F. P. Thompson, 1878.

Grover, Lafayette. *Report of Governor Grover to General Schofield on the Modoc War.* Salem: Mart V. Brown, 1874

Hall, William Hammond. *Report of the State Engineer, Part III: The Flow of the Mining Detritus.* Sacramento: J.D. Young, 1880.

Heartstrand, P. A., et al. "Petition of the Citizens of Siskiyou County, in Relation to the Game Laws of California." *Appendix to the Journals of the Senate and Assembly of the Twenty-second Session of the Legislature of the State of California*, vol. 4. Sacramento: F. P. Thompson, 1878.

"Majority Report of the Committee on Mining Debris." *Appendix to the Journals of the Senate and Assembly of the Twenty-second Session of the Legislature of the State of California*, vol. 4. Sacramento: F. P. Thompson, 1878.

Mendell, G. H. "Report Upon a Project to Protect the Navigable Waters of California from the Effects of Hydraulic Mining." H.ex.doc. 98, 47th Cong., 1st Sess., 1882.

"Mining Debris, California." H.ex.doc. 267, 51st Cong., 2d Sess., 1891.

"Minority Report of the Committee on Mining Debris." *Appendix to the Journals of the Senate and Assembly of the Twenty-second Session of the Legislature of the State of California*, vol. 4. Sacramento: F. P. Thompson, 1878.

"Proceedings of a Military Commission Convened at Fort Klamath, Oregon, for the Trial of Modoc Prisoners" (July 1878). H.ex.doc. 122, 43d Cong., 1st Sess., 1874, 136–77.

Ramsey, Alexander. "To Prevent Injury to the Navigable Waters of California." Letter from the Secretary of War. H. ex.doc. 76, 46th Cong., 3d Sess., 1881.

Raymond, Rossiter. "Mineral Resources of the States and Territories West of the Rocky Mountains." H.ex.doc. 54, 40th Cong., 1st Sess., 1869.

———. "Statistics of Mines and Mining in the States and Territories West of the Rocky Mountains." H.ex.doc. 10, 42d Cong., 1st Sess., 1872.

———. *Statistics of Mines and Mining in the States and Territories West of the Rocky Mountains.* Washington, D.C.: Government Printing Office, 1874.

Redding, Benjamin B., Samuel R. Throckmorton, and J. D. Farwell. *Report of the Commissioners of Fisheries of the State of California for the Year 1880.* Sacramento: F. P. Thompson, 1880.

"Report of the Commissioners of Fisheries of the State of California, 1870 and 1871." *Appendix to the Journals of the Senate and Assembly of the Nineteenth Session of the Legislature of the State of California*, vol. 2. Sacramento: T. A. Springer, 1872.

"Report of the Commissioners of Fisheries of the State of California for the Years 1876 and 1877."

Appendix to the Journals of the Senate and Assembly of the Twenty-second Session of the Legislature of the State of California, vol. 3. Sacramento: F. P. Thompson, 1878.

"Report of the State Engineer." *Appendix to the Journals of the Senate and Assembly of the Twenty-third Session of the Legislature of the State of California*, vol. 5. Sacramento: F. P. Thompson, 1880.

"Second Biennial Report of the State Board of Health of California, for the Years 1871, 1872, and 1873. "*Appendix to the Journals of the Senate and Assembly of the Twentieth Session of the Legislature of the State of California*, vol. 5. Sacramento: G. H. Springer, 1874.

"Testimony Taken by the Committee on Mining Debris, as Reported to the Assembly." *Appendix to the Journals of the Senate and Assembly of the Twenty-second Session of the Legislature of the State of California*, vol. 4. Sacramento: F. P. Thompson, 1878.

"Third Biennial Report of the State Board of Health of California, for the Years 1874 and 1875." *Appendix to the Journals of the Senate and Assembly of the Twenty-first Session of the Legislature of the State of California*, vol. 3. Sacramento: G. H. Springer, 1875.

Thompson, R. W. "Sand Bars and Deposits Near Mare Island." Letter from the Secretary of the Navy. H.ex.doc. 31, 46th Cong., 2d Sess., 1880.

"Transactions of the Agricultural Society of the State of California, 1859." *Appendix to the Journals of the Senate and Assembly of the Eleventh Session of the Legislature of the State of California.* Sacramento: C. T. Botts, 1860.

"Transactions of the California State Agricultural Society, 1863" *Appendix to the Journals of the Senate and Assembly of the Fifteenth Session of the Legislature of the State of California*, vol. 2. Sacramento: O. M. Clayes, 1864.

"Transactions of the California State Agricultural Society, 1870 and 1871." *Appendix to the Journals of the Senate and Assembly of the Nineteenth Session of the Legislature of the State of California*, vol. 3. Sacramento: T. A. Springer, 1872.

United States Census Office. *Agriculture of the United States in 1860.* Washington, D.C.: Government Printing Office, 1864.

————. *Census of the City and County of Los Angeles, California, for the Year 1850.* Los Angeles: Times-Mirror Press, 1929.

————. *The Statistics of Wealth and Industry of the United States, Ninth Census*, vol. 3. Washington, D.C.: Government Printing Office, 1872.

COURT DECISIONS

Bear River and Auburn Water and Mining Company v. *New York Mining Company*, 8 California 327 (1857).

Courtwright v. *Bear River and Auburn Water and Mining Company*, 30 California 460 (1866).

Hoffman, et al. v. *Tuolumne County Water Company*, 10 California 413 (1858).

Irwin v. *Phillips*, 5 California 140 (1855).

Keyes v. *Little York Gold Washing Company* (1879).

Parsons v. *Tuolumne County Water Company*, 5 California 43 (1855).

Robinson v. *Black Diamond Coal Company*, 50 California 460 (1875).

Tartar v. *Spring Creek Water and Mining Company*, 5 California 399 (1855).

Turner and Platt v. *Tuolumne County Water Company*, 25 California 397 (1864).
Wixon v. *Bear River and Auburn Water and Mining Company*, 1224 California 367 (1864).
Wolf et al. v. *St. Louis Independent Water Company*, 10 California 541 (1858).
Woodruff v. *North Bloomfield Gravel Mining Company*, 18 F9 753 (1884).

NEWSPAPERS

Alta California (San Francisco), 1850–52, 1873–78
California Daily Express (Marysville), 1858
Daily California Express (Marysville), 1860
Humboldt Times (Eureka), 1858–62, 1868–70, 1878
Los Angeles Star, 1861–64
Marysville Herald, 1853–54, 1857
Pacific Coast Wood and Iron, 1887–96
Placer Herald (Auburn), 1870–75
Sacramento Daily Union, 1854–64, 1873
Western Watchman (Eureka), 1887–88

PUBLISHED PRIMARY SOURCES

"Annual Review of the Mining Interests of California." *Mining Magazine and Journal of Geology*, 2 (April 1861).
"Argument of J. B. Hobson, of California, in Support of the Law to Regulate Hydraulic Mining in the State of California." Washington, D.C.: Judd and Detweiler, 1892.
Ashburner, William. "On the Profession of Mining Engineering." *Bulletin of the University of California*, 5 (November 1874). Berkeley: Students' University Press.
The Bear River Tunnel Company. Boston: Alfred Mudge, 1881.
Bell, Thomas, et al. *The Mining Debris Question: A Statement by the Miners' Association*. San Francisco, 1881.
Black, George. *Report on the Middle Yuba Canal and Eureka Lake Canal, Nevada County, California*. San Francisco: Towne and Bacon, 1864.
Blanchard, George A., and Edward P. Weeks. *The Law of Mines, Minerals, and Mining Water Rights*. San Francisco: Sumner Whitney, 1877.
Bland, T. A. *Life of Alfred B. Meacham*. Washington, D.C.: T. A. and M. C. Bland, 1883.
Bonner, W. G. *The Redwoods of California: A Glimpse at the Wonder-Land of the Golden West*. San Francisco: California Redwood Company, 1884.
Borthwick, J. D. *Three Years in California*. Oakland, Calif.: Biobooks, 1948.
Bowie, Augustus Jesse, Jr. *A Practical Treatise on Hydraulic Mining in California*. New York: Van Nostrand, 1885.
———. *Hydraulic Mining in California*. 1878.
Bowman, Amos. *Report on the Properties and Domain of the California Water Company*. San Francisco: A. L. Bancroft, 1874.

Brace, Charles Loring. *The New West: California in 1867–1868*. New York: Putnam, 1869.

Brown, J. Ross. *Resources of the Pacific Slope*. San Francisco: H. H. Bancroft, 1869.

Brown's Marysville Directory. Marysville, Calif.: *Daily California Express*, 1861.

By-Laws of the California Lumber Exchange. San Francisco, 1884.

Cadwalader, George. *Address of George Cadwalader, Delivered at Sacramento, February 28 and March 1st, 1882, in the Case of the State of California vs. Gold Run Hydraulic Mining Company*. Sacramento: H.S. Crocker, 1882.

————. *Edwards Woodruff* v. *North Bloomfield Gravel Mining Company, et al.* 1882.

————. *James H. Keyes* v. *Little York Gold Washing and Water Company*. Sacramento: H. S. Crocker, 1879.

California Quicksilver. San Francisco, 1890.

Cary, T. G. *Gold from California, and Its Effects on Prices*. New York: George W. Wood, 1856.

Certificate of Incorporation and By-Laws of the Redwood Lumber Association. San Francisco: Women's Union Print, 1871.

Circular, Descriptive of Placer County, California. Auburn, Calif.: Argus, 1875.

Colville, Samuel. *Colville's Marysville Directory*. San Francisco: Monson and Valentine, 1855.

Cornish, Thomas. *Gold: Importance of Its Past and Continued Production to the Civilized World*. San Francisco: *Alta California*, 1881.

Cronise, Titus Fey. *The Natural Wealth of California*. San Francisco: H. H. Bancroft, 1868.

Cummings, George W. *Report on the Davis Ditch and Mining Company*. Oroville, Calif.: Mercury Print, 1879.

DeGroot, Henry. *Report on the Dutton Creek Mines, Brown's Creek Ditch, Etc*. San Francisco: Bacon, 1879.

Eddy, J. M. *In the Redwood's Realm*. San Francisco: D. S. Stanley, 1893.

Facts Concerning the Quicksilver Mines in Santa Clara County, California. New York: R. C. Root, Anthony, 1859.

Feilner, John. "Exploration in Upper California in 1860." In *Annual Report of the Board of Regents of the Smithsonian Institution, 1864*. Washington, D.C.: Government Printing Office.

G. and O. Amy's Marysville Directory. San Francisco: Monson and Valentine, 1856.

Hague, James D. *The Water and Gravel Mining Properties Belonging to the Eureka Lake and Yuba Canal Company*. Investment prospectus. San Francisco, December 22, 1876. In Huntington Library Collection.

Hale & Emory's Marysville City Directory. Marysville, Calif.: *Marysville Herald*, 1853.

Harris, W. C., et al. *Documents and Reports Relating to Sutter Canal and Mining Company, Amador County, California*. 1870.

Hawley, Walter N. *Report of the Citizens' Debris Committee*. San Francisco, 1881.

Hayes, Albert H. *Report on the Red Hill Hydraulic Gold Mines*. Boston: Alfred Mudge, 1882.

Hendel, Charles W. *Report on the Alturas Gold Mine in Slate Creek Basin, Sierra and Plumas Counties, California*. San Francisco: A. L. Bancroft, 1872.

An Historical Sketch of Los Angeles County, California. Los Angeles: Louis Lewin, 1876.

Hittell, John S. *Mining in the Pacific States of North America*. San Francisco: H. H. Bancroft, 1861.

————. *The Resources of California*. 6th ed. San Francisco: A. Roman, 1874; New York: W. J. Widdleton, 1874.

Irvine, Leigh H. *History of Humboldt County, California*. Los Angeles: Historic Record Company, 1915.

Janin, Louis. *Report on the Excelsior Water and Mining Company, Smartsville, California*. San Francisco, May 16, 1879.

Jennings, Hennen. *The Quicksilver Mines of Almaden and New Almaden: A Comparative View of their Extent, Production, Costs of Work, Etc.* 1886.

Kellogg, A. *Forest Trees of California*. Sacramento: J. D. Young, 1882.

Kit Carson's Autobiography, ed. Milo Quaife. Lincoln: University of Nebraska Press, 1966.

Ludlum, T. B. *Report on the Property Belonging to the Cedar Creek Hydraulic Mining Company, Dutch Flat, California*. April 14, 1880.

Meacham, Alfred Benjamin. *The Tragedy of the Lava-Beds*. Hartford, Conn.: privately printed, 1877.

———. *Wi-ne-ma*. Hartford, Conn.: American Publishing Company, 1876.

Morse, John Frederick. *History of Sacramento*. 1853; Sacramento: Sacramento Book Collectors Club, 1945.

Nordhoff, Charles. *California for Health, Pleasure, and Residence: A Book for Travellers and Settlers*. New York: Harper, 1872.

Odeneal, Thomas. *The Modoc War: Statement of Its Origins and Causes*. Portland, Ore.: Bulletin Printing Office, 1873.

Powell, John J. *The Golden State and Its Resources*. San Francisco: Bacon, 1874.

Powers, Stephen. "A Pony Ride on Pit River." *Overland Monthly*, 13 (October 1874).

———. *Tribes of California*. 1877; Berkeley: University of California Press, 1976.

Preamble, Constitution, and By-laws of the California Lumber Exchange. San Francisco: Dutton and Withington, 1881.

Price, Thomas, and William Ashburner. "Prospectus of the Excelsior Water and Mining Company." 1878.

Prospectus of the Cataract and Wide West Hydraulic Gravel Mining Company. San Francisco: Fluto, 1876.

Pumpelly, Raphael. *Report on the Excelsior Mining and Water Power Company, Smartsville, California*. Boston: T. R. Marvin, 1878.

The Quicksilver Mining Company. New York: Sun Job Printing House, 1868.

The Quicksilver Mining Company. New York: Sun Job Printing House, 1869.

The Quicksilver Mining Company. New York: E. S. Dodge, 1871.

The Quicksilver Mining Company. New York: William F. Jones, 1873.

The Quicksilver Mining Company. New York: D. Murphy, 1874.

The Quicksilver Mining Company. New York: D. Murphy, 1875.

The Quicksilver Mining Company Annual Report. New York: D. Murphy, 1876.

The Quicksilver Mining Company Annual Report. New York: D. Murphy, 1877.

Raymond, Rossiter. *Silver and Gold: An Account of the Mining and Metallurgical Industry of the United States*. New York: J. B. Ford, 1873.

Redwood and Lumbering in California Forests. San Francisco: Edgar Cherry, 1884.

Report of James B. Eads, Consulting Engineer. Sacramento: J. D. Young, 1880.

Riddle, Jeff C. *The Indian History of the Modoc War, and the Causes That Led to It*. San Francisco: Marnell and Company, 1914.

Sacramento Illustrated. San Francisco: Barker and Barker, 1855.

Sierra Lumber Company Prospectus. San Francisco: A. J. Leary, 1882.

Silliman, B., and George D. MacLean. *Reports on the Blue Tent Consolidated Hydraulic Gold Mines of California, Limited*. London: D. P. Croke, 1873.

Simpson, William. "The Modoc Region, California." *National Geographic*, 19 (1874–75).

Smith, Hamilton, Jr. *An Account of the Operations of the North Bloomfield Gravel Mining Company*. San Francisco, January 25, 1875. In Bancroft Library collection.

——. *North Bloomfield Gravel Mining Company Report* (October 1871).

Spencer, F. E. *A Mining Accident at New Almaden, California*. San Francisco, 1888.

Stockton City Directory. Stockton, Calif.: C. M. Hopkins, 1870.

Stockton City Directory and Emigrants' Guide to the Southern Mines. Stockton, Calif.: San Joaquin Republican, 1852.

Stockton City Directory for the Year 1856. San Francisco: Harris, Joseph, 1856.

Stretch, R. H. *Report on the Cherokee Flat Blue Gravel and Spring Valley Mining and Irrigating Company's Property*. New York: Mining Record Press, 1879.

——. "Synopsis of Report on the Cherokee Flat Blue Gravel and Spring Valley Mining Claims Located at Cherokee, Butte County, California," to Messrs. Waldeyer and Geisse. New York, November 7, 1879.

Stretch, R. H., Charles Waldeyer, and Hamilton Smith, Jr. *Reports on the Spring Valley Hydraulic Gold Company, Comprising the Cherokee Flat Blue Gravel and Spring Valley Mining and Irrigating Company's Property*. New York: John J. Caulon, 1879.

Thompson, Thomas H., and Albert Augustus West. *History of Sacramento County, California*. Oakland: Thompson and West, 1880.

Tucker, E. E., George A. Atherton, and Marsden Manson. *Report on a Plan of Sewerage for the City of Stockton, California*. *Stockton Daily Independent*, 1888.

Turner, William M. "Scraps of Modoc History." *Overland Monthly*, 11 (July 1873).

von Geldern, Otto. *An Analysis of the Problem of the Proposed Rehabilitation of Hydraulic Mining in California*. Sutter County, Calif.: January 3, 1928.

Weed, Joseph. *A View of California As It Is*. San Francisco: Bynon and Wright, 1874.

Wells, William V. "The Quicksilver Mines of New Almaden, California." *Harper's New Monthly Magazine*, 27 (June 1863).

Werth, John J. *A Dissertation on the Resources and Policy of California: Mineral, Agricultural, and Commercial*. Benicia, Calif.: St. Clair and Pinkerton, 1851.

Williams, A. L. *Description of the Property of the Yuba Hydraulic Gold Mining Company*. Cincinnati: Moore, Wilstack, and Baldwin, 1867.

Willis, William L. *History of Sacramento County, California*. Los Angeles: Historic Record Company, 1913.

Wood, W.M.R. "California: Its Mining and Industrial Resources." 1864.

The Yuba Levee. San Francisco, 1877.

SECONDARY LITERATURE

Allen, R. H. "The Spanish Land Grant System as an Influence in the Agricultural Development of California." *Agricultural History*, 9 (July 1935), 127–42.

Almaguer, Tomás. *Racial Fault Lines: The Historical Origins of White Supremacy in California*. Berkeley: University of California Press, 1994.

Anderson, Gary C. *Kinsmen of Another Kind: Dakota-White Relations in the Upper Mississippi Valley, 1650–1862*. Lincoln: University of Nebraska Press, 1984.

Bakker, Elna. *An Island Called California: An Ecological Introduction to Its Natural Communities*. 2d ed. Berkeley: University of California Press, 1984.

Bancroft, Hubert Howe. *California Pastoral, 1769–1848*. San Francisco: A. L. Bancroft, 1888.

Blodgett, Peter J. *Land of Golden Dreams: California in the Gold Rush Decade, 1848–1858*. San Marino, Calif.: Huntington Library, 1999.

Boag, Peter. *Environment and Experience: Settlement Culture in Nineteenth-Century Oregon*. Berkeley: University of California Press, 1992.

Brading, David A. *Haciendas and Ranchos in the Mexican Bajío: León, 1700–1860*. Cambridge: Cambridge University Press, 1978.

———. *Miners and Merchants in Bourbon Mexico, 1763–1810*. Cambridge: Cambridge University Press, 1971.

Brechin, Gray. *Imperial San Francisco: Urban Power, Earthly Ruin*. Berkeley: University of California Press, 1999.

Brooks, James F. *Captives and Cousins: Slavery, Kinship, and Community in the Southwest Borderlands*. Chapel Hill: University of North Carolina Press, 2002.

Bunting, Robert. *The Pacific Raincoast: Environment and Culture in an American Eden, 1778–1900*. Lawrence: University Press of Kansas, 1997.

Burcham, L. T. "Cattle and Range Forage in California: 1770–1880." *Agricultural History*, 35 (July 1961), 140–49.

Camarillo, Albert. *Chicanos in a Changing Society: From Mexican Pueblos to American Barrios in Santa Barbara and Southern California, 1848–1930*. Cambridge, Mass.: Harvard University Press, 1979.

Carstensen, Fred, and Diane Roazen. "Foreign Markets, Domestic Initiatives, and the Emergence of a Monocrop Economy: The Yucatecan Experience, 1825–1903." *Hispanic American Historical Review*, 72 (November 1992), 555–92.

Chen, Yong. "The Internal Origins of Chinese Emigration to the United States Reconsidered." *Western Historical Quarterly*, 28 (1997), 521–46.

Chiu, Ping. *Chinese Labor in California, 1850–1880: An Economic Study*. Madison: Historical Society of Wisconsin, 1967.

Cleland, Robert Glass. *The Cattle on a Thousand Hills: Southern California, 1850–1880*. 2d ed. San Marino, Calif.: Huntington Library, 1951.

Cole, David N., and Peter B. Landres. "Threats to Wilderness Ecosystems: Impacts and Research Needs." *Ecological Applications*, 6 (February 1996), 168–84.

Cook, Sherburne. *The Conflict Between the California Indian and White Civilization*. Berkeley: University of California Press, 1976.

Cornford, Daniel. *Workers and Dissent in the Redwood Empire*. Philadelphia: Temple University Press, 1987.

Cox, Thomas. *Mills and Markets: A History of the Pacific Coast Lumber Industry to 1900*. Seattle: University of Washington Press, 1974.

Cronon, William. *Nature's Metropolis: Chicago and the Great West*. New York: Norton, 1991.

Crosby, Alfred W. *Ecological Imperialism: The Biological Expansion of Europe, 900–1900*. New York: Cambridge University Press, 1986.

Cross, Ira B. *Financing an Empire: History of Banking in California*. 2 vols. Chicago: S. J. Clarke, 1927.

Dasmann, Raymond F. *California's Changing Environment*. San Francisco: Boyd and Fraser, 1981.

Davis, Mike. *Ecology of Fear: Los Angeles and the Imagination of Disaster*. New York: Vintage, 1998.

Davis, W. N., Jr. "Sagebrush Corner: The Opening of California's Northeast." In *California Indians*, vol. 5. New York: Garland, 1974.

Eifler, Mark A. *Gold Rush Capitalists: Greed and Growth in Sacramento*. Albuquerque: University of New Mexico Press, 2002.

Engerman, Stanley L., and Robert E. Gallman, eds. *The Cambridge Economic History of the United States*, vol. 2, *The Long Nineteenth Century*. New York: Cambridge University Press, 2000.

Evans, Richard. *Death in Hamburg: Society and Politics in the Cholera Years, 1830–1910*. New York: Oxford University Press, 1987.

Garavaglia, Juan Carlos, and Juan Carlos Grosso. "Mexican Elites of a Provincial Town: The Landowners of Tepeaca (1700–1870)." *Hispanic American Historical Review*, 70 (May 1990), 255–93.

Gates, Paul W. *California Ranchos and Farms, 1846–1862*. Madison: State Historical Society of Wisconsin, 1967.

———. *Land and Law in California: Essays on Land Policies*. Ames: Iowa State University Press, 1991.

———. "Public Land Disposal in California." *Agricultural History*, 49 (January 1975), 158–78.

Gonner, Edward C. K. *Common Land and Inclosure*. London: Macmillan, 1912.

Goodwyn, Lawrence. *The Populist Moment: A Short History of the Agrarian Revolt in America*. New York: Oxford University Press, 1978.

Griswold del Castillo, Richard. *The Los Angeles Barrio, 1850–1890: A Social History*. Berkeley: University of California Press, 1979.

Gutiérrez, Ramón A., and Richard J. Orsi, eds. *Contested Eden: California Before the Gold Rush*. Berkeley: University of California Press, 1998.

Haas, Lisbeth. *Conquests and Historical Identities in California, 1769–1936*. Berkeley: University of California Press, 1995.

Hagen, Olaf Theodore. *Modoc War: Official Correspondence and Documents, 1865–1878*. San Francisco, 1942. In Bancroft Library collecton.

Hammond, John L., and Barbara Hammond. *The Village Labourer, 1760–1832: A Study in the Government of England Before the Reform Bill*. London: Longman, 1912.

Holliday, J. S. *Rush for Riches: Gold Fever and the Making of California*. Berkeley: University of California Press, 1999.

Hornbeck, David. "Land Tenure and Rancho Expansion in Alta California, 1784–1846." *Journal of Historical Geography*, 4 (1978), 371–90.

Horwitz, Morton. *The Transformation of American Law, 1785–1850*. Cambridge, Mass.: Harvard University Press, 1976.

Howe, Carrol B. *Ancient Modocs of California and Oregon*. Portland, Ore.: Binford and Mort, 1979.

Hurley, Andrew. *Environmental Inequalities: Class, Race, and Industrial Pollution in Gary, Indiana, 1945–1980*. Chapel Hill: University of North Carolina Press, 1995.

Hurst, J. Willard. *Law and the Conditions of Freedom in the Nineteenth-Century United States*. Madison: University of Wisconsin Press, 1956.

Hurtado, Albert L. *Indian Survival on the California Frontier*. New Haven: Yale University Press, 1988.

———. *Intimate Frontiers: Sex, Gender, and Culture in Old California*. Albuquerque: University of New Mexico Press, 1999.

Igler, David. "Diseased Goods: Global Exchanges in the Eastern Pacific Basin, 1770–1850." *American Historical Review*, 109 (June 2004), 693–719.

———. *Industrial Cowboys: Miller & Lux and the Transformation of the Far West, 1850–1920*. Berkeley: University of California Press, 2001.

———. "The Industrial Far West: Region and Nation in the Late Nineteenth Century." *Pacific Historical Review*, 69 (May 2000), 159–92.

Isenberg, Andrew C. "The California Gold Rush, the West, and the Nation." *Reviews in American History*, 29 (March 2001), 62–71.

———. *The Destruction of the Bison: An Environmental History, 1750–1920*. New York: Cambridge University Press, 2000.

———. "Environment and the Nineteenth-Century West; or, Process Encounters Place." In William Deverell, ed., *A Companion to the History of the American West*, 77–92. Oxford: Blackwell, 2004.

———. "Historicizing Natural Environments: The Deep Roots of Environmental History." In Lloyd Cutler and Sarah Maza, eds., *A Companion to Western Historical Thought*, 372–89. Oxford: Blackwell, 2002.

Jones, J. Roy. *Memories, Men, and Medicine: A History of Medicine in Sacramento, California*. Sacramento: Society for Medical Improvement, 1950.

Jordan, Terry. *North American Cattle-Ranching Frontiers: Origins, Diffusion, Differentiation*. Albuquerque: University of New Mexico Press, 1993.

Kelley, Robert L. *Gold vs. Grain: The Hydraulic Mining Controversy in California's Sacramento Valley*. Glendale, Calif.: Arthur H. Clark, 1959.

Kelman, Ari. *A River and Its City: The Nature of Landscape in New Orleans*. Berkeley: University of California Press, 2003.

Knack, Martha C. "A Short Resource History of Pyramid Lake, Nevada." *Ethnohistory*, 24 (Winter 1977), 47–63.

Kroeber, A. L. *Handbook of the Indians of California*. New York: Dover, 1976.

Kroeber, Theodora. *Ishi in Two Worlds: A Biography of the Last Wild Indian in North America*. Berkeley: University of California Press, 1961.

Kulikoff, Allan. "The Transition to Capitalism in Rural America." *William and Mary Quarterly*, 3d ser., 46 (January 1989), 120–44.

Lamar, Howard. "From Bondage to Contract: Ethnic Labor in the American West, 1600–1890." In Steven Hahn and Jonathan Prude, eds., *The Countryside in the Age of*

Capitalist Transformation: Essays in the Social History of Rural America. Chapel Hill: University of North Carolina Press, 1985.

Landrum, Francis S., ed. *Guardhouse, Gallows, and Graves: The Trial and Execution of Indian Prisoners of the Modoc Indian War by the U.S. Army*. Klamath Falls, Ore.: Klamath County Museum, 1988.

Laurie, Bruce. *Artisans into Workers: Labor in Nineteenth-Century America*. New York: Noonday, 1989.

Liebman, Ellen. *California Farmland: A History of Large Agricultural Landholdings*. Totowa, N.J.: Rowman and Allanheld, 1983.

Limerick, Patricia Nelson. *Legacy of Conquest: The Unbroken Past of the American West*. New York: Norton, 1987.

MacKenzie, Donald. "Marx and the Machine." *Technology and Culture*, 25 (July 1984), 473–502.

May, Dean. *Three Frontiers: Family, Land, and Society in the American West, 1850–1900*. New York: Cambridge University Press, 1994.

McEvoy, Arthur F. *The Fisherman's Problem: Ecology and Law in the California Fisheries, 1850–1980*. New York: Cambridge University Press, 1986.

McPhee, John. *Assembling California*. New York: Farrar, Straus and Giroux, 1993.

Melosi, Martin. "'Out of Sight, Out of Mind': The Environment and Disposal of Municipal Refuse, 1860–1920." *The Historian*, 35 (1973).

Melville, Elinor G. K. *A Plague of Sheep: Environmental Consequences of the Conquest of Mexico*. New York: Cambridge University Press, 1994.

Merchant, Carolyn, ed. *Green Versus Gold: Sources in California's Environmental History*. Washington, D.C.: Island Press, 1998.

Merrell, James. "Some Thoughts on Colonial Historians and American Indians." *William and Mary Quarterly*, 46 (January 1989), 94–119.

Miller, Crane S., and Richard S. Hyslop. *California: The Geography of Diversity*. Mountain View, Calif.: Mayfield, 1983.

Miller, M. Catherine. *Flooding the Courtrooms: Law and Water in the Far West*. Lincoln: University of Nebraska Press, 1993.

Montejano, David. *Anglos and Mexicans in the Making of Texas, 1836–1986*. Austin: University of Texas Press, 1994.

Mount, Jeffrey F. *California Rivers and Streams: The Conflict Between Fluvial Process and Land Use*. Berkeley: University of California Press, 1995.

Murray, Keith A. *The Modocs and Their War*. Norman: University of Oklahoma Press, 1959.

Namkuong, G., and J. H. Roberts. "Extinction Probabilities and the Changing Age Structure of Redwood Forests." *The American Naturalist*, 108 (May–June 1974), 355–68.

Nash, Gerald D. *State Government and Economic Development: A History of Administrative Policies in California, 1849–1933*. Berkeley: Institute of Governmental Studies, 1964.

Noss, Reed F., ed. *The Redwood Forest: History, Ecology, and Conservation of the Coast Redwoods*. Washington, D.C.: Island Press, 2000.

Orsi, Richard J. "*The Octopus* Reconsidered: The Southern Pacific and Agricultural Modernization in California, 1865–1915." *California Historical Quarterly*, 54 (Fall 1975), 197–220.

Otto, J. S., and N. E. Anderson. "Cattle Ranching in the Venezuelan Llanos and the Florida Flatwoods." *Comparative Studies in Society and History*, 28 (October 1986), 672–83.

Paul, Rodman. *California Gold: The Beginning of Mining in the Far West.* Cambridge, Mass.: Harvard University Press, 1947.

Pease, Robert W. *Modoc County: A Geographic Time Continuum on the California Volcanic Tableland.* Berkeley: University of California Press, 1965.

Phifer, Edward. "Slavery in Microcosm: Burke County, North Carolina." *Journal of Southern History,* 28 (May 1962).

Pisani, Donald J. *From Family Farm to Agribusiness: The Irrigation Crusade in California and the West, 1850–1931.* Berkeley: University of California Press, 1984.

———. *Water, Land, and Law in the West: The Limits of Public Policy, 1850–1920.* Lawrence: University Press of Kansas, 1996.

Pitt, Leonard. *The Decline of the Californios: A Social History of the Spanish-Speaking Californians, 1846–1890.* Berkeley: University of California Press, 1966.

Preston, William. *Vanishing Landscapes: Land and Life in the Tulare Lake Basin.* Berkeley: University of California Press, 1981.

Rawls, James J., and Richard J. Orsi, eds. *A Golden State: Mining and Economic Development in Gold Rush California.* Berkeley: University of California Press, 1998.

Ray, Verne F. *Primitive Pragmatists: The Modoc Indians of Northern California.* Seattle: University of Washington Press, 1963.

Reed, Gregory A. *An Historical Geography Analysis of the Modoc Indian War.* Chico, Calif.: ANCRR, 1991.

Rohe, Randall E. "Hydraulicking in the American West: The Development and Diffusion of a Mining Technique." *Montana: The Magazine of Western History* (Spring 1985), 18–35.

Rohrbough, Malcolm. *Days of Gold: The California Gold Rush and the American Nation.* Berkeley: University of California Press, 1997.

Rosenberg, Charles. *The Cholera Years: The United States in 1832, 1849, and 1866.* Chicago: University of Chicago Press, 1987.

Salvatore, Ricardo D. "Modes of Labor Control in Cattle-Ranching Economies: California, Southern Brazil, and Argentina, 1820–1860." *Journal of Economic History,* 51 (June 1991), 441–51.

Saxton, Alexander. *The Indispensable Enemy: Labor and the Anti-Chinese Movement in California.* Berkeley: University of California Press, 1971.

Schoenherr, Allan A. *A Natural History of California.* Berkeley: University of California Press, 1992.

Schryer, Frans J. "A Ranchero Economy in Northeastern Hidalgo, 1880–1920." *Hispanic American Historical Review,* 59 (August 1979), 418–43.

Schultz, Stanley K., and Clay McShane. "To Engineer the Metropolis: Sewers, Sanitation, and City Planning in Late Nineteenth-Century America." *Journal of American History,* 65 (1978), 389–411.

Schwantes, Carlos A. "Protest in a Promised Land: Unemployment, Disinheritance, and the Origin of Labor Militancy in the Pacific Northwest, 1885–1886." *Western Historical Quarterly,* 13 (October 1982), 373–90.

Spence, Clark C. *British Investments and the American Mining Frontier, 1860–1901.* Ithaca, N.Y.: Cornell University Press, 1958.

———. "The Golden Age of Dredging: The Development of an Industry and Its Environmental Impact." *Western Historical Quarterly,* 11 (October 1980), 401–14.

Steinberg, Theodore. *Nature Incorporated: Industrialization and the Waters of New England*. New York: Cambridge University Press, 1991.

Takaki, Ronald. *Strangers from a Different Shore: A History of Asian Americans*. Boston: Little, Brown, 1998.

Taylor, Joseph E., III. *Making Salmon: An Environmental History of the Northwest Fisheries Crisis*. Seattle: University of Washington Press, 1999.

Thompson, E. P. *The Making of the English Working Class*. New York: Vintage, 1963.

Thompson, Kenneth. "Insalubrious California: Perception and Reality." *Annals of the Association of American Geographers*, 59 (March 1969), 50–64.

———. "Riparian Forests of the Sacramento Valley, California." *Annals of the Association of American Geographers*, 51 (September 1961), 294–315.

Turner, Frederick Jackson. "The Significance of the Frontier in American History." American Historical Association *Annual Report* (1893), 199–227.

Turner, Michael. *Enclosures in Britain, 1750–1830*. London: Macmillan, 1984.

Turner, Stan. *The Years of Harvest: A History of the Tule Lake Basin*. 3d ed. Eugene, Ore.: Spencer Creek Press, 2002.

Unruh, John D. *The Plains Across: The Overland Emigrants and the Trans-Mississippi West, 1840–1860*. Urbana: University of Illinois Press, 1979.

Vale, Thomas P. "Forest Changes in the Warner Mountains, California." *Annals of the Association of American Geographers*, 67 (March 1977), 28–45.

Warren, Louis. *The Hunter's Game: Poachers and Conservationists in Twentieth-Century America*. New Haven: Yale University Press, 1997.

Watson, Harry L. "Conflict and Collaboration: Yeomen, Slaveholders, and Politics in the Antebellum South." *Social History*, 10 (October 1985), 273–98.

Webb, Walter Prescott. "The American West: Perpetual Mirage." *Harper's Magazine*, 214 (May 1957), 25–31.

Weber, David J. *The Spanish Frontier in North America*. New Haven: Yale University Press, 1992.

Wells, Allen. "Family Elites in a Boom-and-Bust Economy: The Molinas and Peons of Porfirian Yucatán." *Hispanic American Historical Review*, 62 (May 1982), 224–53.

West, Elliott. *The Way to the West: Essays on the Central Plains*. Albuquerque: University of New Mexico Press, 1995.

White, Richard. "Indian Peoples and the Natural World: Asking the Right Questions." In Donald L. Fixico, ed., *Rethinking American Indian History*, Albuquerque: University of New Mexico Press, 1997.

———. *Land Use, Environment, and Social Change: The Shaping of Island County, Washington*. Seattle: University of Washington Press, 1980.

———. *The Middle Ground: Indians, Empires, and Republics in the Great Lakes Region, 1650–1815*. New York: Cambridge University Press, 1991.

———. *The Organic Machine: The Remaking of the Columbia River*. New York: Hill and Wang, 1995.

Williams, John Hoyt. "Black Labor and State Ranches: The Tabapi Experience in Paraguay." *Journal of Negro History*, 62 (October 1977), 378–89.

Williams, Michael. *Americans and Their Forests: A Historical Geography*. New York: Cambridge University Press, 1989.

Wood, W. Raymond. "Plains Trade in Prehistoric and Protohistoric Intertribal Relations." In W. Raymond Wood and Margot Liberty, eds., *Anthropology on the Great Plains*. Lincoln: University of Nebraska Press, 1980.

Worster, Donald. "Hydraulic Society in California: An Ecological Interpretation." *Agricultural History*, 56 (July 1982), 503–15.

———. *Rivers of Empire: Water, Aridity, and the Growth of the American West*. New York: Pantheon, 1985.

Wright, Doris Marion. *A Yankee in Mexican California: Abel Stearns, 1798–1848*. Santa Barbara, Calif.: Wallace Hebberd, 1977.

Wrightson, Keith. *Earthly Necessities: Economic Lives in Early Modern Britain*. New Haven: Yale University Press, 2000.

Zhu, Liping. *A Chinaman's Chance: The Chinese on the Rocky Mountain Mining Frontier*. Niwot: University Press of Colorado, 1997.

DISSERTATIONS AND THESES

Dahl, Albin Joachim. "British Investment in California Mining, 1870–1890." Ph.D. dissertation, University of California, Berkeley, 1961.

Fedewa, Philip. "Abel Stearns in Transitional California, 1848–1871." Ph.D. dissertation, University of Missouri, 1970.

Graybill, Andrew. "Instruments of Incorporation: Rangers, Mounties, and the North American Frontier, 1875–1910." Ph.D. dissertation, Princeton University, 2003.

Melendy, Howard Brett. "One Hundred Years of the Redwood Lumber Industry, 1850–1950." Ph.D. dissertation, Stanford University, 1952.

Pulling, Hazel Adele. "A History of California's Range-Cattle Industry, 1770–1912." Ph.D. dissertation, University of Southern California, 1944.

Stanford, Everett Russell. "A Short History of California Lumbering." M.S. thesis, University of California, Berkeley, 1924.

Wattenburger, Ralph Thomas. "The Redwood Lumbering Industry on the Northern California Coast, 1850–1900." M.A. thesis, University of California, Berkeley, 1931.

Weidberg, Dorothy. "The History of John Kentfield and Company, 1854–1925, a Lumber Manufacturing Firm of San Francisco." M.A. thesis, University of California, Berkeley, 1940.

Acknowledgments

I began my research for this book at the Huntington Library in San Marino, California. I am grateful to the Huntington for supporting my work and to the archivists for their indispensable help. I later continued my research at the Bancroft Library in Berkeley, California, and at the California State Library, California State Archives, and Sacramento City Archives, all in Sacramento. I am grateful to the staffs of these institutions for their assistance, and to Princeton University for supporting my research. At Princeton, I was also blessed with two talented research assistants, Manuel Berrelez and John Matsui.

Much of the book was written in Erfurt, Germany, where I had the good fortune to spend one year as a Fulbright Scholar. It seems an unlikely place to write a book about California, but as it turned out an ideal one. My colleagues at the University of Erfurt were unfailingly helpful and ever willing to discuss ideas. I am grateful to them all, but especially to the cheerful encouragement and friendship of Ulla Lehmkuhl.

I completed the book shortly after joining the faculty at Temple University. The Department of History at Temple has created an intellectual environment supportive of new scholarship. I thank Temple University for its support of this project and its confidence in its author.

My work has benefited, in numerous direct and indirect ways, from conversations with many fellow historians. These include David Abraham, William Breitenbach, Peter Brown, Kurk Dorsey, David Freund, Harold James, Bill Jordan, Kevin Kruse, David Rich Lewis, Jim McPherson, Ken Mills, John Murrin, Ted Rabb, and Marc Rodriguez.

A number of scholars read and commented on one or more chapters. I am grateful to Karl Appuhn, Emily Brock, Rosanne Currarino, William Deverell, Jolie Dyl, Sarah Elkind, Andrew Graybill, Nicholas Guyatt, Albert Hurtado, David Igler, Ari Kelman, Matt Klingle, Emmanuel Kreike, Arthur McEvoy, J. C. Mutchler, Jared Orsi, Harold Platt, Sara Pritchard, Arthur Schmidt, Frans Schryer, Peter Siskind, Steven Stoll, Ellen Stroud, Peter Thorsheim, Jay Turner, Greg Urwin, and Louis Warren.

I presented earlier versions of parts of the book at a number of conferences and seminars. I am grateful in particular to the participants in the conference on "New Directions in Environmental History" at the University of New Hampshire in April 2001; the participants in the Atlantic Cultural History Colloquium at the University of Erfurt in the spring of 2002; the participants in the history and sociology workshop at the University of Pennsylvania in February 2003; the members of Louis Warren's graduate seminar in western history at the University of California at Davis in the spring of 2003; and the contributors to the "Nature of Cities" conference at Princeton University in December 2003.

Thomas LeBien of Hill and Wang is a model editor. His encouragement and incisive critiques were indispensable in transforming this project from a manuscript to a book.

I could not have written this book, or done much of anything else for that matter, without the support of family and friends: Mike Angell and Jennifer Harper, Bruce Buttny, Jim and Terry Denegre, Tom and Jean Faszholz, Franz-Josef and Elisabeth Gödde, John and Lynn Hillman, Eric Isenberg, Greg Lind, Bernd Lorenzen, Art McEvoy, Ken and Libby Mills, Joel and Edwina Schorn, Kim and James Sprague, Lisa and Rüdiger Thurm, and Louis and Spring Warren. My wife, Petra Goedde, and our children, Kai, Elena, and Noah, were always with me as I worked, even—indeed, especially—when I was thousands of miles from them doing research in California. No matter how far distant, my parents will always be with me, too. This work is for them.

Index

―◆―

Page numbers in italics refer to illustrations.